Aural Skills Acquisition

AURAL SKILLS ACQUISITION

The Development of
Listening, Reading, and Performing Skills
in College-Level Musicians

———————— Gary S. Karpinski ————————

OXFORD
UNIVERSITY PRESS

2000

OXFORD

UNIVERSITY PRESS

Oxford   New York
Athens   Auckland   Bangkok   Bogotá   Buenos Aires   Calcutta
Cape Town   Chennai   Dar es Salaam   Delhi   Florence   Hong Kong   Istanbul
Karachi   Kuala Lumpur   Madrid   Melbourne   Mexico City   Mumbai
Nairobi   Paris   São Paulo   Shanghai   Singapore   Taipei   Tokyo   Toronto   Warsaw

and associated companies in
Berlin   Ibadan

Copyright © 2000 by Oxford University Press, Inc.

Published by Oxford University Press, Inc.
198 Madison Avenue, New York, New York 10016

Oxford is a registered trademark of Oxford University Press

Library of Congress Cataloging-in-Publication Data
Karpinski, Gary S. (Gary Steven)
Aural skills acquisition : the development of listening, reading, and performing skills in
college-level musicians / Gary S. Karpinski.
p.   cm.
Includes bibliographical references and index.
ISBN 0-19-511785-9
1. Ear training.   2. Sight-reading (Music)   3. Music in universities and colleges.
I. Title.
MT35.K186   2000
781.4'2—dc21   99-057684

1 3 5 7 9 8 6 4 2

Printed in the United States of America
on acid-free paper

*To my mother
and the memory of my father*

Acknowledgments

It is due in large part to the faith and persistence of Maribeth Anderson Payne, executive music editor at Oxford University Press, that this book exists at all. Our early conversations about the various paths a book like this might take have helped to shape the entire project. Her encouragement to continue my work studying aural skills acquisition as a scholarly discipline motivated me to return to this topic even after pursuing several other long and deeply involving projects.

I owe a debt of gratitude to many others who helped in various ways. To the dozens of professors and teaching assistants who have taught aural skills with me over the years, thank you for being such wonderful colleagues, listening to my ideas, critiquing them, and providing many valuable ideas of your own. To Mary Arlin, Richard Ashley, Ann Blombach, John Buccheri, Carol Krumhansl, Alice Lanning, Suzanne La Plante, Steve Larson, Alissa Leiser, Elizabeth West Marvin, Joe Palca, Janet Palumbo, Joel Phillips, Lee Riggins, Carl Schachter, John Sloboda, Paulina Stark, and David Williams, thank you for your prompt replies to requests for reprints and other sources. To Pamela Juengling, music librarian at the University of Massachusetts at Amherst, and to Ann Maggs, music library assistant at Amherst College, thank you for your generous help in finding and obtaining materials. To Sigrun Heinzelmann, thank you for your meticulous, responsible, and intelligent research assistance. To Andrew Davis, Hali Fieldman, Richard Kram, and Mary Wennerstrom, thank you for your careful attention in reading portions of early drafts of the manuscript.

Special thanks are due to Michael Rogers, whose support and encouragement for over a decade have inspired and sustained me. His thoughtful reading of the manuscript and his well-reasoned suggestions made this a much better book.

Special thanks also go to David Butler for his enormously helpful comments on the manuscript. His intimate knowledge of the field proved to be an invaluable resource.

I owe the greatest debt to my wife, Jean, for her unflagging support and sage advice, and to my young children, Julia and Alex, for being understanding about my commitment to this project with a maturity and grace that far exceed their years.

The following pieces of music were reprinted from other sources:

"No. 3" from *Ten Easy Pieces* by Béla Bartók. © Copyright by Editio Musica Budapest. Copyright renewed. Used by permission of Boosey & Hawkes, Inc., U.S. Agent.

"My Love" from *Candide* by Leonard Bernstein. © 1955, 1957, 1958, 1976, 1952, 1990, 1994 by Amberson Holdings LLC. Copyright renewed. The Leonard Bernstein Publishing Company LLC, Publisher, Boosey & Hawkes, Inc., Sole Agent. Used by Permission.

"Sunrise" from *Grand Canyon Suite* by Ferde Grofe. © 1932, 1943 (copyrights renewed) EMI Robbins Catalog, Inc. All Rights Reserved. Used by Permission. Warner Bros. Publications, U.S. Inc. Miami, FL 33014.

"No. 1" from *Lasske Tance* (Lachian Dances) by Leoš Janáček, Oboe part. © Copyright by Bärebreuter-Verlag. Used by permission.

Contents

Part I: Listening Skills

Aural Skills Acquisition

Introduction

Purpose

The purpose of this book is to explore how college-level musicians acquire the various skills involved in two broad areas of musical behavior: (1) listening and (2) reading and performing. Music listening skills cover a wide range of activities, from listening to general characteristics, to the complex activities involved in various kinds of dictation, to attention to finer features such as tone quality and intonation. Reading and performing skills are equally complex and numerous, involving mechanics such as vocal technique and eye movements, the code-interpreting tasks involved in reading notation, and production skills such as tonal orientation and maintenance of a steady pulse. Many adages have circulated for years surrounding the reciprocal nature of these two sets of skills. For example, Schumann ([1848] 1967) wrote: "You must get to the point that you can hear music from the page"[1] (p. 402), and, "A perfect musician should be able to picture a piece, at first hearing . . . as though he had the score in front of him"[2] (p. 413). Smith (1934) noted that "the musician must learn to 'hear with the eye, and see with the ear' " (p. 58). Benward and Carr (1999) refer to the "hearing eye" (p. xi), and Benward and Kolosick (1996b) invoke the "seeing ear" (p. ix). Butler (1997) speaks of "an intrinsic and unbreakable link between music performance skill and music listening skill" (p. 44). Indeed, although the bipartite division of this book separates listening skills from reading and performing skills, readers will find that much of what is presented in one half will be applicable in the other as well.

---

1. "Du muß es so weit bringen, daß du eine Musik auf dem Papier verstehst!"
2. "Ein vollkommener Musiker müsse imstande sein, ein zum erstenmal gehörtes . . . wie in leibhaftiger Partitur vor sich zu sehen."

An important goal in the development of musical skills is the ability to think *in* music. Best (1992) distinguishes thinking *in* music from other musical activities, particularly thinking *about* music: "If I can truly think in music, I may well depend less on verbal and visual languages as proxies for this primary responsibility. Thinking in music should thus precede and direct whatever else I do musically" (p. 4). Serafine (1988) goes so far as to define music as "the activity of *thinking* in or with sound" (p. 69) and excludes thinking that "may be *about* but not *in* music" (p. 70). Elliott (1996) makes a similar distinction: "It is possible to think about music, discuss music, and express ideas about music without 'understanding' music" (p. 71). Developing musicians who study rudiments, harmony, counterpoint, form, and other subdisciplines of music theory without previous or concurrent training in the appropriate kinds of aural skills are usually condemned to thinking *about* music without learning how to think *in* music.

This book is about thinking *in* music. Music listeners who understand what they hear are thinking in music. Music readers who understand and auralize what they read are thinking in music. This book investigates the various ways musicians acquire those skills.

Methodologies

Butler and Lochstampfor (1993) reported the following:

> A cursory examination of references cited in the literature of aural training pedagogy suggests that there is very little correspondence between research activities in music cognition and pedagogical activities in aural training: although there are important individual exceptions, there simply does not seem to have been a widespread effort to identify, gather, evaluate, and synthesize experimental results from the research area of music cognition so that they may be applied directly to aural training in our college music programs. (p. 6)

There is indeed a gap between the disciplines of music cognition and aural skills training. One of the goals of this book is to help bridge that gap.

To that end, this book draws heavily on experimental research performed by musicians and psychologists. Much of this research focuses narrowly on isolated behaviors (as good science often does), but it is incumbent on musicians to interpret the results of these studies and apply what can be learned from them to the development and use of everyday listening, reading, and performing skills. Therefore, many of the discussions in this book take the form of a kind of humanistic metaanalysis of various scientific studies of musical behaviors. By bringing together the data and conclusions of various scientists working on isolated aspects of a particular skill, we can often discover ways of improving and honing that skill for better use in musical contexts.

But as Butler and Lochstampfor (1993) note, "Experimental research is not the only route. In the last decade, a lot of attention has turned toward qualitative—rather than quantitative—research methods: case studies, ethnographic studies, autobiographical protocols" (p. 16). These and other studies (of learning theory and human intelligence, for example) also inform this volume. And I have included first-person accounts from my own case studies where such materials illuminate specific topics with particular clarity.

This book also draws on centuries of wisdom from music theorists of the past. Thus, where appropriate, readers will find ideas about aural skills pedagogy drawn from, amplified through, or clarified by theoretical principles in the works of such theorists as Guido of Arezzo, Gioseffo Zarlino, Franchinus Gaffurius, C. P. E. Bach, Jean-Philippe Rameau, Arnold Schoenberg, and Heinrich Schenker.

Certain approaches in this book are based on some of the best and most provocative recent work in tonal music theory. Thus, readers will find approaches to aural training based on theoretical models such as hypermeter and recent research in Schenkerian theory. This serves the dual purpose of building strong bonds between theory and aural skills on the one hand and preparing students for future study of these disciplines on the other.

This book also draws on the writings of various pedagogues in aural skills, music theory, other disciplines within music, and teaching in general. Much of the territory covered here has been traversed at one time or another by one or more of these writers, so their approaches and findings are examined here.

Where appropriate, specific textbooks are acknowledged as progenitors of effective approaches, cited for their inclusion of important ideas or techniques, or critiqued for contents that run counter to important findings. The contents and behaviors of various instructional computer software products are examined in a similar vein. These discussions are not meant as formal reviews, nor are they directed personally at the authors of these books and software (I have great respect for anyone who writes an aural skills textbook or program). Rather, they are drawn in as practical illustrations that can make certain issues very real, particularly to aural skills instructors.

In addition, passages from the writings of certain significant musicians—performers, conductors, composers—are included to help demonstrate the relevance of certain aural skills in various practical contexts. These musicians often exhibit an intuitive musical grasp of principles that psychologists and pedagogues come to know through very different paths in their own disciplines.

Organization

Aural skills have often been divided into two broad categories: ear training and sight singing. This book's two main headings reflect a slightly different approach: "Listening Skills" and "Reading and Performing Skills."

Listening skills are essential to musicians because music exists fundamentally in the aural domain. It is important that musicians develop *musical* listening skills. As Elliott (1993) remarked, in order to understand and appreciate music, listeners require "the same kinds of knowing as the performer" (p. 69). That kind of knowing is perhaps most importantly contextual in that it operates on real music in real time (as opposed to isolated elements such as intervals). And training in music listening should be considered a central part of musical development. As Gromko (1993) concluded, "Perception of musical sound should be a primary purpose of music teaching" (p. 46).

Reading and performing are grouped together in the second part of this book because these two types of skills are necessary for and important goals of sight singing. They are in fact two separable (but typically intertwined) sets of skills. Music-reading skills are those involved in code interpretation. Performing skills are those necessary to produce the sounds indicated by that code. Each type of skill can be used separately (for example, one can read music silently on the one hand and perform music without notation on the other), but they are typically practiced together during aural skills training. In addition, much of what is discussed in the second half of this book is aimed at *literate* reading and performance—in other words, reading and performing through, with, and for musical understanding. I take it as axiomatic that it is not enough to produce the right sounds. Musically meaningful reading and performance simultaneously stem from and foster an understanding of such factors as key, meter, and harmonic function.

Scope

For all but a few brief (essentially parenthetical) digressions, this book confines itself to music that is metric and tonal. I have made this restriction for two reasons. First, the types of music central to most music curricula—common-practice-period classical music, Western European folk music, Western commercial popular music, and even most jazz— exhibit these features nearly ubiquitously. Second, the perception, reading, and performance of metric and tonal music involve more than enough skills to examine in a single volume. Although there is much to say about aural approaches to nonmetric and nontonal music from before and after the common-practice period and from some non-Western cultures, they are subjects for yet another book.

The skills this book examines range from the extremely basic to the complex. Lest readers be concerned by the elementary nature of the skills at the former end of that scale, let me offer two justifications:

1. Many universities, colleges, and conservatories report that entering students often suffer from deficiencies in aural skills. For example, Wennerstrom (1989) reported that at the Indiana University School of Music "a continuing problem is the entrance level of the freshman. Students are particularly ill prepared in aural skills and sightsinging" (p. 163). Earlier generations were not immune to this problem. The Juilliard School of Music (1953) listed ten characteristics typical of the incoming student, among which was that "he has an untrained ear. In most cases, no attempt has been made to train the ear" (p. 48). Juilliard also refers to students (particularly singers) "who cannot sing at sight the simplest diatonic melody" (p. 43).
2. By developing strong basic skills and by correcting the basic causes of aural difficulties (not merely addressing the symptoms), we establish a solid foundation on which to build further skills with ease and fluency.

These two factors alone are more than sufficient to warrant beginning with such basic skills and materials.

Individual musicians have individual degrees of facility and difficulty with each of the many skills this book examines. Therefore, it is possible—for example—for one musician to experience difficulties in recalling short musical passages whereas another might remember such passages but find it difficult to infer a tonic from any of them. Each of the dozens of aural skills in this book is treated separately (while still keeping sight of the role it plays in context with the others), eschewing a one-size-fits-all approach to listening or reading. The workings and functions of each of these skills are examined, means of assessing and diagnosing specific skills in individual musicians are discussed, and various approaches to instilling and improving each skill are presented.

Readership

This book should be relevant to a variety of readers. Aural skills instructors should find much in its pages to inform (and perhaps inspire) their teaching. Teachers and students of music theory pedagogy should find more than enough material here to stimulate their discussions and lead them to further readings. Members of the music education community will find that this book is informed by some of their research and that it might even suggest new studies as well as affect certain classroom applications. Psychologists and musicians who perform research in music perception and cognition might find new questions to investigate, new paths to pursue, or perhaps simply be pleased and inspired to see their research applied in practical settings.

My hope is that all of these readers will gain something from this book, some will adopt things they learn from it in their teaching, and others will be spurred on by it to perform further research (in the form of experiments, clinical trials, ethnographic studies, or whatever). If my most hopeful expectations come to pass, new findings from teachers and researchers will make this volume outmoded in short order.

Conclusion

Over thirty years ago, Chittum (1967) concluded that "the day is past when teachers can say, 'you either have an ear or you don't.' The pedagogy of aural development is, however, in its infancy, and the future will bring refinements of techniques along with a greater insight into the mechanisms that impede aural development" (p. 73). Thirty years of research and publications have brought us many refinements and much insight. More will certainly come in the future. What remains is to implement what we have learned.

PART I

LISTENING SKILLS

Developing the ear is
of the utmost importance
—Robert Schumann
([1848] 1967, 400)

Identification of Basic Features

This chapter examines basic features of music that listeners can learn to identify at the earliest stages of study. The essential difference between the listening skills discussed in this chapter and those discussed in the next is that those in this chapter are not absolutely necessary for immediate progress whereas those in the next chapter lay an essential groundwork for the progressive curriculum discussed from there on. One might therefore consider the skills in this chapter to be "optional," and—in some senses—they are. However, as part of any well-rounded musician's training, the ability to articulately discriminate among various differences in the following features is fundamental. These topics may be addressed in advance of the materials in the subsequent chapters or may be covered concurrently with them.

Texture

One of the most fundamental listening skills is the ability to discriminate among various basic musical textures—the contemporaneous strands of musical activity and how they interact. Thus, instruction and evaluation of this skill can begin in the earliest days of training. It seems unwise to begin a curriculum with intervals or scales and to progress through melodic dictation, two-voice dictation, and harmonic dictation without ensuring that students can differentiate the various textural conditions that give rise to the need to apply such listening skills in the first place.

The classic tripartite division into *monophonic*, *homophonic*, and *polyphonic* textures can serve as a useful point of departure.[1] Listeners

---

1. Perhaps not surprisingly, Ellis (1995) found that novice listeners tended to have much more difficulty discriminating between homophonic and polyphonic textures than between either of these two and monophony.

must be provided with ample numbers of examples of each of these three textures in order to build familiarity with them. Directed listening assignments that involve responses to specific questions can provide a framework for exposure to these examples. Such questions might focus on more general information, such as "What makes the parts 'independent'?" and "How do these 'independent' parts relate to one another?," and on specific quantifiable details like "How many instruments/voices do you hear?" or "How many independent parts?" or "Does the number of parts remain constant throughout this passage?"[2] Other important related areas of exploration include types of motion (contrary, oblique, similar, parallel), the relative densities of various textures, and perhaps even syllabic versus melismatic text setting.

Monophonic examples might include samples of plainchant, instrumental ensemble unisons (for example, the first few measures of No. 13 from Mozart's Thirteen German Dances, [K. 605, No. 3]), or solo vocal or instrumental literature. Homophony might be represented by a chorale (particularly, at first, entirely homorhythmic passages such as mm. 1–4 of Bach's "Valet will ich dir geben" [No. 30]) or other homorhythmic passages in various genres and styles (such as the opening bars of Brahms's Symphony No. 4, mmt. 4). Polyphonic examples can be drawn from any canon, ricercar, invention, sinfonia, or fugue; polyphonic passages from other works are also illustrative.

But the division into monophony, homophony, and polyphony is only a point of departure. Perhaps most important, there is the issue of homophony: how it appears in at least two forms: (1) "true" homophony, wherein all voices move with essentially identical rhythms; and (2) "melody and accompaniment," characterized by a rhythmically independent melody set against other homophonic voices. Listeners should learn to distinguish homophony in general from other textures and homorhythmic homophony from melody and accompaniment. In addition, other textures fall essentially outside the traditional three. One such texture is heterophony, in which one strand of texture embellishes the material of another simultaneous strand. Another is not a single condition but rather a plasticity of texture: *Freistimmigkeit*, in which a generally polyphonic texture is blurred by the relatively free addition and subtraction of voices and the occasional use of more homophonic elements.

Finally, for listening to take place on any level of sophistication beyond the mere pedantic, listeners must come to understand that these textures interact, overlap, and blend with one another in various ways. Many compositions do not maintain a single textural condition, even within single movements, so that a textural understanding of such works be-

---

2. However, instructors should be aware of David Huron's (1989) findings that even expert musicians have difficulty determining the number of voices in passages with more than three concurrent voices when all parts have similar timbres.

comes a dynamic process of perceiving changing conditions. In addition, more than one texture can be operative at any given time. A passage might join a melody, a homorhythmic chordal accompaniment, and a running bass (for example, "Oft She Visits" from Purcell's *Dido and Aeneas*), thereby creating more complex relationships among those layers of texture.

Timbre

It is also important for listeners to be able to discriminate among various instrumental and vocal timbres.[3] Training in this area can begin with monophonic examples of various instruments and voices and progress through diverse combinations of timbres. Timbres may be categorized into certain standard classifications. For example, the organologist's groupings of idiophones, chordphones, aerophones, and membranophones can serve to connect timbres aurally with distinct means of sound production. (One might consider adding electrophones to this list, although some electrophones can aurally mimic certain acoustic timbres, thereby obfuscating the true nature of their sound source.) Similarly, learning to aurally identify the traditional Western orchestral divisions of strings, woodwinds, brass, and percussion can help orient listeners along those lines. Voices can likewise be grouped according to type, first according to gender and then at least into the subdivisions soprano, alto, tenor, and bass. In all these manners, listening tasks and assessments can take the form of identifying timbres solely in terms of their membership in such broad classifications.

Listeners can practice more finely honed timbral discrimination through learning to identify various instruments and voices in ensemble settings. Later in the curriculum this skill can be intertwined with transcription work wherein listeners are required to identify the individual instruments that are producing the separate lines they are transcribing. In general, it is important to contextualize timbral listening, at the very least presenting listeners with musical phrases rather than single notes, since listeners use a variety of cues to determine timbre. In a study of college students' perceptions of timbre, Kendall (1986) found that "accuracy using whole phrases was significantly greater than when using single notes" (p. 210).

---

3. For a musical introduction to the acoustical bases of timbre, see Levarie and Levy (1980, 63–65). The literature on and scientific principles that underlie timbre and timbral perception are discussed in Handel (1989, 169–73), Campbell and Greated (1988, 141–64), and Butler (1992, 64–77, 129–42). Butler's two chapters are accompanied by fifteen sets of listening examples on compact disc, which form an excellent starting point for the exploration of timbre. The sound sheets that accompany Pierce (1983) also contain a few examples of this type.

Special instrumental timbres can also be explored through specifically designed exercises and transcription. These special timbres include various string techniques such as pizzicato, snap pizzicato, col legno, and sul ponticello; muting of various instruments; stopped horn; and—if desired—the vast array of extended techniques developed during the past century.[4]

Even more refined timbral listening can be practiced, listening for such parameters as waveforms, overtones, envelopes, transients, and formants, particularly with the use of synthesized sounds (see, for example, Risset and Wessel 1999). At this point, distinctions can be made between *timbre* and *tone source* identification (Roederer 1995, 152–53), leading to a reexamination of the very definition of timbre itself (see Butler 1992, 64).

Tessitura and Register

The two main types of pitch solmization—fixed and movable—and their various subspecies are octave-neutral. In other words, they do not specify the octave in which any particular pitch occurs. Thus, a perfectly executed solmization of any given aural stimulus could map equally well into any register. It is therefore incumbent on listeners to attend to the specific register of what they hear. This kind of activity can be introduced during the earliest days of pitch training, at least once the notions of the octave and octave equivalence have been presented.[5]

Just how listeners discern registral placement is quite a complicated matter. As Butler (1992) notes, "Octaves are easily confounded: often, even people with absolute pitch can label chromata [pitch class[6]] with amazing accuracy, but err when identifying the octave within which the tone is placed" (p. 62). Listeners' familiarity with any given sound source has a direct effect on their ability to determine registral placement. For example, oboists will be much more adept at judging the octave of a pitch played on an oboe than that of one played on a French horn. Short of requiring students to log hours on each and every instrument, listening to recordings and performances while reading scores provides an excellent source of this familiarity across a broad range of instruments.

4. See Adolphe (1991, 13, 18, 19) and Pratt (1998, 71–83) for further suggestions that concern listening to instrumental and vocal timbres.

5. An interesting survey of the literature on the perception of octave equivalence appears in Handel (1989, 344–47). See Thurlow and Erchul (1977) for interesting evidence that not all Western listeners (both trained and untrained) perceive pitch similarity at octave multiples.

6. In standard pitch-set terminology, a single pitch class subsumes all pitches equivalent under enharmonicism and octave equivalence. Thus, for example, all C♯s and D♭s in any octave belong to the same pitch class.

Several types of listening activities can attune listeners to the registral placement of what they hear. One such activity is a simple drill and response, for which listeners are presented melodies (at least at first with relatively narrow ranges) whose general range they are to identify. This can begin, if necessary, with simple identifications such as "low," "middle," and "high." More specific registers can be identified by octave designation or by approximate placement on an appropriate staff. Such activities can and should be carried out with the sounds of various instruments and voices. General designations for registers are particularly useful and enlightening in these contexts. Listeners should be able to identify the differences between chalumeau and clarion clarinet registers, or pedal tones and the brilliant upper range on the trombone, or the G and E strings on the violin, or perhaps even "chest" and "head" voice (although this is much more dependent upon individual singers and their choices of tone production for particular notes). Later, when full-fledged dictation is practiced, dictations can be given without starting pitch or clef. In this way, listeners must also try to determine the proper octave in which to place the pitch classes they hear and identify.

Tempo

Let us divide tempo identification into two broad categories, *static* and *dynamic*. Static tempo—the unchanging speed of a pulse—can be identified in two different manners. One means of identifying static tempi uses the somewhat broad, rather subjective indications collectively known as *tempo*: terms in Italian, German, French, and English such as *Allegro, Langsam, Animé,* and *Moderately.* Overlapping at times and somewhat subjective, such tempo indications do not always apply neatly as right and wrong answers (was that *Andante* or *Moderato*?). In addition, some tempo indications that are either more suggestive of mood than speed (*Misterioso; With quiet grace*) or merely vague in and of themselves (*Mesto*). Nevertheless, discussions can surround which indications might be most suitable or evocative for a listening excerpt, and quizzes and tests might ask for an "appropriate" tempo indication or a choice from a carefully selected group of tempi. A second means of identifying static tempi is that of the metronome marking ("M.," "M.M.," or "MM," for "Maelzel Metronome"). Such markings take a form such as "$\bnotehalf = 80$," which indicates that the half-note beat unit progresses at a rate of eighty per minute.

Once a particular level of pulse is agreed upon (see chapter 2), most listeners can learn to make very accurate judgments about the metronomic value of a particular static tempo.[7] This kind of tempo judgment

7. For a review of the standard literature on static tempo perception, see Brown (1979).

involves matching a musical stimulus against some memory or memories for preexisting tempo, and most listeners are capable of recalling repeatedly heard performances within 8% of their original tempo (Levitin and Cook 1996). Thus, memories of several particular compositions, each performed at a particular tempo, can serve as a points of reference for determining various tempi. Learning to count seconds ("one thousand, two thousand, . . .") can serve as an additional point of reference.[8] Continued involvement in tempo judgment activities is worthwhile: research by Madsen (1979) shows that listeners "improve in assessing tempi with repeated trials" (p. 63).

Even when a performance includes expressive tempo fluctuations it seems that listeners manage to infer a steady pulse frequency that approximates the single statistically average tempo for the entire performance (Repp 1994). As Gabrielsson (1988) put it, "If you measure the performance of a phrase and calculate its average tempo, you may find that this average tempo in fact never appears at any position in the phrase—it is an average of a continuous variation. But as a listener you find it quite natural and adequate" (p. 33).

Dynamic tempo conditions—changes in tempo—may also be represented in both linguistic and numeric terms. One variety of tempo change might be referred to as a "quantum" change: an immediate, abrupt change from one tempo to another. Language used to indicate this type of change includes the following:

- The insertion of a new tempo indication after another has been in force (e.g., *Allegro* after a *Largo* section);
- An instruction relative to the prevailing tempo (e.g., *Plus lent; doppio movimento;* ♩=♪);
- An instruction to return to a previous tempo (e.g., *tempo primo*)

Numeric indications of immediate tempo changes take the form of a new metronome marking inserted in the music. Perception of quantum changes in tempo has been investigated by Wapnick (1980), who found that "the perception of tempo change is not very precise" (p. 11) and that such perceptions tend to cluster around perceived doublings and halvings of the original tempo.

Another variety of tempo alteration involves a gradual change of the rate of pulse. This type simply indicates a speeding up (e.g., *accelerando*) or slowing down (e.g., *ritardando*) of the tempo over some span of time, usually terminating in a specific new tempo. Ellis (1991) offers a concise survey of the scientific literature on the perception of gradual changes in tempo and reports the results of an experiment that found that the

---

8. George Pratt (1998, 54–56) discusses this technique in further detail.

minimum percentage of tempo change necessary for detection by most musically experienced listeners falls in the narrow range between 5% and 8%, with the exception of extremely slow starting tempi (MM48 in his study), which required a nearly 12% change to be noticed. With these perceptual thresholds in mind, exercises and tests can be devised that ask for suitable indications for listening excerpts, which will help to instill listeners with appropriate terminology and symbols for the temporal events they hear.

Dynamics

Traditional terms and symbols for dynamics can be presented and discussed in relation to exemplary listening excerpts. As with tempo, both sudden and gradual changes in dynamics can be heard and labeled with appropriate means (*p, ff, cresc.*, etc.).[9]

Whereas musicians commonly refer to an absolute form of measuring tempo—the metronome marking—they make no routine deference to any absolute measurement of dynamics. Such fixed means—measurement in decibels, phons, or sones—are typically left to the realm of scientists and engineers. Nevertheless, it is additionally instructive and illuminating to introduce the concept of amplitude and acoustical and psychoacoustical measurements of loudness at the earliest stages of learning. The causes and effects of actual and perceived differences in musical dynamics can be explored in this way.[10]

Articulation

Yet another musical feature that can be addressed in advance of the pitch and rhythm materials in the following chapters is articulation. Sensitive listeners should be able to discriminate among various types of articulation—general varieties and some of those specific to certain instruments.

At the broadest levels, listeners can discriminate between passages played legato and staccato. An infinite world of gradations between these two extremes can be explored; at the least, two intermediate articulations can be introduced—leggiero (or non legato) and portato.

Listeners can also learn to identify the presence or absence of accents and to discriminate among their various types: for example, the simple

9. An excellent discussion of this appears in Read (1979, 249–59).
10. For a more detailed discussion, see Butler (1992, 78–88). Also see Howe (1975, 5–6, 20–22), Backus (1977, 91–106), Levarie and Levy (1980, 60–63), Roederer (1995, 85–99), and Radocy and Boyle (1997, 89–99).

dynamic accent (i.e., >), *sf, fp*, and even the agogic accent. Further investigation can be guided into the causes of various accents, such as dynamics, rhythm, meter, harmony, pitch, contour, and expressive timing.[11]

Instrument-specific articulations can also be explored at this stage. Among these are various types of bowing and pizzicato on string instruments, diverse kinds of tonguing on wind instruments, and assorted percussion articulations such as the roll and choke.

Conclusion

Although none of the features discussed in this chapter is essential for further progress in an aural skills curriculum, they are all important aspects of musical composition and performance that every educated musician should be able to identify and discriminate among aurally. Whether they are covered prior to the pitch and rhythm materials in the following chapters or studied together with them, these features should be a part of every curriculum in aural training.

---

11. See Lerdahl and Jackendoff (1983, 17) and Kramer (1988, 86–87) for categorization of accents into three types (stress, rhythmic, and metric) and the differentiation between *types* of accents and their *causes*.

Preliminary Listening Skills

M any courses of study in aural skills begin with "basic" musical components such as scales, intervals, and chord identification.[1] This chapter proposes a model for the beginning of a curriculum in aural skills that starts with more fundamental concepts and skills and builds— like a mathematics text—on few assumptions and develops each new idea from previously assimilated ones. The curriculum makes no assumptions about prior training in music notation but, rather, relies on certain musical abilities and aptitudes in order to build listeners' skills and knowledge.

Pulse and Meter

The discussions of temporal features that follow apply only to music that is metric (thereby excluding such ametric musics as chant, some non-European folk music,[2] and some graphically scored works that have appeared since the 1950s). Meter and rhythm are addressed in that order intentionally to point up the learning sequence advocated herein: apprehension of metric characteristics (and, even before that, pulse) necessarily precedes that of rhythm. Particular attention will be paid to making various temporal features palpable to listeners and to diagnosing, developing, and testing listeners' metric and rhythmic skills.

---

1. See, for example, the two most popular texts for listening skills according to the survey conducted by Pembrook and Riggins (1990). They are (1) any of the first three editions of Benward and Kolosick (1991) and (2) either edition of Horacek and Lefkoff (1989).

2. For example, the *honkyoku* repertoire for the Japanese *shakuhachi*.

Perception of Pulse

Of all the abilities involved in temporal aspects of music listening, perception of the pulse is perhaps the most fundamental. From it derive the sensation of meter, the notion of beat, and the measurement of rhythmic durations.

We need a simple and unpolluted method for testing pulse perception. Although we are often tempted to equate "test" with "paper and pencil," in the case of pulse perception paper and pencil are ineffective tools for the job.[3] Instead, we can measure listeners' *physical* responses to pulse. Madsen, Duke, and Geringer (1986) were thinking along similar lines when they wrote that "perception of a beat or duration might be better differentiated by having subjects perform (conduct) rather than take a pencil and paper test" (p. 108), but conducting should *not* be used at this stage, since it combines pulse perception with the hierarchical organization of pulses into meter. Clapping works well, since it is meter-neutral (if done evenly). Tapping a level surface such as a desktop is also appropriate and can logically and smoothly progress into conducting when meter perception is assessed (Karpinski 1990, 213–14). Thus, early testing (say for an entrance or placement exam or very early evaluation within a course of study) might be given individually in person. Such individuals can be asked to "clap steadily" along with some music. Although there are many possible wrong answers, there are always several correct ones, depending upon which level of pulse a given individual chooses.[4]

Notwithstanding the necessity to test pulse perception without written responses, when one is progressing beyond such initial testing in this area it is necessary to make a transition to written symbols. To examine listeners' perceptions of pulse, meter, and rhythm as interrelated but separate features of music, there is a need to separate what listeners understand of what they hear from their ability to notate what they have understood. For this purpose, we can use a kind of protonotation—first proposed in Karpinski (1990)—for representing meter and rhythm without regard to particular notational manifestations tied to individual beat units. Thus, the meter signs and rhythm symbols of traditional Western notation can be avoided for a time, in favor of concentrating on perception of the pulse, meter, and rhythmic proportions.

3. See Gardner (1985, esp. pp. 3–4) and Boyle and Radocy (1987, 97–98) for critiques of paper-and-pencil testing.

4. Radocy and Boyle (1997, 126–30) survey experimental studies on pulse and tempo perception, which show that listeners tend to gravitate toward a pulse level in the approximate range of 60 to 120 beats per minute, conceptually doubling or halving rates of stimuli when necessary to fall within this range. For further discussion of how these various levels interact, see "Hypermeter," later in this chapter.

Example 2.1. Beethoven, Symphony No. 7, mmt. 2, mm. 3–10, three common responses to the request to "clap steadily" along with the music.

This is where the first component of such a protonotation system comes into play: a series of vertical lines can be used to represent pulses. Example 2.1 shows mm. 3–10 from the second movement of Beethoven's Seventh Symphony, which—it is assumed here—would be presented aurally to listeners who have no recourse to the notation. Three likely responses to the request to "clap steadily along with the music"[5] are printed above the score, with vertical lines replacing the claps.[6] Each of these responses represents a different level of pulse. Each is correct, and individuals who can infer such steady pulses without additional cues (such as notation or "preparatory beats") are ready to apply the technical term "pulse" to their experience and to begin exploring how these levels relate and create meter and hypermeter.[7]

At this point, we might define "pulse" as a "regularly recurring feeling of musical stress." The word "regularly" is included to avoid confusion with the varying rhythms that also vie for subjects' attentions at this stage. The word "stress" is included to represent the *feeling* of emphasis subjects have already experienced (created by repetitive rhythms, melodic shape, dynamics, articulation, harmonic changes, or whatever).

5. In fact, these three responses are taken from those frequently elicited from subjects in the classroom.

6. Compare the similar symbology in Kramer (1988, e.g., pp. 102, 107, and 129).

7. This experiential approach to meter is based in part on various theoretical notions of metric structure and hypermeter. See Cooper and Meyer (1960), esp. pp. 2–11, 42, 60–87, and 88–99); Cone (1968, esp. pp. 39–43; he coined the term "hypermeasure" on p. 40); Komar (1971, esp. pp. 49–69 and 151–61); Yeston (1976); Schachter (1976; 1980; 1987); Lerdahl and Jackendoff (1983), particularly with regard to "metrical structure"; Kramer (1988, esp. pp. 81–107 and 112–20); and Rothstein (1989). Some of these ideas are implemented in Karpinski (1981) and Steele and McDowell (1982). Adolphe (1991, 23) suggests some broad instructions for listening to various levels of pulse.

Example 2.2. Beethoven, Symphony No. 7, mmt. 2, mm. 3–10, primary and secondary pulses incorporated into one horizontal series of vertical lines.

Perception of Meter

If two of the adjacent levels of pulse in Example 2.1 are isolated—say, the upper two—then some interesting and useful relationships can consequently be made evident. It can be noted that pulses that coincide between the two levels regularly convey a greater amount of stress than the others (since they acquire stress from two levels, not just one). Once these two types of pulse have been experienced by a listener, technical terms may be attached to them: "primary" for those pulses that regularly evoke more stress and "secondary" for those that evoke less. The vertical lines can be adjusted accordingly to accommodate this information and incorporate the two levels into one horizontal series of differentiated pulses, with larger lines indicating primary pulses and smaller ones indicating secondary pulses, as shown in Example 2.2.[8]

At this point, we can provide listeners with a definition derived from these experiences as follows: music that exhibits any such regular differentiation into primary and secondary pulses has *meter*.[9] Conducting can also be introduced at this point, since it is a musical and practical means of responding to and representing meter. The duple pattern is all that is needed here, but as other meters are explored other appropriate patterns can be added.

8. See Karpinski (1981; 1990, 202) and Johnson-Laird (1991, 91–92) for earlier implementations of this symbology. Compare the similar graphic representation of five "metric time levels" in Jones (1990, 203).

9. Similarly, Yeston (1976) requires the presence of at least two levels of pulse in his definition of meter (pp. 65–67), as do Lerdahl and Jackendoff (1983, 19). As for the specific musical features that *result* in metric perception, see Dawe, Platt, and Racine (1994), which includes a literature review. Also see the survey in Lee (1991, 63–75), which includes synopses in the form of a table (p. 64).

Example 2.3. Beethoven, Symphony No. 3, mmt. 1, mm. 631–38.

It is important to note that all of this—primary and secondary pulses and a sense of meter—can be heard without recourse to a score. These are characteristics heard and felt by listeners before being seen in notation.[10] However, few aural skills textbooks isolate meter perception as a separate fundamental skill. As a small exception, Fish and Lloyd (1964) offer one exercise in "finding the meter of a composition" through listening to recordings or live performances (pp. 34–35). In contrast, most do not address the issue at all; and when they undertake dictation, they supply meter signs, bar lines, and a total number of measures for each dictation.

At this point, the fundamental distinction between duple and triple meters can be broached. A brief reexamination of the music in Example 2.2 yields the fact that primary and secondary pulses occur in pairs, thereby leading to the definition of duple meter. There are—as mentioned previously—several "correct" levels of perceivable pulse, certainly more than two for this excerpt. This means that there are also several possible "correct" perceptions of the meter. (More on this shortly.)

Example 2.3 shows a melody from Beethoven's Third Symphony accompanied by two levels of attendant pulse. Note that these two (carefully chosen) levels of pulse relate to each other in a 3:1 proportion. Thus, every third pulse is a primary pulse (as shown in Example 2.4), leading to an experientially based definition of triple meter.

We can begin to derive units of measurement at this point. The current discussion uses the term "pulse" to refer to a point in time. In this usage, a pulse has no duration and cannot, therefore, be used to measure anything in and of itself. Instead, pulses act as points of demarcation in our measurement of musical time. Durations between successive pulses—introduced here by definition as *beats*—can serve as units of that measurement.[11]

10. See Steedman (1977), Longuet-Higgins and Lee (1982), and Miller (1993) for information on the cues listeners use to infer pulse and meter.
11. Compare Lerdahl and Jackendoff's (1983) use of the term "beat." As part of their definition, they state that "beats, as such, do not have duration" (p. 18), thus using the term "beat" for what we call pulse here.

Example 2.4. Beethoven, Symphony No. 3, mmt. 1, mm. 631–38, primary and secondary pulses incorporated into one horizontal series of vertical lines, showing triple meter.

The current discussion uses the term "beat" only as a measurement of duration in music. Thus, it would be incorrect to refer to "feeling the beat" (where the term "pulse" should be used) or to say a "tango beat" (where the term "rhythm" should be used; see the following discussion). We can, however, refer to primary and secondary beats (those beats that begin with primary and secondary pulses, respectively).

We can now begin to recognize the significance of pulse groupings and use those as units of measurement as well. We call the duration from one primary pulse to the next a *measure*. The number of beats per measure is a consistent characteristic of individual meter types: two beats per measure in duple meter, three beats per measure in triple meter, and so on.

At this stage, listeners are armed with enough experience, concepts, and technical terms to move on to discussions of hypermeter and rhythm. But it is also possible to proceed with more complicated meters directly from this point, so we will delay the introduction of hypermeter and rhythm until later, in order to discover how other meters grow out of basic duple and triple ones.

Avoiding all other meters (even quadruple meter) up to this point has caused us to focus on the fundamental nature of duple and triple metric conditions and the essential difference between the two. This leads to the following principle, which will guide discussions of meter and hypermeter throughout this book:

> Any relationship between two adjacent levels of pulse is either duple or triple at its simplest; otherwise, there is an intervening level that divides that larger number into some combination of twos and/or threes.[12]

12. Lerdahl and Jackendoff (1983) note that "time-spans between beats at any given level must be either two or three times longer than the time-spans between beats at the next smaller level" (p. 20). Lester (1986) makes a similar restriction: "In tonal music . . . for all practical purposes we may consider recurring duple and triple groupings as the only ones" (p. 46).

Example 2.5. Schubert, Symphony No. 9, D. 944, opening, showing three levels of pulse incorporated into quadruple meter.

Quadruple meter is a simple case in point. In order to achieve four pulses for every primary pulse, one must admit *three* levels of pulse: one at the unit or beat level, another that groups those units into pairs, and yet another that groups that middle level into further pairs.[13] Example 2.5 shows the opening of Schubert's Symphony No. 9, D. 944, above which its three levels of pulse are shown in a composite set of vertical pulse lines that distinguish among the three levels—weakest pulses (2 and 4), stronger pulse (3), and primary pulse (1)—through vertical length.

Of course, there is no way to audibly distinguish whether anything with three (or more) adjacent levels of duple pulses has been notated in duple or quadruple meter. Schubert could have just as easily written the notation shown in Example 2.6. And Beethoven could have just as easily written the notation shown in Example 2.7.[14]

Although the path frequently operates in the reverse, from duple to quadruple, it does not always do so. Music notated in duple meter might not be correctly rebarred in quadruple. Consider Example 2.8, a folk tune notated in $\frac{2}{4}$. It could not properly be rebarred in $\frac{4}{4}$ simply by eliminating every other bar line: the triple hypermetric structure of the music would require rebarring in $\frac{3}{2}$. Similarly, Bartók's "Slovak Young Men's Dance" (Example 2.9) would defy rebarring in $\frac{4}{4}$ because of its asymmetrical hypermetric structure.

13. Of quadruple meter, Lerdahl and Jackendoff (1983) state that "the lengths of time-spans multiply consistently by 2 from level to level" (p. 20). Lester (1986, 47) includes quadruple meter with compound meters because both types of meter signatures indicate the interactions among three or more levels of pulse (two or more levels of interaction).

14. This is not to say that there are not other reasons for composers' choices of particular meter signs—reasons subtly communicated to readers and performers. Note, as extreme examples, meters such as $\frac{1}{4}$ in Varèse's *Intégrales* and $\frac{8}{4}$ in Bartók's Fifth Quartet. See Read (1979, 159–63) for an extensive list of such interesting meter signs. To this date, I am unaware of any studies that test the audibility of duple versus quadruple meters from performances. To the extent that works in duple meter are audibly indistinguishable from works in quadruple meter in that they exhibit duple hypermetric grouping, such studies would arguably be of little practical value.

Example 2.6. Schubert, Symphony No. 9, D. 944, rewritten in duple meter, representing only two adjacent levels of duple pulse.

Since the preceding discussion has included the notion of how three adjacent levels interact, it is possible to introduce the concept of compound meter as the next logical consequence of the current line of inquiry. Example 2.10 shows the French carol "Un Flambeau, Jeanette Isabelle."

Previously we found that quadruple meter exhibits three levels of pulse: one at the unit or beat level, another that groups those units into pairs, and yet another that groups that middle level into further pairs. But here, in the case of the folk melody in Example 2.10, we see an eighth-note-level pulse, another that groups those units into *threes*, and yet another that groups that middle level into pairs. Those three levels of pulse may be represented as shown in Example 2.11.

Such notation, which shows beats as combining by threes into pulses that themselves combine by some larger grouping into measures, represents *compound meter*. The folk melody "Un Flambeau, Jeanette Isabelle" is in *compound duple* meter since its measures are divided into pairs of threes (and in contrast we refer to simple duple, simple triple, etc.).

The same process may be employed to arrive at compound triple meter, wherein a beat level is grouped into threes and yet another level groups that middle level into *threes*. Example 2.12 shows the Canadian folk song, "Un Canadien Errant" written in triple meter.

Example 2.7. Beethoven, Symphony No. 7, mmt. 2, mm. 3–10, rewritten in quadruple meter, representing three adjacent levels of duple pulse.

Jé - sus- Christ s'ha - bille   en   pau - vre: Fai- tes- moi la   cha - ri -   té!

Example 2.8. French folk song, "Jésus-Christ s'habille en pauvre."

Example 2.9. Bartók, "Slovak Young Men's Dance," *Ten Easy Piano Pieces*, No. 3, mm. 1–19.

Example 2.10. The French carol "Un Flambeau, Jeanette Isabelle" in triple meter.

Example 2.11. The French carol "Un Flambeau, Jeanette Isabelle" with three levels of attendant metric structure represented.

Example 2.12. The Canadian folk song "Un Canadien Errant" in simple triple meter.

Example 2.13. The Canadian folk song "Un Canadien Errant" with three levels of attendant metric structure represented.

The three levels of pulse in the Canadian folk melody may be represented as shown in Example 2.13. The three levels represent the *compound triple* nature of the melody. This process may be extended to compound quadruple, compound quintuple, and so on.[15] It is important to note that—as in the relationship between quadruple and duple meters—a compound meter is audibly indistinguishable from the triple meter that forms its measure divisions.

Although it is possible to proceed with discussions of more complex meters (such as asymmetrical, variable, or mixed ones) at this point, we will instead explore how still further levels of pulse interact.

Hypermeter

It might seem pedagogically appropriate to reserve a topic such as hypermeter—one that appears mostly in the pages of journals aimed at an audience of scholars[16]—for more advanced levels of study, but it is quite appropriate to flow naturally from the relationships discovered while investigating the interactions between only two or three levels of pulse to the larger-scale relationships unveiled by the study of many such layers. Lerdahl and Jackendoff (1983) remark that "typically there are at least five or six metrical levels in a piece" (p. 21). These range from what John Buccheri has called the "fastest tappable pulse"[17] to large levels of metric

---

15. The extended compound groupings 15, 18, and even 21 are unusual but not unheard of. See Read (1979, 160–63) for references to notable appearances of such meters.

16. See the references under "Perception of Pulse" earlier. Also see the survey in Smyth (1992) and the critical assessments in Krebs (1992) and Hasty (1997, 48–58).

17. In a presentation to the College Music Society Institute for Music Theory Pedagogy Studies in Aural Skills, Missoula, MT, June 1992. He first referred to "tappable pulses" in Buccheri (1990, 131).

structure where "the listener's ability to hear global metrical distinctions tapers and finally dies out" (Lerdahl and Jackendoff 1983, 21).[18]

If we return to the opening measures of the second movement from Beethoven's Seventh Symphony as an example, we can extend the simple metric principles discussed earlier to broader levels of organization. Recall the principle set forth in "Perception of Meter," that "any relationship between two adjacent levels of pulse is either duple or triple at its simplest; otherwise, there is an intervening level that divides that larger number into some combination of twos and/or threes." In the excerpt from the Seventh Symphony, each and every level groups into the next larger one in a duple fashion. In this manner, as shown in Example 2.14, eighth notes pair into quarters, quarters into measures of $\frac{2}{4}$, measures into pairs of hypermeasures, and so on, creating two-, four- and eight-measure groups (and even larger ones for some listeners).

At this juncture, listeners should be exposed to other possible combinations of two- and three-group levels. In theory, any level can manifest itself as duple or triple; in practice, most Western music admits triple groupings at smaller levels much more readily than at broader ones.[19] Consider Example 2.15, the violin's opening phrase in Franck's Sonata in A Major for Violin and Piano. In this music, the two fastest levels group into threes, whereas all subsequently broader levels group into twos.

Such structures are eminently audible, and such audition is easily assessable through extensions of the clapping and tapping techniques discussed earlier under "Perception of Pulse." Conducting also serves as a useful assessment tool, with the ictus capable of falling on various levels of pulse from the submetric through hypermetric.

Further discussion of hypermeter is reserved until chapter 5, as part of an examination of more advanced activities.

Rhythmic Dictation

Listening to and notating rhythms without pitch comprise an activity with a long-standing tradition of its own. Most of the fifty-eight lessons in White (1935) contain some rhythms "for practice and dictation." The Eastman Series's *Teachers Dictation Manual* by McHose (1948) is organized into four broad parts: "Rhythmic Dictation," "Melodic Dictation," "Harmonic Dictation," and "Harmonic Counterpoint." McHose advises

---

18. Some theorists have argued that hypermeter operates on quite deep structural levels; others have questioned the significance of hypermeter altogether. See Krebs (1992) for an examination of both sides of the issue. For our purposes it is sufficient that subjects are capable of perceiving many levels of metric structure and drawing musical conclusions from where and how those levels form into larger groups.

19. According to Kramer (1988), "It is certainly possible, though less than common, to establish three-beat hypermeasures as normative on some level" (p. 107).

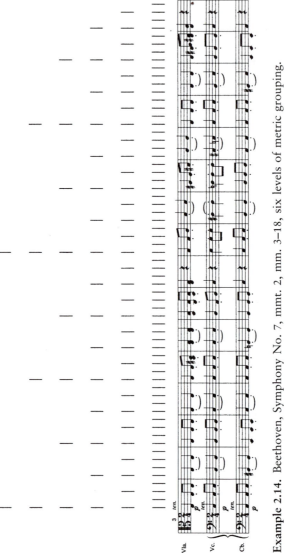

Example 2.14. Beethoven, Symphony No. 7, mmt. 2, mm. 3–18, six levels of metric grouping.

Example 2.15. Franck, Sonata in A Major for Violin and Piano, mmt. 1, mm. 5–12.

that "rhythmic dictation precedes melodic and harmonic dictation" and "although rhythmic dictation is concerned only with developing the recognition of meter and time values, the instructor should realize that he is establishing the foundation for melodic and harmonic dictation" (p. 3). Over one-quarter (twelve out of forty-two) of the dictation exercises in Hindemith (1949) are for rhythm alone (see pp. 185–231). A recent example of rhythmic dictation is Benward and Kolosick (1996a): each of its sixteen units contains one or two sections titled "Rhythmic Dictation." This is also a popular component in computer-assisted instruction software, such as *Practica Musica* (Kirkland, WA: Ars Nova), *MusicLab* (Redmond, WA: Musicware), and the software that accompanies Benward and Kolosick (1996a).

Whereas there is no inherent pedagogical problem per se with such isolated rhythmic dictation, one must consider its efficiency as a means toward developing comprehensive listening skills. One variety of rhythmic dictation asks listeners to notate from a purely rhythmic stimulus. This will have little direct application for all but unpitched music.[20] Another asks listeners to notate only the rhythms of melodies. In such instances, the stimulus is now contextual, but the response is still somewhat acontextual. But as students develop their listening skills, they should be striving to remember whatever portion of a musical passage they are working out at any given time, *including both its rhythms and pitches*. This means that in taking purely rhythmic dictation they will discard whatever pitches they have remembered after each listening. Because of this, it seems more musical and more responsive to the innate behavior of musical memory to contextualize rhythmic listening, understanding, and notation as part of the broader study of melodic dictation. Metric and rhythmic cognition play an integral role as part of this more comprehensive process—particularly as practitioners begin to grapple with each remembered section of music. Therefore, discussions of rhythmic memory, understanding, and notation will be delayed until they can be dealt with in melodic contexts in chapter 3.

Pitch

The discussions of pitch-related skills that follow in this chapter apply almost exclusively to tonal music, and—not surprisingly, considering the preliminary nature of the skills being addressed—to largely diatonic music as well.

---

20. Instructors should consider the degree to which unpitched music might play a role in the academic and professional careers of their students and adjust the amount of this activity accordingly.

Pitch Matching

This examination of pitch matching is separate from that of pitch memory because they are in fact two different skills. Pitch matching involves producing a sound to match a stimulus *while* that stimulus is sounding; pitch memory involves some delay (a rather short one for our purposes here) between the stimulus and the response.

Pitch matching does not necessarily involve any memory but, rather, entails a feedback loop that operates during concurrent stimulus and response: subjects sing (or play) to match a given pitch. At its coarsest, it is a matter of reaching a tolerable proximity to a target—something within fifty cents of it at the very furthest. At its finest, it is a specific type of intonation—at the unison or at some octave replication.[21]

In attempting to develop the aural skills of a subject who finds it difficult to reach the tolerable proximity mentioned earlier (one who sings an E when presented with an A, for instance), it is important to bear in mind that this difficulty is a symptom for which there might be one of several causes. First, problems in vocal production might impede what would otherwise work properly. There are individuals who might be capable of matching pitches but whose voices behave unpredictably. Such individuals often report a feeling of responding incorrectly without knowing in what way and can even identify with some accuracy those instances when they are correct. One must be careful of such self-reporting, however. Students seem to jump at the opportunity to blame their voices for other problems;[22] the actual percentage of adult musicians whose vocal production truly impedes their pitch-matching abilities is probably quite small.[23]

Second, some individuals have had little or no experience with matched pitches in general (those percussionists without experience on pitched instruments come particularly to mind here). In such cases, rather than have a student make repeated unsuccessful attempts at matching pitches, one remedy is to have the *student* first sing a note,

21. Both types are distinguished from scale-degree matching, which is more appropriately assessed and developed during work on music reading and performing. See especially "Inculcating Scale and Solmization" in chapter 6 and "Interval and Scale-Degree Strategies" in chapter 7.

22. Note, for example, the frequent number of coughs from an otherwise "healthy" sight-singing student while struggling with a difficult passage. However, see the survey of studies on vocal production and its effects on pitch discrimination in children in Shuter-Dyson and Gabriel (1981, 64–65, 217–20).

23. See the section titled "Vocal Production" in chapter 6 for some suggestions on improving the use of the voice as a tool in aural skills training. For an excellent (but now slightly dated) review of the literature on pitch-singing difficulties in general, see Welch (1979).

which an instructor then matches.[24] After the feeling of pitch matching is established in this manner, the instructor can tell the student to follow the matched pitch as the instructor moves higher or lower via portamento. After this, moves can be made by step or skip. Finally, the *instructor* should initiate pitches within that range for the student to match.

Third, there may be psychological factors at work. Davies and Roberts (1975) noted that "it would seem wise . . . not to label a child as a monotone or even as a 'poor pitch singer' too early, since secondary difficulties associated with the classification may persist after the child is capable of singing in tune" (p. 35). This also extends into adulthood. In one case study at the University of Massachusetts, a student who had been labeled a "nonsinger" in grade school still suffered from that experience through her undergraduate training. Instructors should be sensitive to the fact that aural skills classrooms are generally not conducive environments for dealing with such problems, nor can private meetings between student and instructor always get to the heart of the matter. If such psychological difficulties are strongly suspected, the best course of action may be to refer such students to psychological counseling.

Certainly such gross difficulties in pitch matching should already have been dispensed with for any level of musical training beyond the most basic. Nonetheless, as Pembrook and Riggins (1990) noted, "Ear training teachers indeed are grappling with vexing pedagogical questions" (p. 240). Among those are the causes and remedies for students with deficiencies in pitch matching.

As far as the finer aspects of pitch matching are concerned, one must bring to bear one or more of the intonation-improving techniques pedagogues and researchers have developed over many generations.[25] Perhaps the most ubiquitous is attention to the *beats* that are produced by two slightly mistuned pitches.[26] The frequency of these beats changes as a result of the difference in frequency between two mistuned pitches. Two very closely mistuned notes will produce extremely slow beating (for example, A440 and A442 will beat twice each second). Butler (1992) aptly describes the phenomenon as the mistuning increases: "As the pitches of the two tones are moved apart, the frequency of the beating increases;

24. Compare the technique of finding and working with a "personal note" in Roberts and Davies (1976).

25. Salzberg (1980) provides synopses of various techniques along with an excellent literature review. Note that the current discussion is focused narrowly on intonation during pitch matching and not on the intonation of various intervals, the perception of which is a much more complicated phenomenon; see Siegel and Siegel (1977) and Wapnick, Bourassa, and Sampson (1982).

26. For information on the acoustical causes of the phenomenon of beats, consult any good introductory text on acoustics—such as Backus (1977, 49–51), Levarie and Levy (1980, 67–68), or Campbell and Greated (1988, 36–37, 60–61)—or a good introductory text on music perception: Butler (1992, 56).

before the beats fuse into a perceived third ('subjective') tone, they take on what many listeners describe as a 'rough' sound" (p. 56). Sensitivity to beats and roughness is an integral part of intonation.

The phenomenon of beats seems to be particularly apparent between sustained sound sources with simple timbres produced at the unison. Combinations of more complex timbres complicate matters. For instance, Campbell and Greated (1988) state that "beating between complex tones is less straightforward to analyse, since many pairs of component pure tones can be beating simultaneously" (p. 37). This is important to consider because a common method of testing pitch matching—in the aural skills classroom, for vocal auditions, and so forth—involves asking individuals to sing to match a pitch produced on a piano. Voice and piano both produce relatively complex tones, and the differences in timbre between them are great. In addition, the piano produces sounds that begin to decay immediately after their attack. Thus, the intensity of the feedback loop diminishes proportionately and a point is reached at which it produces no usable feedback. While effortless matching of various sound sources (particularly the piano, which remains omnipresent in many educational settings) is an important goal, in some cases it becomes necessary to facilitate what might otherwise be an impossible task. One way is to ask students to match pitches voice-to-voice: an instructor vocally models a pitch, which a student then attempts to match.[27] The gender match between instructor and student plays a role in the success of this method. Obviously, cross-gender pitch matching (female instructor with male student or vice versa) can involve replication at the octave—a slightly more complicated task. Another option is to place a student's face quite close to an audio speaker that is producing a steady sustained pitch, which the student is to match. The interference beats become quite pronounced under these circumstances.[28] However, it is possible that musicians do not use beat discrimination in judging intonation in real musical contexts. On the basis of subjects' judgments of intonation in two-part musical fragments, Rasch (1985) concluded that "beats do not play a role of much importance in the judgement of the intonation of our musical fragments" (p. 456).

Visual feedback has been shown to have a positive lasting effect on pitch-matching and intonation skills. Several studies have tested the efficacy of such techniques. For example, Welch (1989) found that two groups that received real-time visual feedback training over the course of a single school term "recorded a significant improvement in their vocal pitch matching ability compared to the control group" (p. 85). This feedback can take the form of the tried-and-true stroboscopic tuner; its sim-

---

27. Compare the technique wherein an instructor matches a student's pitch first, discussed in the immediately preceding text.

28. I would like to thank Monte Tubb for suggesting this technique.

pler, less expensive, and more portable descendant, the match-needle tuner; or one of several software-controlled computer input devices.[29] Visual and aural feedback, like that provided by the *Pitch Master*, has also been shown to be effective in improving pitch accuracy (Brick 1984). Directed study with such equipment can increase sensitivity to and accuracy in pitch matching and intonation.

Verbal feedback is also very effective. Salzberg (1980) provided subjects with specific contingent verbal information about intonation between trials. These subjects "performed with the most accurate intonation," significantly better than subjects who received no feedback, better than those who listened to recordings of their first trials, and better than those who were presented with model performances. Similar results are reported in Albert (1967). Welch, Howard, and Rush (1989) found that "a combination of verbal and visual feedback may be the optimum form of qualitative feedback" (p. 156).

Interestingly, Salzberg (1980) found that model performances of excellent intonation presented between trials did not help at all. She concluded that university music majors "had already internalised the correct models, and additional models did not further improve the perception of intonation" (p. 47).

Finally, it should be noted that many musicians who have reached the university, college, or conservatory level demonstrate only small improvements in intonation skills. Fogarty, Buttsworth, and Gearing (1996) concluded that "much of the 'steep' part of the [intonation] learning curve has already been covered by the time these students commence the study of music at a university level" (p. 169).

Pitch Memory

A delay between stimulus and response in pitch reproduction logically involves some kind of memory. Of particular interest here is *short-term* pitch memory—on the order of a few milliseconds to perhaps several minutes[30]—for it serves as the basis for so much of the cognitive musical processes that follow. In discussing tasks in which subjects are to distin-

---

29. Stroboscopic tuners—popular in teaching wind players—are made by Peterson, among others. Match-needle tuners are marketed by many manufacturers, including Korg, Roland, and Matrix. Commercial computer pitch-tracking devices with software aimed at developing intonation range from *Sing!* and *Music Lab* (Redmond, WA: Musicware,) to *SmartMusic* (Eden Prairie, MN: Coda Music Technology).

30. An experiment by Kauffman and Carlsen (1989) implied that "short-term memory is at least 180 s in length with music" (p. 11). Some recent models replace the idea of short-term memory with "working" memory, which accounts for both storage and processing of information. See Berz (1995) for a literature review and proposal that regards working memory in music.

guish between two tones (rather than reproduce the first) Crowder (1993) wrote that "to perform a delayed same-different task absolutely requires that the first stimulus be preserved in some form—remembered—until the second stimulus arrives" (p. 123).[31]

Two basic types of activities can be used to test memory of individual pitches. The first is *recognition*, and the second is *recall*. Recognition requires subjects to listen to a single pitch and then—after some delay or interference—to a second pitch. They respond by identifying whether the second sound had the same pitch as the first. This is an instance of the classic "same-different" recognition tests used frequently in various fields of cognitive studies. The delay might be a short silence or range to one on the order of several minutes; it might be filled with some interference such as spoken numbers or even more pitches.[32] Whereas most conditions had little effect on listeners' performance of the task, if the delay was filled with further pitches then performance dropped significantly (Deutsch 1970a; 1970b). This drop in performance—known generically in various types of memory studies as "interference" or, more specifically, "retroactive interference" or "retroactive inhibition"[33]—has profound implications in aural skills training and music listening in general. Those individuals who are significantly afflicted by retroactive inhibition have great difficulty remembering pitches, motives, and melodies that are followed by more musical material.[34]

The second activity that can test memory of individual pitches—recall, or the ability to reproduce pitches—is perhaps more immediately practical in much aural skills training: it is more common that musicians and music students find it necessary to *reproduce* a pitch than merely to identify whether some later pitch is the same as an earlier one. Many of the learning sequences and diagnostic procedures advocated in these pages depend upon students' abilities to reproduce pitches. In particular, recalling portions of dictation materials, responding to modeled patterns, and establishing keys from given pitches all rely heavily on this skill.

Just as important as memory for single pitches, perhaps more so, is listeners' abilities to remember melodies. This skill is crucial to much aural training, other types of music training, and many musical pursuits in general. Pembrook (1987) put it thus: "Melodic memory is an impor-

---

31. Pitch memory seems to be separate from other types of brain functions: researchers (for example, Deutsch 1970b) have shown that pitch memory is coded in a nonverbal way. More generally, compare Gardner's model of musical intelligence, which he views as separate from other intelligences (see Gardner 1985 and 1993).

32. See the survey in Deutsch (1999, 391–400).

33. See, for example, Deese and Hardman (1954) and Jenkins and Dallenbach (1924). Put another way, the mere passage of time does not cause forgetting, but the influx of competing information does; see Reitman (1971).

34. For further information on the musical implications of retroactive inhibition, see the discussions in the following chapter, which specifically addresses dictation skills.

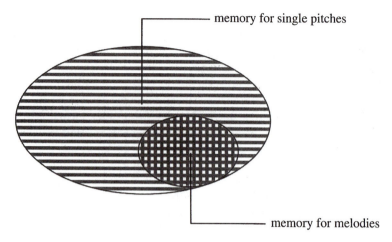

Figure 2.1. A Venn diagram that represents a speculated relationship between memory for single pitches and for melodies.

tant skill for musicians to possess. Whether it is used as the basis for taking dictation, recognizing the return of a theme in the recapitulation section of a piece, or providing the basis for improvisatory excursions from a given 'riff' as is common in jazz performance, melodic memory needs to be exercised. Techniques that help augment individuals' abilities in this area can only strengthen musicians and the field of music as a whole" (p. 157).

One might posit a simple superset/subset relationship between (1) those subjects capable of remembering single pitches with consistent accuracy and (2) those subjects capable of remembering melodies with equal aplomb—a relationship like the one shown in Figure 2.1.

In reality—depending, of course, on the difficulty of the melody (a subject addressed in chapter 3)—the relationship manifests itself as two intersecting sets, as shown in Figure 2.2. *A* represents those who can remember single pitches. *B* represents those who can remember melodies. *A*∩*B* represents those who can do both. *B*' (the complement of B—all A not in B) represents those who can remember single pitches but not melodies. *A*' (the complement of A—all B not in A) represents those who can remember remember melodies well but not single pitches. Why does this final class of listener exist at all? To answer this question, it is sufficient to note at this point that two important factors listeners use in remembering pitches are context and contour.[35] Single pitches presented

35. See the discussion later in this chapter. For a good survey and discussion of experimental studies of these factors, see Sloboda (1985, 177–87). A more recent discussion appears in Dowling (1994). An even more recent survey—and experimental

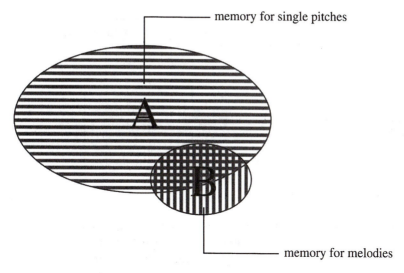

memory for single pitches

memory for melodies

Figure 2.2. A Venn diagram that shows the actual relationship between memory for single pitches and for melodies.

in isolation possess neither. Although less complex than the combinations of tones that make melodies, isolated pitches afford none of the referential features created by context and contour. Knowing this, we find it understandable that certain subjects can reproduce melodies with flavor and character after having balked at reproducing individual notes *in campo aperto*.[36]

Memory of Pitch Collections

After hearing a passage of diatonic music, well-trained listeners should be able to reproduce the pitch classes that make up its pitch collection. This is a basic skill, essential for any substantial work in the diatonic system, crucial as a point of reference in tonal music, and similarly useful for application to listening experiences in other pitch collections, such as whole-tone and octatonic. Evidence of this recall usually takes the form of singing a scalar pattern, ascending, descending, or both. For example,

evidence that listeners use contour, interval, and scale-degree information in remembering diatonic music—can be found in Freedman (1999).

36. Serafine (1988) remarks that "it appears that the perception of single pitches does not necessarily precede the perception of groupings of multiple pitches. In other words, the discernment of single pitches is not the prerequisite to the perception of musical wholes" (p. 63). The significance of this skill is explored further in the section titled "Short-Term Melodic Memory" in chapter 3.

a.

b.

Example 2.16. (a) Stimulus melody; (b) Listener response.

when presented with the melody shown in Example 2.16(a), certain listeners respond with the scale shown in Example 2.16(b).

In this example, in addition to indicating a recall for a pitch collection, listeners informally indicate an inference of tonic by starting and ending the scalar response on that pitch. The reader will note, however, that the current discussion—of recalling a pitch collection—is separated from the one addressed in the next section: inference of the tonic. The two do not necessarily go hand in hand.[37] It is not uncommon for individuals to be able to reproduce the pitch classes of a collection without being able to identify a tonic. As a separate skill such listeners frequently exhibit memory for pitch collections (without regard to a tonic) by singing unidirectional scalar patterns, beginning on various scale degrees, and trailing off or truncating rather than ending with a meaningful pitch (Example 2.17).

---

37. Butler and Brown (1994) make the scale–collection distinction: "It should be emphasized that there is an important difference between *scale* and *pitch set* [i.e., collection]: while pitch sets are not necessarily ordered or grouped in any certain way, scales are conventionally ordered within an octave span, and also ordered so that they form a ladder-like arrangement. The order of tones in any scale is a matter of convention and convenience, but it does not impose any necessary order on the pitches as they may be used in a piece of music" (p. 199).

However, Butler and Brown do not make a clear distinction between collection and *tonic*. Listeners have inferred a diatonic collection when they discern (consciously or intuitively, directly or indirectly) the position of the two diatonic half steps. Within any diatonic collection, the music may lead listeners to hear certain members of that collection as exhibiting pitch centrality. Within common-practice-period tonality, that centrality is manifested as a sense of *tonic*; in medieval and Renaissance modality, it is a sense of *final*. Any diatonic collection is capable of harboring various different finals and tonics. Within any diatonic collection, the tonicization of one of its pitch classes is a product of ordering, structural placement, metric organization, and other factors. Nor do Butler and Brown fully address the tonic implications of scales. More than being merely "ordered within an octave span," the terminal pitches of an octave-bounded scale are culturally imbued with a sense of tonic due at the very least to the overwhelming number of scales practiced and learned indelibly by musicians during their studies.

a.

b.

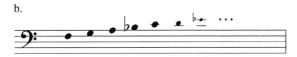

Example 2.17. (a) Stimulus melody; (b) Listener response.

What processes are involved in recalling the collection of a musical passage? In some ways, it seems that such recall should entail a simple expansion of pitch memory: from memory of a single pitch to memory of all pitches in a passage. But it may be that a process is at work here similar to that posited by Brown and Butler on tonic inference: that listeners can often infer the collection of a diatonic passage "swiftly and apparently without conscious effort" (Butler 1992, 119).[38] In fact, bringing "collection inference" into this discussion might help to clear up some of the ambiguities in the literature on tonic inference.[39]

Butler's conclusion has been that "the listener makes the perceptual choice of most-plausible tonic on the basis of style-bound conventions in the time ordering of intervals that occur only rarely in the diatonic set; that is, minor seconds (or enharmonics) and the tritone" (Butler 1989, 238). One could probably substitute the term "diatonic collection" for "tonic" in that passage (pace Butler) and arrive at another truth, one that begins to clarify the separate nature of collection inference: the listener makes the perceptual choice of most-plausible *diatonic collection* on the basis of style-bound conventions in the time ordering of intervals that occur only rarely in the diatonic set; that is, minor seconds (or enharmonics) and the tritone.

No formal studies have been carried out on the ability to *reproduce* the pitches of a diatonic collection independent of the tonic and serial order of melodic presentation.[40] However, Krumhansl and Kessler (1982) did ask for some pitch-collection *recognition* in an experiment in which subjects were instructed to judge "how well, in a musical sense, each

38. Their references are mainly to tonic inference, but the analogy holds.

39. Recently (e.g., in 1998) Butler has begun to distinguish between "diatonicity" and "tonal meaning." Cross, Howell, and West (1985) distinguished between "scale" (i.e., collection) and key for their studies of "scalar conformance." See the discussion immediately following under "Inference of Tonic."

40. Williams (1975) presented subjects with pitch series scattered randomly across the *chromatic* collection. There are other similar studies.

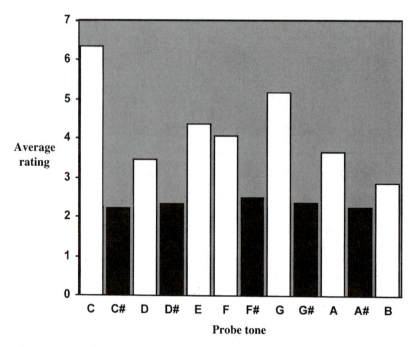

Figure 2.3. Probe tone ratings for C major after Krumhansl and Kessler (1982, 343) and Krumhansl (1990, 30). Used with permission.

probe tone fit into or went with the musical element just heard"—a scale, a "tonic triad chord," or a three-chord cadence (p. 342). While such experiments are justifiably targets of criticism,[41] they form a start for the purposes of determining what pitches subjects recall from a musical stimulus. Figure 2.3 reproduces the C-major profile from this experiment.[42] Note that the diatonic pitch classes C, D, E, F, G, A, and B (the white bars) form peaks (that is, they were recognized more often as "fitting" with the stimulus) and that the chromatic pitch classes C♯/D♭, D♯/E♭, F♯/G♭,

41. For example, Butler (1989) criticized this study, noting that "direction and contour, repeated tones, implied harmonic succession, and serial position of the tones" could all likely affect subjects' judgments (p. 228). If this experiment is regarded as a test of tonal hierarchy and tonic inference such factors do indeed pollute the results. But if it is regarded as a simple test of short-term memory for pitches in the diatonic collection the results seem straightforward enough.

42. Note that this figure represents the data (which are discrete, not continuous) in the form of a bar chart instead of a line graph, with white bars representing diatonic pitches and black bars representing chromatic ones. Also note how this color scheme maps directly onto the piano keyboard. The data are taken from Krumhansl (1990, 30).

Example 2.18. Schumann, Symphony No. 3, mmt. 5, mm. 17–19.

G#/A♭, A#/B♭ (the black bars) form valleys on the graph (that is, they were recognized less often as "fitting" with the stimulus). In addition, note that no chromatic pitch class was rated higher than any diatonic pitch class: the highest-rated chromatic pitch class, F#, received a 2.52 rating; the low-estrated diatonic pitch class, B, received 2.88. Nothing surprising here: given a set of seven elements to remember, human subjects tend to remember them rather well (Miller 1956).

However, consider the fact that the subjects in this study "had received instruction on musical instruments and voice for an average of 10.9 years" and "performed for an average of 12.0 years in instrumental groups and 2.1 years in choral groups" and were "playing music an average of 3.1 hours per week and listening to music for 23.3 hours per week" (Krumhansl and Kessler 1982, 341). How are we to account for the fact that not all diatonic probe tones received a perfect rating and not all chromatic ones received no score at all? Perhaps these results indicate that not all musicians are perfect at the task of recalling diatonic collections. But these results might also be a product of the vague instruction to judge how well "each probe tone fit into or went with the musical element just heard," in the sense that a chromatic pitch might just as easily "fit" or "go" after a diatonic passage. Consider, for instance, how well D♭ "fits" after the passage in the three-flat diatonic collection shown in Example 2.18. If it had not "fit" in *some* sense, would Schumann have written it?

Other studies also use tonal (presumably diatonic) series for recognition tasks rather than reproduction. In one such study, Long (1977) noted that "pitches embedded in the tonal melodies were much easier to remember than pitches embedded in the atonal ones" (p. 280). Williams (1980) came to a similar conclusion. Cross, Howell, and West (1985, 132–139) summarize several experiments designed to test recognition of and memory for nondiatonic pitches (at which subjects performed significantly well, even when given only minimal diatonic cues). None of these experimenters asked subjects to *reproduce* all or as many of the diatonic pitch classes as they could.

In clinical settings, I have encouraged subjects to freely explore singing the pitches they have heard in a melody. I have discovered a few principles from their experimentation. First, to avoid mere repetition of the melody, I instruct them to sing in a scalar fashion. Second, to avoid some of the

Example 2.19. Stimulus melody for recall.

tonic-implying influence of a simple ascending scale, I ask them to choose a high pitch in the passage and sing *down* by scale from it on any neutral syllable,[43] continuing until *I stop them*. These qualifications—that subjects descend, and do so without syllable labels, and without their own intended terminal pitch—help (at least in part) to avoid serial ordering and tonic inference as parts of the unique process of reproducing a diatonic collection.

Some individuals balk at singing pitches as a collection extracted from a melody; others, even after recalling the melody correctly, sing incorrect pitches for the collection. In a typical response of the latter sort, a listener would—for example—hear a melody in G major, choose a B as a starting pitch, and then sing the pitches of a descending B-major scale. This inability to extract the pitches of a melody as an abstract list is a fundamental failure that can cause a complete breakdown in the learning sequence. If it can be remedied at all, that will be achieved through repetitive modeling on the part of an instructor and careful guidance in painstakingly comparing the pitches in a melody with a cautiously measured note-by-note response.

Inference of Tonic

Refer now to Example 2.19. One student's response to the request to "sing back" this seven-note melody was completely accurate with regard to pitches and rhythms. However, he balked at applying syllables. I offered him the opportunity to spell the letter names of the pitches directly in the key of D♭ What follows is a transcript of his subsequent responses:

STUDENT [sings the melody correctly on neutral syllable *la*]
    GSK . . . suppose I were to tell you that that was in the key of D♭ Could you tell me what the notes are?
STUDENT [after thirty-second pause] It was in what key again?
    GSK D♭
STUDENT D♭. Would it be G♭, D♭, F, D♭, . . . E♭ . . . That's not what I needed to do.
    GSK OK, try it again.

---

43. This has further advantages in tonic inference, as noted in the next section.

STUDENT	OK, I know what I want to do. A♭, D♭, . . . G♭, D♭, . . . F, D♭.
GSK	Sing the tune again.
STUDENT	[sings the melody correctly on neutral syllable *la*]
GSK	All right, and so then the pitches would be . . . again . . . Say what you said.
STUDENT	I don't think I have it right. I was trying to go from *sol* to *do*. . . .
GSK	Well, try those syllables out, what you were thinking of. Try it on syllables.
STUDENT	OK, I tried to go [sings] "*Sol, do, fa, do, mi*, . . . *fa, sol.*"
GSK	Now, rethink what you were doing. What's the one thing you didn't do?
STUDENT	Didn't establish the key.
GSK	That's right. So where is *do?*
STUDENT	[sings high *do* correctly]
GSK	. . . and low *do*—that might help you, too.
STUDENT	[sings low *do* correctly]
GSK	That's right. So where does it start?
STUDENT	*Mi.*
GSK	Yes . . . and so?
STUDENT	[sings] *Mi, sol, re, sol, do, mi, sol.*
GSK	Excellent. Good.

If all we were to have from this student were a notated response, there would be no way of discerning the nature of his errors. His initial response would have begun with the pitches G♭, D♭, F, D♭, and E♭; his subsequent "correction" would have begun with A♭, D♭, G♭, D♭, F, and D♭. Such answers could have easily been caused by errors in memory, as well as notation. However, the interview transcribed here reveals that the fault lay in his understanding of the scale-degree functions of the pitches and that the underlying cause of that was a single error: his failure to properly infer the tonic.

Inference of the tonic is at once magical to behold and diabolical to understand. At its most facile, the process seems intuitive.[44] Many listeners can infer tonics from passages—often remarkably short, even isochronous ones[45]—yet cognition researchers have struggled to explain just how this feat is accomplished. Among the most recent—and to my mind most elegant and accurate—explanations of the process is one put forward by Helen Brown and David Butler. In a series of papers and publications over nearly two decades, Brown and Butler have refined a "theory of intervallic rivalry," which Butler (1989) summarizes: "Any

44. Butler (1989) wrote that "tonally enculturated listeners can recognize the tonal center in an unfamiliar tonal composition almost instantly, and without visible effort" (pp. 237–38).

45. The term "isochronous" refers to events of equal duration that occur at regular intervals.

tone will suffice as a perceptual anchor—a tonal center—until a better candidate defeats it" (p. 238).[46]

Brown and Butler concluded that the presence of the rarest interval classes[47] (ics) from the diatonic collection—ic1 and ic6—and the temporal ordering of pitches are significant factors in determining how listeners infer the tonic of a passage. But, as suggested previously under "Memory of Pitch Collections," it is possible that listeners use ics 1 and 6 as cues to ascertain the diatonic collection, whereas they use the temporal ordering (and perhaps structural, metric, and registral positioning) of the pitches to infer the tonic. Indeed, West and Fryer (1990) found that changes in order of the seven diatonic pitch classes cause listeners to infer pitches other than the major-mode tonic as a tonal center. And Brown, Butler, and Jones (1994) found that the temporal ordering of merely the three pitches of a major triad can influence listeners to infer different tonics. Note that neither ic1 nor ic6 is present in a major triad. The absence of ic6 renders ambiguous the triad's diatonic membership status: it could be a subset of three different diatonic collections.[48] In the specific case of Brown, Butler, and Jones's stimulus, [C–E–G] could belong to the one-sharp collection, the one-flat collection, or the no-sharp/flat collection. The ordering <C–E–C–G> caused listeners to prefer C as the most appropriate completion tone. The ordering <C–G–E–C> caused listeners to prefer F as the most appropriate completion tone. When either of these orderings was followed by <F>, the collection's ambiguity was reduced by one-third, since the F eliminated the possibility of the one-sharp collection. Nonetheless, without the presence of either B or B♭ to make certain the embedding diatonic collection, listeners rated F as less appropriate following the first ordering and more appropriate following the second. What this suggests is that the process of tonic inference operates in part independently and on the basis of different criteria from the perception of diatonic collections.[49]

46. Most of this research is summarized in Butler and Brown (1994).

47. In standard pitch-set terminology, there are seven interval classes (ics) in all, numbered 0 through 6 (representing semitones). A single interval class subsumes all intervals equivalent under enharmonicism, inversion, and octave equivalence. Thus, for example, ic4 includes all major thirds, diminished fourths, minor sixths, augmented fifths, major tenths, etc.

48. This book adopts the following working definition for "diatonic collection": any seven-member segment of the cycle of perfect fifths. You may also think of a diatonic collection as any collection given by a "standard" key signature. This assigns *chromatic* status to the raised sixth and seventh scale degrees in minor. Compare René Van Egmond and Butler (1997), who include harmonic minor and ascending melodic minor as diatonic collections.

49. See Huron and Parncutt (1993) for a synopsis of *structural* and *functional* approaches to understanding tonic inference (pp. 154–55) and for some interesting—and more successful—modifications of Krumhansl's tone profile studies.

But there are listeners who have difficulty with tonic inference. As Marvin and Brinkman (1999) noted, "The abstraction of the tonic pitch [aurally] from a musical surface is a common ability among musicians, but one in which errors are made" (p. 405). Some listeners are unable to respond after hearing certain passages; others respond, but with incorrect pitches. There are even listeners who must resort to explicit analysis of what they have heard in order to begin trying to calculate which pitch might be a tonic.[50]

So how should listeners go about developing their ability to determine the tonic of a passage? Initially, they should undergo some testing and drills on their ability to sense tonal closure. This can take the form of asking listeners to identify musical phrases that end with open cadences and those that end with closed cadences. However, given the limitations of interpreting binary responses, such exercises are circumscribed in their usefulness. Here are some further suggestions:

As mentioned previously in "Memory of Pitch Collections," the act of singing *down* from any pitch within a given diatonic collection is useful in guiding listeners to the tonic of a musical passage. Once listeners have heard a melody, they should choose any relatively high pitch within the passage and begin to sing down by step on any neutral syllable through the pitches of the diatonic collection. The descending direction has a specific benefit in this context: many music students seem to have been conditioned, through years of practicing multitudinous scales, to interpret descending stepwise motion as progressing toward a final tonic.[51] In my clinical experience, a majority of students who initially experience difficulties inferring tonics find that this descending scalewise technique works immediately. A particularly telling and rewarding sign is the illumination on students' faces when they slow down and arrive on the tonic, as if guided there by some power outside their control.

The minority of students who are still incapable of inferring tonics after working on such techniques have a musically fatal shortcoming that must be remedied if they are to pursue further study. They can begin to make up for years of missed or misdirected acculturation by intensive listening to strongly tonal music, particularly excerpts that do not modulate. In addition, they can practice copious amounts of solmization using

---

50. In my clinical experience, I have frequently encountered students who—upon initially failing to identify the tonic of a passage—turn to searching for the half-step dyads in the collection in order to proffer one or both of the upper members of those dyads as tonic.

51. Over a half-millennium ago, Gaffurius ([1496] 1968) recognized the power of descent to create closure: "A descent from high to low causes a greater sense of repose" (p. 50). Larson's "musical gravity" similarly accounts for this phenomenon. Larson defines musical gravity as "the tendency of an unstable note to *descend*" (see, for example, Larson 1997, 102, and 1993a, 70).

Example 2.20. A melody and mental encoding for its step/leap directional contour.

a functional system wherein a single syllable is always assigned to the tonic.[52]

Perception of Melodic Contour

Although it might seem logical to progress directly from tonic inference to scale-degree identification, an important intermediate step—one curricula often leave implicit—is discernment of melodic contour.[53] An important reason behind making this explicit is simple: if listeners are unable to determine the contour of a melody they have retained in short-term memory, they will have great difficulties calculating the scale degrees associated with its pitches.[54]

The current discussion assigns special status to two aspects of contour in diatonic melodies: (1) direction and (2) step-verse-leap motion. If a listener can accurately determine both of these, then scale-degree identification is greatly facilitated. One must carefully identify the scale degree of an initial pitch, follow the direction of stepwise passages, and carefully identify the scale degrees that follow leaps. For example, once listeners have heard and remembered the short melody shown in Example 2.20, its contour could be mentally encoded as shown below the music (with + representing ascending motion, − representing descending motion, s

---

52. See the following discussion under "Solmization Systems for Preliminary Listening Skills."

53. Two exceptions make the barest mention of melodic contour. Henry and Mobberley (1986) comment that two pages of diatonic patterns "are intended to focus students' attention on the direction of a stepwise melodic pattern. Each pattern involves six pitches and each has a distinct contour. As a preliminary exercise, students could listen to the patterns and draw their contours" (p. 58). Fish and Lloyd (1964) instruct that, for one set of stepwise exercises, "after several repetitions the class should be able to sing back the melody, while imitating its rise or fall by motions of the hand" (p. 20).

54. For the most part, the current discussion considers only note-to-note contour relations. However, listeners do make judgments about contour relations among nonadjacent notes (see Quinn 1999), and these can be taken into account during training as well.

representing motion by step, and 1 representing motion by leap, each separating pitches represented by •).

Listeners can write these symbols to convey their understanding of a melody's contour. Those who find such a symbology cumbersome may try the more intuitive (if less specific) techniques of tracing the shape with a hand in the air and drawing horizontal lines to represent the relative heights of the pitches.[55] Added benefits can be derived from performing this task silently in the mind. One study (Davies and Yelland 1977) found that such work improves the ability to recall a recently heard tonal sequence and draw its melodic contour. In fact, work that requires listeners to silently rehearse and manipulate familiar tunes can help develop aural skills in general. This process of hearing music mentally in the absence of the physical sound will hereafter be referred to as "auralizing."[56]

Contour can affect melodic memory. A dramatic example can be seen in one element from a diagnostic examination designed for use at two universities.[57] For this examination, examinees were to sing back brief melodic fragments as demonstrations of their short-term melodic memories. The most frequently and consistently incorrectly recalled fragment is the isochronous pitch string shown in Example 2.21(a), followed by the most common incorrect response in Example 2.21(b).

We can speculate about the causes for this response. The incorrectly recalled pitch falls precisely in the middle of the seven pitches. This places it as far as possible from the primacy and recency effects. However, many other seven-note stimuli do not produce such a high error rate for pitch 4 as that caused by this pitch string. Therefore, there must be some other force at work that causes the error. One possible explanation comes from what Larson (1993a) calls "musical inertia"—the tendency for listeners to think of a pattern of musical motion to continue in the same fashion—but without further study of this problem we can only speculate as to its causes.

55. I have profitably employed the former as a diagnostic tool in individual meetings with students and the latter as a part of entrance and diagnostic examinations.

56. Martin (1952) defined the verb "auralize" somewhat similarly as "to form a mental impression of sound not yet heard" and noted that "auralize" and "auralization" are "the counterpart in hearing to the terms 'visualize' and visualization' in seeing" (p. 416). It seems that the term "auralize" first appeared early in the twentieth century. Matthay (1913) referred to "the ability keenly to visualise, or auralise things apart from their actual physical happening outside of us" (p. 10). Robinson (1918, 20) defined "auralized" as "conceived by the ear," perhaps more similar to Larson's "to *hear as*," which he defines as "to give meaning to a sound by (subconsciously) assigning it to a category" (Larson 1993a, 70). Compare Edwin Gordon's neologism "to audiate," which he defines as to "hear *and comprehend* music for which the sound is no longer or may never have been physically present" (Gordon 1993, 13). These uses (Robinson, Larson, and Gordon) combine auralization and understanding—which the current definition of "auralize" allows us to examine as separate phenomena.

57. Used at the University of Oregon since 1988 and the University of Massachusetts since 1997.

a.

b.

Example 2.21. (a) A stimulus melody; (b) Most common incorrect recall.

In an analogous situation, it is helpful when beginning two-voice listening skills to develop listeners' skills at discerning the relative contours formed between two lines, expressed as the four basic types of contrapuntal motion: parallel, similar, oblique, and contrary. Demonstrations of these types of motion may be presented after listeners have mastered the basics of monophonic contour; subsequent drill and testing may take the form of contour following (through physical motion, drawing, or symbology) and multiple-choice responses that use the names of the four basic types of contrapuntal motion.

Identification of Scale Degrees

All of the pitch skills discussed thus far—matching and remembering pitches, recalling pitch collections, inferring tonics, and understanding melodic contour—are essentially preliminary to our next subject: aurally identifying scale degrees.[58] Inference of tonic and discernment of contour (particularly with regard to step-versus-leap motion) work together in listeners' minds as a framework for identifying the scale degrees of a melody's pitches. Once listeners have correctly inferred a melody's tonic and assessed its contour, they are then ready to determine its scale degrees. In the case of Example 2.20, they can ascertain the scale degree of the starting pitch ($\hat{3}$), follow the descending stepwise motion for the next two pitches ($\hat{2},\hat{1}$), determine the scale degree after the first leap ($\hat{5}$), follow the turnaround stepwise motion for the next two pitches ($\hat{6}$, $\hat{5}$), determine the scale degree after the next leap ($\hat{7}$), and resolve to the tonic pitch via ascending step ($\hat{1}$).

---

58. In a sense, listeners who have inferred a tonic have already identified a scale degree: $\hat{1}$.

But that scenario rests on the assumption that listeners can fluently and almost intuitively identify the scale degrees of pitches within a tonal context. An ultimate goal is for listeners to develop that sense, to hear the 3̂-ness of a 3̂, for instance. However, not all listeners begin their studies with this skill already in place. How can this skill be developed?

One method is inculcating listeners with a functional solmization system.[59] The constant association of a consistent set of labels with individual scale degrees will, in time, lead many listeners to link those scale degrees with their labels. Listeners for whom such links are not yet automatic and immediate can use a technique that will allow them to mechanically calculate the scale degree of any pitch in relation to the tonic. This technique consists of mentally isolating the unidentified pitch and the tonic, connecting the two by scale (singing the members of the diatonic collection on a neutral syllable), and figuring the scale degree of the unidentified pitch on the basis of its distance in diatonic pitches from the tonic. In practice, most people who use this technique perform better if they connect the scale *from* the unidentified pitch *to* the tonic rather than the other way around. This procedure allows listeners to travel from the unknown to the known—a much safer strategy for any traveler than trying to go from the known to the unknown. In many clinical settings, I have heard listeners isolate an unidentified pitch, sing the tonic, and then attempt to sing a scale from the tonic to the unidentified pitch only to sing right past their target—precisely because the target is unknown and therefore more capricious and ephemeral in memory. If listeners sing from the unidentified pitch through the pitches of the diatonic collection to the tonic, their (we hope, by this stage, reliable) sense of the tonic will guide them safely home. All that they need to do is keep track of the number of scale degrees traversed during this process in order to identify the previously unidentified pitch from which they started. Whereas this technique may seem rather mechanical and detached, it has the distinct advantage of being more accurate. And as listeners become more familiar with the tonal functions of the pitches they traverse, they can begin to identify the scale degrees of pitches on that more meaningful and immediate basis.[60]

In order to obtain more drill and practice in identifying scale degrees, several types of activities can be helpful. One involves playing a melody and asking listeners to identify the scale degree of either the starting pitch or the ending pitch. Another consists of establishing a key through a melody or chord progression and then playing isolated pitches for listeners to identify one by one while they retain the tonic in memory.[61] Yet

59. See "Solmization Systems for Preliminary Listening Skills" later for further description and discussion of these systems.

60. See Karpinski (1990, 215–16).

61. Several software packages—for example, the software that accompanies Benward and Kolosick (1996a)—include drills of this variety.

another asks listeners to work out all the scale degrees from various familiar melodies from memory without the aid of an instrument or notation.

Identification of Intervals

Interval identification is perhaps the most ubiquitous of all the atomistic ear-training activities. One need only scan certain introductory texts (for example, Horacek and Lefkoff 1989[62] or Ottman and Dworak 1991), sample one of the ubiquitous computer-assisted-instruction interval drills (such as the interval components of *Common-Practice* [Boston, MA: LeadingTone Software], *Practica Musica* [Kirkland, WA: Ars Nova], or dozens of others), or survey colleagues who teach beginning aural skills (as Pembrook and Riggins 1990 did; see esp. p. 237) to glean some sense of the frequency with which intervals are drilled, practiced, and tested. Rogers (1984) observed that "many schools and ear-training manuals spend enormous amounts of time (weeks, months, and even semesters) and space (chapters and even volumes) on interval identification" (pp. 104–5).

It *is* possible to obtain the pitches in a melody by calculating the intervals between each of its temporally adjacent notes. In order to do this, one must be given the name of the first pitch and be proficient at identifying melodic intervals. Although this approach is certainly feasible, it does bring with it several drawbacks when working with tonal music.

First, it causes errors to accumulate serially—that is, a mistake on one interval will cause *all* subsequent pitches to be incorrect by the magnitude of that mistake. As Lake (1993) noted, "A scale-degree strategy is most suitable for tonal melodies. A typical problem for an interval thinker is to misjudge a leap and then remain off by a step; thinking scale degrees, however, allows quick reorientation after such a mistake" (p. 57).

Second, a preponderance of experimental evidence shows little connection between the ability to identify intervals acontextually and the ability to do so in a tonal context. Shatzkin (1981), after surveying a dozen experimental studies of contextual and intervallic perception, noted "significant context effects" and remarked that "it is surprising that both research and ear training methods still concentrate on interval perception outside, rather than inside, a context" (pp. 111–12). Wapnick, Bourassa, and Sampson (1982) found that musicians were significantly more accurate at discriminating among and labeling intervals in a melodic context

---

62. The first 101 of the 479 pages in volume 1 are devoted to acontextual interval training. In contrast, compare Steele and McDowell (1982), in which singing and dictation are practiced using scale-degree numbers for 211 pages (nearly half the book) before intervals are introduced.

Andante grazioso

Example 2.22. Mozart, Piano Sonata in A Major, K. 331, mmt. 1, mm. 1–4.

than in isolation. Hantz (1984) offers two elegant examples of how tonal context affects interval perception (in equal temperament):

1. An interval that spans six semitones, the two pitch members of which exchange their scale-degree functions depending on context. For example, the pitches C and G♭ function as $\hat{7}$ and $\hat{4}$, respectively, in the context of a D♭ tonic, whereas their enharmonic equivalents C and F♯ (which sound the same as C and G♭ out of context) function as $\hat{4}$ and $\hat{7}$ in the context of a G tonic.
2. An interval that spans three semitones, which can be heard as a minor third or an augmented second. For example, G♯ and B function as $\hat{3}$ and $\hat{5}$ in E major, whereas A♭ and B function as $\hat{6}$ and $\uparrow\hat{7}$ in C minor.[63] In each, according to Hantz, "the two intervals are palpably, perceptually different" (p. 253).

Third, it seems that listeners remember and understand tonal music in terms of diatonic collections and scale-degree functions. Shepard and Jordan (1984, 138-144) found that Western listeners map the pitches they hear onto members of an "internalized musical scale." This occurs even if those pitches fall well outside Western tuning systems. Dowling and Harwood (1986) summarize a number of studies that point toward melodic memory mechanisms that encode "a sequence of relative pitch chromas (pitch levels in a tonal scale) rather than a set of intervals between tones" (p. 142).

Finally, we must consider the kind of musical thinking we wish to foster through aural training. Should we train listeners to calculate lists of intervals between successive pitches? This seems somewhat analogous to, say, training literature majors to list all of the phonemes or the number of letters in each word of a Shakespeare soliloquy? Such inventories would be true and eminently knowable, but would they be worthwhile and meaningful? Similarly, imagine listeners mentally encoding the opening melody from Mozart's Piano Sonata in A Major, K. 331, mmt. 1 (shown in Example 2.22) like this:

---

63. Special symbols will be used hereafter to represent the chromatic alteration of diatonic scale degrees. The symbol ↑ will be used to raise a scale degree one semitone, and the symbol ↓ will be used to lower a scale degree one semitone.

<+m2, −m2, +m3, P1, −P4, +M2, −M2, +m3, P1, −P4, P1, +M2, P1, M2, +m3, −M2, −m2, −M2>.

One step toward understanding some musical meaning of such a passage comes from knowing the *functions* of its pitches. And the tonal, melodic, and harmonic functions of pitches rest, at least in part, on their scale degrees. Thus, encoding the opening of K. 331 as this:

$$\hat{3}, \hat{4}, \hat{3}, \hat{5}, \hat{5}, \hat{2}, \hat{3}, \hat{2}, \hat{4}, \hat{4}, \hat{1}, \hat{1}, \hat{2}, \hat{2}, \hat{3}, \hat{5}, \hat{4}, \hat{3}, \hat{2}$$

seems, on functional grounds, to be a much more meaningful activity.

Dowling (1986) found that "the scale steps of melodic pitches are inseparable from their tonal functions, which in the diatonic tonal system carry their musical meanings. Thus, it seems reasonable to suppose that the moderately experienced listeners have access via scale-step representation to deeper levels of musical meaning than inexperienced listeners using surface-level interval representations" (p. 294). Thomson ([1969] 1975) concluded that "attempting to imagine the two pitches of an interval exclusive of any context beyond themselves is like trying to imagine two points in vision without spatial reference. Rigorous attempts at either seem equally fruitless; both must occupy positions in some form of auditory or visual background of space-time" (p. x). Rogers (1984) asserted that "success in melodic dictation does not depend on mastery of intervals or other fragments. Tonal dictation—and, surprisingly, even nontonal material to a large extent—can be hindered, in fact, by overreliance on a note-to-note type of hearing because it detracts from larger-scale connections that are both more important musically than surface details and also more important pedagogically because they make the learning of hearing easier" (p. 110).[64]

Some interval training, despite being placed early in the learning sequence, relies on fluency with functional scale degrees—perhaps more than some of its practitioners recognize or acknowledge. This kind of approach involves the association of specific intervals with familiar melodies.[65] This is such a common practice that any criticism of it in these pages probably risks alienating readership. Nonetheless, injunctions to learn to hear intervallically—for example, to hear all major sixths as the opening two pitches of "My Bonnie Lies over the Ocean"—warrant closer

---

64. For more on the subject of intervallic versus functional listening, see Rogers's (1984) other comments (pp. 110, 112, and 114–15) and Rogers (1983).

65. A classic example appears in Boatwright (1956): "A great help in learning intervals is to find examples among known melodies which can be instantly recalled. No list is given here because every person should have his own melody repertoire as a basis" (p. 15, fn.). White (1981, 35), calls for linking well-known tunes with specific intervals, too, and offers a list of eight "common ones" for intervals from the minor third through the minor seventh.

Example 2.23. Schumann, Piano Quintet, Op. 44, mmt. 4, mm. 115–18 (rehearsal F in the Peters edition).

scrutiny. Can listeners learn to hear *all* major sixths this way? *Should* they? The specific functional context for the opening two pitches of "My Bonnie Lies over the Ocean" is $\hat{5}$–$\hat{3}$. How here should listeners hear the first two pitches of the theme shown in Example 2.23, which function as $\hat{4}$ and $\hat{2}$? Scale degrees $\hat{4}$ and $\hat{2}$ form another major sixth, but it is counterintuitive and antimusical to ask listeners to associate them with the opening of "My Bonnie Lies over the Ocean," which functions quite differently.[66] Indeed, the simple distance between pitches has very little musical meaning compared to the position within the scale held by the pitches that form that distance. This means that, for instance, there are *several* major sixths worth knowing—each with its own attendant scale degree functions.[67] Intervals change their function and consequently their effect, affect, and meaning in different contexts. Coupled with the overwhelming empirical evidence that acontextual interval study results in little carryover into functional contexts, such questions about which specific context to study logically lead away from interval study in general and toward the study of individual scale-degree function instead.

In light of these concerns, it might be easy to conclude that interval training should be expunged altogether from the curriculum. But intervallic information is not altogether unimportant. Ottman (1956) found a strong correlation between accuracy at interval identification and achievement in sight-reading (although it is impossible to tell from his study which came first). Marvin (1995) concluded that "students need to develop a flexible memory retrieval system that is capable of both interval and scale degree information" (p. 44). Lake (1993) was more specific with

66. Rogers (1984) similarly warned of "the fallacy in assigning one particular effect or meaning for each interval, which specific melody references tend to foster" (p. 106).

67. The figured-bass theorists may have been among the first to recognize the special qualities of individual scale-degree functions with their notion of the "rule of the octave." Fétis attributed certain characteristics to specific scale degrees (see Fétis [1840] 1994, 159, for example). Schoenberg ([1934] 1975) defined "tonality" as "the particular way in which all tones relate to a fundamental tone, especially the fundamental tone of the scale" (p. 270). Zuckerkandl (1973) makes the argument via the fugue subject from Beethoven's Op. 110: "A man who hears [this] merely as three equal steps, three gradually ascending fourths, and fails to hear how the same acoustical interval takes on a new meaning as it ascends from $\hat{1}$–$\hat{4}$ through $\hat{2}$–$\hat{5}$ to $\hat{3}$–$\hat{6}$ . . . such a man does not hear music" (p. 114).

regard to which system is more applicable to particular types of musical materials: "Although some teachers concentrate solely on one or the other approach, the ideal strategy is a flexible one, utilizing intervals and scale degrees depending on the demands of the melody"; he also observed that an intervallic strategy works best for tonally vague and atonal melodies (p. 58).[68] Considering this, it seems wisest to move interval study to a point much later in the learning sequence and a time somewhat before tonally vague and atonal melodies are to be encountered.

But intervallic approaches should not be delayed for too long. Even before reaching tonally vague and atonal materials, listeners might find that certain figures (for instance, a skip to and from a chromatic pitch) present challenges for which—momentarily—interval measurement offers itself as the most direct tool for decoding the musical structure. Far better to be armed at such a time with the necessary tools and learn to use them flexibly than to be locked into a single approach. For functional tonal music, however, scale degrees remain the single most important feature of pitch. As Alldahl (1974) noted, "As important as the interval experience is, more important is the understanding of degree functions in a scale" (p. 114).

Identification of Scale Types

Yet another relatively acontextual activity is the identification of scale types. This typically involves the performance of a scale that listeners are to identify as "major," "minor" (perhaps including its several forms, e.g., "harmonic"), or possibly one of the various Church modes. Although not as amusical as the two-note stimuli used for interval training, scalar drills carry with them their own assumptions that (perhaps tacitly) serve to separate them from contextual tonal and modal perception.

The most fundamental of such assumptions is that the beginning and ending pitches in a scale are somehow (by presumption, declaration, fiat?) its tonic.[69] There are two flaws in this assumption: (1) not all scalar *passages* in actual musical contexts begin or end on their tonic,[70] and (2) not

---

68. Intervallic strategies do indeed play a much more important role in atonal music, but the current discussion is centered on tonal music. For two different approaches to atonal aural training, both of which are internally consistent and quite sound pedagogically, see Edlund (1964) and Friedmann (1990).

69. Computer-assisted instruction software frequently makes this assumption. Many such programs play a scale in order to establish tonic. For an example, see the scale-degree identification drills in the software that accompanies Benward and Kolosick (1996a).

70. Consider, as two examples, (1) the opening theme to the fourth movement of Beethoven's First Symphony ($\hat{5}$, $\hat{6}$, $\hat{7}$, $\hat{1}$, $\hat{2}$, $\hat{3}$, $\hat{4}$, $\hat{5}$, etc.) and (2) the second theme in the third movement of Brahms' First Symphony ($\hat{3}$, $\hat{2}$, $\hat{1}$, $\hat{7}$, $\hat{6}$, $\hat{5}$, $\hat{4}$, $\hat{3}$, etc.) (mm. 33ff.). Neither begins or ends on its tonic, but the function of each is clear because of its respective context.

all listeners inherently interpret such starting and ending pitches as tonics.[71] But if this assumption is made explicit to students, such exercises can at least serve as a means of drilling and testing memory for pitch collections and as a kind of precursor to truly contextual inference of the tonic,[72] in addition to serving as a series of interval stimuli that lead toward modal identification and labeling.

Solmization Systems for Preliminary Listening Skills

Among the tonal skills discussed in this chapter—pitch matching, pitch memory, memory of pitch collections, inference of tonic, perception of melodic contour, and identification of scale degrees—two benefit substantially from the application of solmization syllables. Those two are inference of tonic and identification of scale degrees; of the others, pitch matching and pitch memory are acontextual, memory of pitch collections should be carried out as a task of recall rather than analysis, and perception of melodic contour is best expressed in terms of shape through physical motion, drawing, or symbolic representation. Thus, we are left with the two functional skills: inference of tonic and identification of scale degrees.

Only two of the handful of solmization systems used widely for Western music explicitly model the tonal functions of the tonic and the scale degrees that relate to it.[73] Those systems are (1) scale-degree numbers, in which the tonic in all modes is sung as "1," and (2) the variety of movable-*do* in which the tonic in all modes is sung as "*do*." Each of these systems attaches an internally consistent label to the tonic regardless of mode or transposition level of the tonic. In addition, each system attaches a unique label to every scale degree regardless of transposition level.

Through constant association, 1 or *do* becomes a convenient, almost intuitive name for the tonic. Once learned, it quickly facilitates communication about tonic inference (see, for example, the previous discussion under "Inference of Tonic") and establishes a point of reference for hearing and performing tonal music. Likewise, the internal consistency of scale-degree labels in each system—once learned—provides a means of

---

71. Although many listeners have already been conditioned by this point in their instrumental or vocal studies to assume that the terminal pitches of the scales they perform are tonics.

72. No empirical studies have tested the efficacy of using scalar listening drills to develop *contextual* tonic inference.

73. This is not to say that other solmization systems do not have their place, only that they are inappropriate for modeling the tonal functions of the tonic and the scale degrees that relate to it. See the various discussions of the different applications of diverse solmization systems in later chapters.

examining perception of scale-degree functions and a tool with which to decode the symbols of tonal pitch notation.

Absolute Pitch

Listeners who possess absolute pitch (AP) must be treated in special ways. We should begin by understanding some of what is known about AP—what it is and what it is not. At its simplest, AP is the ability to identify the pitch class of a sound without comparison to any reference pitch.[74] In this way it is fundamentally different from functional relative pitch (RP—the ability to identify pitches with reference to a tonality) and interval identification (the ability to identify the distance between two otherwise acontextual pitches, a nonfunctional type of RP). In addition, some listeners use other cues that enable them to mimic AP. Some use the sensations of vocal placement—particularly at the extremes of their ranges—as points of reference. Others use instrumental timbre, including the intensity of particular formants or other instrument-specific cues such as registral changes (for example, the clarinet's "break" is one such cue). Such skills are not to be construed as AP; listeners with AP can recognize the "C-ness" of all Cs in a manner analogous to the way the color-sighted can recognize the blueness of all blues without reference to other colors.[75]

What special needs do students who possess AP have? Marvin (1995) notes that "absolute pitch musicians . . . need to develop a flexible system—one that uses not only the pitch-class information readily available to them, but also interval and scale-degree information that they often must be trained to use" (p. 44). In other words, AP listeners should develop the same kinds of relative listening strategies non–AP listeners use. Functional strategies are particularly important: tonal music derives a great deal of its meaning from these functions; identifying a series of unrelated pitches does not promote the understanding of this meaning. Marvin (1995) writes:

> If we ask AP students to listen to a harmonic progression and write Roman numerals only—without benefit of staff paper—they are often completely unable to do this, because they have not been

74. For more complete background discussions of the nature of absolute pitch, see Ward (1999), Takeuchi and Hulse (1993), Miyazaki (1989), and Costall (1985).

75. In recent years researchers have complicated our understanding of AP, redefining it as perhaps a group of related skills. Terhardt and Ward (1982) report that some subjects score at the level of chance on transposition-level recognition tasks, but that their responses are almost always within a half step of the target pitch. Levitin (1994) reports that *one in four* subjects recalled popular tunes at their exact pitch. Butler (1992) notes that "some people appear to have absolute pitch when the tones possess a certain timbre; that is, what might be called 'absolute oboe' or 'absolute piano.' Others seem to have 'absolute A' or 'absolute B-flat' " (p. 50).

trained to hear harmonic function. These students tend to transcribe letter names as quickly as possible, then return to their transcriptions and analyze for Roman numeral function. Even in the simplest of tasks, like interval identification, they tend to write (or think) letter names first and then analyze for the correct label. (pp. 54–55).

Miyazaki (1992) found that some AP listeners rely on AP to the exclusion of relative thinking. And any discrepancy between learned absolute pitches and a sound source can present great difficulties for those with AP: mistuned audio playback equipment; dictations to be written in keys other than what has been heard; regional and cultural differences in tuning; Baroque tunings; nonequal temperament; reading, singing, or playing in transposition; recognizing transposed motivic relationships in nontonal contexts (Mangeot 1953, 14; Butler 1992, 50; Miyazaki 1992; 1993; Marvin 1995, 58). In addition, it has been shown that many AP listeners can identify white-key pitch classes more fluently than they can black-key pitch classes (Miyazaki 1989; 1990; Takeuchi and Hulse 1991). Finally, it seems that many with AP find that at some time during midlife their perception of AP begins to "shift," eventually mapping once-learned pitch-class names onto incorrect pitches (Vernon 1977; Ward 1999, 280–81).[76]

What pedagogical accommodations ought to be made to meet these needs? Certainly a de-emphasis on notation with a concomitant emphasis on scale-degree numbers or movable-*do* solmization and Roman numerals will help AP listeners to develop their functional RP skills. Transposition of sight-singing and dictation materials should also be frequently employed. AP listeners can also benefit from increased training in keys with many sharps or flats and materials with many chromatic pitches to overcome their slower responses to black-key pitch classes.[77] Developing functional RP in those who possess AP will not only arm them with an effective strategy for dealing with the midlife "perceptual shift" that awaits them, but it will also help them hear tonal function—an essential feature of the language of tonal music.

As to whether individuals without AP can be trained to develop it, substantiation is unclear. After surveying the literature on the subject, Miller (1989) concluded that "there is very little strong empirical evidence bearing on the issue" (p. 63).[78]

76. This midlife perceptual shift seems to affect all listeners in the sharp direction—that is, if presented with the sound of A440, they would perceive it as B♭ a semitone higher. The effect seems to widen as subjects get older: I have spoken with musicians over seventy years of age who report their AP shifting by as much as a third.

77. See Marvin (1995, 58–59) for a more detailed description of such activities.

78. Although the book's focus is savants, this passage is about the etiology of AP in the general population.

Several main theories exist that attempt to explain how AP is acquired. One holds that AP is purely inherited. See, for example, Révész (1913), Seashore (1938), and Bachem (1940).

Another holds that it is an entirely learned skill. Early studies—Meyer (1899) and Mull (1925)—are questionable with regard to experimental method. Meyer used only two subjects (including himself) and achieved accuracy rates of 64% and 60% for the respective subjects over thirty-nine pitches (accuracy rates hardly qualifying as AP). He also noted that "we did not continue these experiments further, because the value of the acquired facility did not seem to us to correspond to the expense of time. Now, after several years have passed we have lost the greater part of what we had acquired, by the want of continued practice" (p. 516). Mull played a reference pitch for her twelve subjects with only a "short but effectual period of auditory distraction" immediately before trials (p. 478). Her subjects improved from 40.4% to 82% in recognizing middle C out of a set of nine pitches. Two further experiments used subject groups of four and two respectively—too small for obtaining valid results. A more recent study—Lundin and Allen (1962)—purported to show improvement in AP, but the authors seem to have accepted answers within a semitone on either side of the correct pitch as accurate. They began their study with only five subjects, a mere three of whom completed the training. Among those three, their improvements in percentage of correct pitch identification were as follows: (1) 54% to 100%, (2) 42% to 96%, and (3) 17% to 42%. Even though a subject base of three is not statistically valid, the results from the first two subjects are quite tantalizing. Another study—Brady (1970)—is unacceptable due to the fact that Brady used himself as his only subject and he achieved a success rate of only 65%, allowing for 97% "correct within ±1 half step" (p. 883). Cuddy (1970) used sets of only nine pitches—surely not enough to test AP judgment—and her reports of greater accuracy at the extreme ends of the frequency scale would seem to indicate that listeners were using pitch height and not chroma as a cue. In addition, some listeners freely reported that they "tried to concentrate on one tone in the series, kept 'imagining' the tone throughout the training and tests, and used the tone as a reference to judge other tones" (p. 269). These subjects were clearly using their powers of RP, and not developing AP at all. Yet another study—Rush (1989)—is somewhat problematic in that it did not test for pitches beyond those used in the training set (a commercial product) and found only moderate improvement in its subjects (with none moving clearly from the realm of non–AP possessors to that of AP possessors). Miller (1989) remarked that "such attempts have met with limited success, for the most part" (p. 44). Takeuchi and Hulse (1993) concluded that these studies are "not strong evidence that AP can be learned by adults" (p. 358).[79]

79. Also see the discussion in Ward (1999, 283–86).

Other theories suggest that most or all individuals are born with the ability, but that the development of RP pitch through acculturation or training suppresses and eventually eliminates AP. For example, nearly a century ago Copp (1916) argued that we are born with a predisposition for what she called "Positive Pitch," but that it will not develop unless properly conditioned.

Recent research postulates a critical childhood learning period (like that for language acquisition) during which AP may develop in some or perhaps all of the population if certain conditions are experienced. Crozier (1997) trained preschool and adolescent subjects for a period of six weeks and found that improvements in tests of AP were largely confined to the preschool group, who—after training—performed at a level "typically associated with AP possession" (p. 116). Only marginal improvement was found among the adolescents. Ward proposed that "everyone has the capacity to develop AP behavior but that it must be reinforced early in life and also subsequently or else it will be trained out by experience with RP" (Ward 1992). A team led by Nelson B. Freimer is focusing on the combination of genetics and environment. Their preliminary conclusion: "[Our] data suggest that both early musical training and genetic predisposition are needed for the development of AP" (Baharloo et al. 1998, 224).[80]

The jury is still out, in fact sequestered, concerning the genesis of AP. Certainly the question of whether AP can be acquired by adults remains unanswered. It seems, however, that the question, from the viewpoint of developing aural skills in general, is this: which musicians would end up with the most practical, musical skills—those trained for a certain number of months or years to improve their ability to identify absolute pitches or those trained for the same amount of time to develop their sense of RP? This question is perhaps too complex to answer with an experiment, but we act as if we have already answered it when we make certain pedagogical choices. For example, Levin and Martin (1988a) instruct students to use a tuning fork as a reference from which to sing A440 before all exercises. "Over a period of time," they write, "you will discover that your accuracy will improve until you have virtually 'memorized' the sound of A440" (p. 10). Multer (1978) called this "the beginning, it is hoped, of what will develop as far as possible in the direction of absolute pitch (for students who lack it)" (p. 33). We must decide whether the kinds of experimental results associated with such attempts warrant the devotion of time and effort to them.

---

80. See also Sergeant (1969) and Sergeant and Roche (1973).

3

Melodic Dictation

Melodic dictation seems to stand as an important focal point of undergraduate music training. Most aural skills texts—if they address listening at all—feature melodic dictation. For example, the first half of Kraft (1999) is devoted to melodic dictation, and the first sections in all sixteen units of Benward and Kolosick (1996a) are labeled "Melodic Dictation." Some universities, colleges, and conservatories offer entire courses titled Dictation; others—with course titles such as Ear Training or Aural Skills—nonetheless typically advertise melodic dictation prominently in their course descriptions. Working with melodic dictation can help to develop some very important musical skills such as musical attention, extractive listening, short-term musical memory, musical understanding, and notation. Because of its widespread use and the various skills it can develop, melodic dictation warrants close and extensive scrutiny.

The Inadequacies of Melodic Dictation

Although melodic dictation might take many forms—in terms of length, number of playings, duration between playings, playing in whole or in part, and so on—they all share the common objective that melodies, aurally experienced, be translated into music notation. Whereas notation is laudable as a final result, and an important tool, it is also frequently an inadequate means of determining perceptual and cognitive problems.

Example 3.1(a) shows a dictation melody that was presented to a class of fifty freshman-level university music majors. Example 3.1(b) shows a diplomatic transcription of one student's response to that stimulus.[1]

---

1. Students were given the following information: treble clef, C tonic, and eighth-note beat unit (no starting note or complete meter sign). The melody was performed

a.

b.

Example 3.1. (a) Dictation melody; (b) Student response.

It might seem—based on the music notation used to respond to this test—that this response contains but a small error (perhaps due only to carelessness). However, music notation alone can offer a rather unclear view into the perceptual and cognitive operations of the musical mind. Example 3.2 presents that same student's entire response, complete with a kind of protonotation (shown above the staff) that he was using to represent the meter, rhythms, and scale-degree functions of what he heard prior to translating that into actual music notation.[2]

We are now privy to some of the inner workings of his mind as he progressed from hearing this melody to writing it down. If we view the protonotation as a stage in and of itself, we see that—although the meter and rhythms are interpreted flawlessly—the scale-degree functions of the

Example 3.2. Student response to melody in Example 3.1(a), including protonotation.

at a tempo of approximately ♪ = 120. Three playings were given, with one minute between playings and two minutes after the final playing.

2. Durations are represented by horizontal lines drawn in relation to the vertical pulse lines. Scale-degree functions are indicated by first letters of movable-*do* solmization syllables, with "D" = *do* = 1̂, "R" = *re* = 2̂, and so on. The use of protonotation to represent the understanding of rhythm and pitch is examined at length later in this chapter.

pitches are almost entirely incorrect. In fact, the single pitch (the final note) that looked like a careless error upon examining only the music notation turns out to be the solitary scale degree that was perceived correctly!

This is all the data we have from this subject. We have no concurrent self-reporting commentary, no follow-up interview. Nonetheless, we can speculate a bit further about the nature of his errors without treading on much unsafe territory. It is possible that two errors have formed for the first three measures—a kind of double negative. The first error involved misidentification of the scale degrees.[3] The second error could be (and here we have no guide except common sense) one of clef: it is likely that this subject has mentally substituted bass clef for treble. Every syllable maps correctly onto a bass clef reading of his notation. Thus, in this instance, two wrongs *have* made a right: the errors have canceled each other out for twelve of the thirteen pitches.

The single example here, while perhaps exceptional in some ways, is nonetheless representative of many dictation responses in that the final product in the form of notation is not illuminating enough to reveal what went wrong (or even what went right) without access to the entire process. As Pembrook (1986) noted, "Without specific inquiries (such as having the student sing back the 'perceived' melody), any categorization of inaccurate reports as a function of improper perception or misuse of the notational system is mere speculation" (p. 239).

A Model for Music Perception and Cognition during Dictation

A simple model for music perception[4] can account for many such errors by separating the process of taking dictation into four broad phases (some of each with a number of their own subphases): hearing, short-term melodic memory, musical understanding, and notation.

Hearing

To start with, musical hearing involves the physical motion of the tympanic membrane and associated structures and its conversion to neural impulses that the brain interprets as sound. There are various physical

---

3. Without additional data—self-commentary, interview, etc.—we cannot know whether this misidentification was a result of one of several factors such as improper memory, inability to infer the tonic, and inability to identify the starting scale degree in relation to the tonic.

4. Presented in detail in Karpinski (1990).

and neurological conditions that can interfere with hearing, degrading the quality or quantity of material that reaches the auditory stream.

Equally important is each listener's *attention* to the auditory stimulus: listeners must be able to attend to a passage of music (or some portion thereof) with enough concentration to ensure that it will reach their short-term memory. According to LaBerge (1995), "attention modifies auditory input at the earliest stages of cortical processing, well before auditory information reaches cortical regions of higher cognitive processing" (p. 20).

Whether through boredom, lack of discipline, test anxiety, attention deficit disorder, or any of a number of other causes, the failure to focus musical attention during dictation (or any other directed musical listening, for that matter) has ruinous consequences for the rest of the process. There are extreme cases in the form of listeners with attention deficit disorder who, during dictation, have let entire playings pass by without the slightest sensory intake, reporting that it was "as if nothing was played at all." Similar reports have come from students who were experiencing test anxiety.

Although physical and mental causes of interference with hearing are beyond the traditional jurisdiction of aural skills instruction, dictation (and other musical training) can often serve as an initial point of diagnosis for these conditions. Subsequent to such a preliminary diagnosis, instructors should follow up with a referral to an appropriate specialist or agency—an audiologist or center for learning disorders, for example. In any case, it is important to recognize that without attentive hearing there is no listener in the world who can succeed at the ensuing stages of memory, understanding, and notation.

Short-Term Melodic Memory

As noted earlier, certain internal machinations remain concealed in the absence of some form of self-reporting beyond the typical music-notation type response to dictation and even beyond protonotation. Therefore, in a series of interviews with student/subjects, I recorded verbal and sung responses to various requests such as simple repetition of melodies, identifying scale degrees, and spelling such passages in various keys.

In several interviews, the stimulus shown in Example 3.3(a) was used. One student—who was known to have excellent notational skills—was asked to repeat what he had heard by singing it (a technique hereafter referred to as "singing back"). Example 3.3(b) shows his response.

When asked to attach syllables to his response, this student produced the appropriate syllables for his incorrect memory of the melody: "Mi–sol–re–sol–do–re–mi." There is little doubt that this student would have written the "proper" notation for these incorrect final pitches as well.

a.

b.

Example 3.3. (a) Stimulus melody to test musical memory; (b) Student's sung response.

This is a relatively benign example of how listening can break down at the memory stage. There are much worse examples of musical memory gone awry. Consider the melody shown in Example 3.4(a), and one student's sung response to this melody, shown in Example 3.4(b).

This is just one example of the many kinds of listeners who often display an ability to recall the shape (and sometimes even general harmonic function) of a melody within a diatonic context without proper placement within the scale. Many times, these listeners report such feelings as "I know it, but I can't remember it"; "I can remember it, but I just can't repeat it"; or "I know that's not right, but I can't get it."[5] Such reports point to evidence for two separate memory encoding mechanisms: one that encodes the contour of a melody—its direction and step-versus-leap shape—and another that encodes specific pitches, at least of starting notes of stepwise groups. The first, contour, operates accurately much more frequently. The second is more capricious, and some individuals find that it operates accurately much less frequently. Dowling (1978) concluded that "contour is an abstraction from the actual melody that can be remembered independently of pitches or interval sizes" (p. 346). DeWitt and Crowder (1986) showed that the mind exhibits "a trend toward differential retention of contour and interval information with contour information more easily encoded and recognized at short [one-second] delays" (p. 271).[6] Dowling (1994) noted that "contour is most important in memory for novel melodies tested after brief delays [thirty or forty seconds]" (p. 188). Consequently, we are left with instances

---

5. Davies and Yelland (1977) reported similar responses: "Sometimes a version is sung incorrectly, and then afterwards subject will say, 'I sang it wrong,' or words to that effect. . . . Furthermore, such subjects are frequently unable to specify how the sung version was incorrect" (p. 8).

6. See also Dowling and Bartlett (1981).

a.

b.

Example 3.4. (a) Stimulus melody to test musical memory; (b) Student's sung response.

when individuals' memory for melodic contour is crystal clear while their memory for specific pitches or intervals has failed them *at the same time*. It is these two conflicting mental conditions that contradict each other and result in the kinds of self-contradictory statements reported earlier.[7]

It seems that many listeners form accurate memories for melodies through encoding a *combination* of specific pitches and contours. The listener who produced the incorrect memory in Example 3.4(b) encoded contour properly but the starting pitch improperly. The combination of these two produces a response that traces the shape of the original, but on incorrect pitches.

Listeners who produce such responses often benefit from drill and practice specifically designed to develop retention of starting pitches. For example, dictation-length melodies can be provided as stimuli to which such listeners can reply by singing only each starting pitch. Listeners who have difficulty even with this simple procedure can work at matching the starting pitches of melodies almost immediately as they are played (provided these listeners are competent at matching pitches in general). They must become acclimated to latching onto the starting pitch of a melody but allowing enough attention to encode contour as well. In practice, this becomes a balancing act among memory for the very first pitch, the starting pitches of all stepwise groups, and melodic contour.

Listeners who produce such contour-following incorrect-pitch responses often retain the original diatonic collection. It seems that tonal music provides the diatonic collection as a supporting framework during this activity. Diatonicism restricts the myriad possible melodic pitch and

---

7. For an excellent, pedagogically oriented summary of research on various melody-encoding strategies, see Marvin (1995, 34–45).

interval combinations and can guide the ear through its unique placement of semitone demarcations. In addition, tonality provides *function*, which—to the sensitized listener—can act intuitively or consciously as a guide in aiding memory for such general features as tension and resolution and such specific features as scale degree and harmonic function. Deutsch (1977) put it this way: "The differences between attempting to recall a musical sequence in a familiar tonal system as compared with a set of notes chosen at random, is equivalent to the difference between trying to recall a sentence as compared with a set of nonsense syllables" (p. 114). And as Hantz (1984) noted, "In such cases it is easy to see why tonal imitations (same-contour-different-interval cues) might be regarded as 'same'; they conform to a higher order regularity—that of preserving the tonality of the standard" (p. 260).[8]

In addition, stylistic norms—instilled through acculturation (and thus varying significantly from listener to listener)—form a kind of "musical grammar" that affects listeners' expectations and therefore their memories. Oura and Hatano (1988) concluded that "in order to memorize any melody efficiently, a large amount of knowledge highly specific to that style of music seems to be needed" (p. 104); in Western tonal music, much of that highly specific knowledge is of the tonal system itself. As Handel (1989) noted, "It might be expected that sequences [of pitches] that are musically 'correct' (i.e., those that fit musical grammars) would be easiest to remember and reproduce. Moreover, reproduction errors for sequences that do not fit musical conventions might tend to create a sequence that is more musically correct. The reproductions would be more 'grammatical'" (p. 344). Since listeners are guided by their expectations in forming musical memories, they must learn to react quickly and effectively to melodic figures that contradict those expectations and not "compose" more "grammatical" memories. Davies (1978) concluded that people engaged in actively listening to music are constantly "making guesses as to what is likely to happen next. This looking into the future is not merely guesswork, but is more in the nature of a prediction based on the data currently available" (p. 74). Listeners' expectations of what might come next often affect their ability to remember or understand what they have heard. If a melody follows a course that closely matches listeners' expectations, they are more likely to remember and understand it. Conversely, unexpected melodic events are more difficult to process (see Unyk and Carlsen 1987). Indeed, as Dowling (1990) noted, "A listener having perceptual experience with a certain style or a particular

---

8. See Davidson and Welsh (1988) for a summary of studies that show that "tonal patterns are easier to process, recognize, and recall than atonal patterns" (p. 261). As Dowling (1993) noted, musically experienced listeners—even those with only a moderate amount of experience—have "an implicit scheme of tonal-scale pitch categories built into their auditory systems, which is essential to musical understanding at the level of pitch coding" (p. 16).

piece literally hears a different set of music events than does a listener lacking that experience" (p. 149). It is possible, then, that the more music listeners learn, and the more *about* music they learn, the wider their field of expectations will be and they will therefore experience fewer expectancy violations and consequently fewer errors in memory and understanding.[9]

Listeners can also rely on a kind of "melodic anchoring," a cognitive means of processing melodic pitches into hierarchical relationships determined—at the very least—by consonance-dissonance status, temporal order, and relative duration (Barucha 1984; Laden 1994). This helps organize pitches into what may be more easily memorized structures.

Although the case is clear that developing melodic memory is an important goal, the question remains as to whether certain activities concomitant to memory and dictation help or hinder progress. In an experiment designed to isolate the role that singing back plays in melodic memory, Pembrook (1987) examined the accuracy of subjects on a same/different melodic discrimination task. One group of subjects heard pairs of melodies (some matching pairs, some not) with a two-second delay between the members of each pair, a second group heard the melody pairs with a nineteen-second delay, and a third group was instructed to sing the melody during this delay. Interestingly, this third group scored significantly lower on the same/different discrimination task. The reason for this is clear: 89% of the sung responses were incorrect. As Pembrook (1986) noted, "If students cannot sing what they have heard, asking them to sing may provide a 'self-composed' inaccurate model from which to dictate, especially for longer melodies" (p. 260). If one factors out those incorrect vocal responses, the same/different responses for the remaining 11% of trials that were sung correctly yielded a 91% accuracy rate—much higher than under any of the other conditions. Pembrook (1987) wrote: "Obviously, when people did sing correctly there was an overwhelming tendency to recognize an ensuing melody as either same or different" (p. 165). The results of this study tell us at least two things: (1) singing back, if used as a diagnostic tool, can *interfere* with the memory process; and (2) if listeners can be trained to sing back melodic segments accurately, their melodic memories will be similarly enhanced. Pembrook (1986) also noted that listeners, when singing back melodies, may attempt to sing more notes than they can remember. "If such is the case, it would behoove aural skills teachers to refrain from compelling students to sing beyond their memory limits" (p. 257).

Memory indeed plays an essential role in the sequence of skills executed while taking dictation. The degree to which listeners can remember what they have heard bears directly on their success in carrying out sub-

9. See Dowling and Harwood (1986, 124–44) for further discussion of melodic expectancy and a survey of related literature.

sequent steps in the process. Extreme cases of difficulty with musical memory result in extremely poor performance in dictation. As McHose (1948) noted over a half-century ago, "One must realize that the average student's memory is not accurate," and, "The author urges the instructor not to be too hasty in requiring the student to place the notation on the staff. The student should not be allowed to write the notation until he can sing back the exercise on a neutral syllable. The author has found that in certain specific cases it was necessary to provide a tutor to work on this one problem. It was not a lack of talent; the difficulty was caused by an undeveloped memory" (p. 3).

McHose was incisive in his observation that memory should be isolated as a separate stage in the dictation process. However, in stating that "the student should not be allowed to write the notation until he can sing back the exercise on a neutral syllable," McHose was not cognizant of two important aspects of short-term musical memory. First, on successive hearings, listeners show little or no improvement at recalling longer and longer portions of melodies longer than the limits of their short-term memories.[10] Second, yet another important concomitant skill dictation can help to develop is listeners' abilities to *selectively* remember portions of music taken from a larger context. This is an important skill for musicians to possess. Adept listeners use it frequently while they perceive music as it passes in time. It enables them to attend to particular musical figures, features, or relationships while further music continues to sound. Performers and conductors use this skill constantly during rehearsal. Teachers use it frequently in both the studio and the classroom. Music students use it in a variety of settings, not merely for taking dictation.

For dictations longer than a listener's short-term limit, the phenomenon of "retroactive interference" comes into play.[11] Example 3.5(a) shows a longer stimulus played for a college aural skills student. When asked to sing back that entire melody, the student gave the response shown in Example 3.5(b).

Like many developing listeners, the student was unable to retain a completely accurate aural image of such a long melody upon first hearing. Although her response was quite musical, she missed seven of the fourteen pitches (and, perhaps most important, the harmonic implications in m. 2). Many such listeners find their melodic memories restricted to somewhere between five and nine notes—equivalent to George Miller's (1956) "magical

10. Sloboda and Parker (1985) found that—on successive repetitions of long melodies (the example central to their report contains twenty-nine notes)—"subjects do not show an improvement in performance over the six trials on any of our measures. Some recalls get longer, but they do not get any better" (p. 160). Pembrook (1987) remarked that many aural skills texts that "malign the writing-while-hearing approach seemingly have recognized the dual processing problem without considering the [short-term memory] storage limitation problem" (p. 156).

11. See the discussion in chapter 2 under "Pitch Memory."

a.

b.

Example 3.5. (a) Dictation melody; (b) Student response.

number seven plus or minus two." One experimental study that tested Miller's limit in a musical context is reported in Marple (n.d.). Marple found that "the retention of new musical materials for most children and adults falls within the expected limits for short term memory as defined by Miller" (p. 78). Marple also found that melodic memory increased to somewhere between six and ten notes if rhythmicized: "It would appear that rhythm added to a musical phrase enables a person to retain one additional melodic bit in short term memory" (p. 78). Thus, it is *easier* to remember both pitches and rhythms than to remember pitches alone. Tallarico (1974), Long (1977), and Pembrook (1983) found similar results, with the limit falling somewhere between seven and eleven notes. One final note: aural memory for melodic material is subject to limitations referred to as the "primacy" and "recency" effects—the tendency of subjects to remember initial and final items in a series more often than those in the middle.[12]

Only one or both of two strategies can extend the capacity of short-term musical memory: (1) extractive listening and (2) chunking.

EXTRACTIVE LISTENING   Extractive listening is a combination of focused attention and selective memorization. To demonstrate the simplicity, utility, and power of extractive listening, consider the following responses from the student in Example 3.5—presented with another novel melody (shown in Example 3.6(a))—when instructed to remember halves of the melody after successive listenings. Example 3.6(b) shows her sung response after one listening. Example 3.6(c) shows her sung response after the second listening to the entire melody.

What she has acquired here is not merely a new strategy that will enable her to take better dictation (and why should pedagogues be interested in developing droves of dictation takers?) but, more important, a

12. See Roberts (1986) for recent confirmation of these effects in music.

a.

b.

c.

Example 3.6. (a) New dictation melody played for student from Example 3.5; (b) Her sung response after one listening, following instructions to remember halves of the melody after successive listenings; (c) Her sung response after the second listening, following instructions to remember halves of the melody after successive listenings.

fundamental musical skill—the ability to focus attention on a selected segment of a musical stimulus and *remember* that segment despite the inhibitive nature of surrounding musical material.

There are many developing listeners for whom this is a difficult task.[13] Such listeners can improve their extractive listening skills through activities specifically designed to focus on retaining the memory of one musical stimulus while another continues to sound. One useful technique requires listeners to advance through several progressive levels, being certain to attain competency at any one level before progressing to the next: (1) singing back short (six-to-ten-note) melodies, to be sure that their short-term memory is reliable when not interfered with;[14] (2) singing back the

13. In two decades of teaching aural skills at the university, college, and conservatory level, I have found retroactive interference to be the single most common cause of difficulties in taking dictation.

14. *MacGamut* (Columbus, OH: MacGamut Music Software International) has a feature that allows users to hear only the first or second half of a melodic dictation. Listeners who use this feature constantly may never develop extractive listening skills. But listeners who are instructed to use it sparingly to ensure that their short-term memory is reliable when not interfered with can use this feature profitably.

first six to ten notes of a melody immediately after those six to ten notes have sounded but during the sounding of the interfering material, so as to effectively drown out the interfering material; (3) singing as in level (2), but this time sotto voce, so as to allow the sound of the interfering material to strike the ears while maintaining focus on the fragment to be remembered; and (4) silently auralizing the fragment to be remembered while the interfering material continues to sound. Another interesting drill involves remembering a musical fragment that is unrelated to the interfering material (for example, different styles, meters, keys, timbres, etc.). This helps to differentiate the two stimuli (and simulates the typical interference experienced in many less than acoustically perfect music buildings).

Let us take a look at extractive listening in action while a subject takes dictation. Example 3.7(a) shows a first-semester dictation melody. Example 3.7(b) shows, after each of three playings, (1) a transcription of the subject's sung recall and (2) a diplomatic transcription of the subject's written response.

Note that this subject recalled a good but slightly flawed rendition of the first two measures of the original dictation after playing 1 and accurately notated that flawed recall (compare his version of m. 2, beat 1, with the original). He used playing 2 to correct his memory of m. 2 and add one unrhythmicized pitch from m. 3 (which he, tantalizingly, sang incorrectly but notated correctly), although he carelessly allowed a notational error to creep into m. 2, beat 3. The third playing allowed him to (1) correct the notational rhythmic error in m. 2 and (2) focus his memory primarily on the second half of the melody, producing a flawless recall for these eight pitches and rhythms (but executing several notational errors[15]).

Listeners who develop their extractive listening skills find that not only do they succeed better at taking dictation, but also their music listening proficiency improves in a variety of settings. Their aural acuity in the concert hall, classroom, and ensemble becomes much more flexible and manageable. Their ability to focus attention and retain specific musical information becomes extremely valuable while listening, performing, studying, conducting, composing, and teaching.

CHUNKING   As musical understanding increases, so does musical memory. Listeners who can hear and immediately understand such features as scalar passages, triads, repetitions, sequences, modulations, and

---

15. See the beaming in m. 3 and the rhythmic notation of the first two pitches in m. 4. It may be reassuring to know that when asked, "How many beats long are each of the first two notes in measure 4?" he immediately exclaimed "Oops! . . . One beat," and corrected these rhythms to eighth notes.

a.

b.

Example 3.7. (a) A first-semester dictation melody; (b) One subject's successive responses after each of three playings.

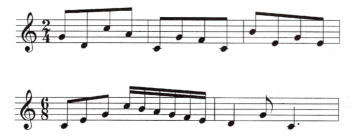

Example 3.8. Two melodic fragments of contrasting chunkability.

rhythmic patterns have a leg up on those listeners still listening without immediate comprehension. Such immediate comprehension affords listeners the opportunity to encode music in meaningful chunks, thereby dramatically reducing the number of memorable "bits" in a passage. Marple (n.d.) reported that "a relatively small percentage of persons are capable of chunking melodic materials at first hearing in order to exceed Miller's [7 ± 2] limits" (p. 80), but Potter (1990) reported that the most proficient dictation takers do indeed use chunking (p. 68). Dowling (1973b) found that *rhythmic* grouping aids listeners in chunking. Deutsch (1980) found that when such rhythmic grouping aligns with hierarchical pitch structures (for example, a three-note sequence grouped rhythmically in threes) melodic memory is enhanced significantly over ungrouped or nonhierarchical materials.[16] Oura (1991) developed a successful model for melodic pitch memory (in college music majors) that involved "reduced pitch patterns"—prototypical melodic figures that serve as chunk-like building blocks in forming efficient memories for melodies.[17]

The effects of chunking can be quite dramatic. For example, the two melodic fragments in Example 3.8 each contain the identical number of statements of each pitch (2 C4s; 1 D4; 2 E4s; 1 F4; 3 G4s; 1 A4; 1 B4; 1 C5),[18] but the second melody is much more easily memorable because it is grouped serially and rhythmically so as to foster chunking.

16. Also see Deutsch and Feroe (1981) for a formalization of these findings.

17. Karpinski (1990, 198) addresses some of the implications of chunking in melodic dictation for both instructors and students.

18. Here and elsewhere, this book adopts the USA Standard system of octave designation, without subscripts or superscripts, wherein "C4" represents middle C. See Butler (1992, 198) for a graphic comparison of octave designations.

a.

b.
after playing 1

after playing 2

after playing 3

Example 3.9. (a) A melody for dictation; (b) Diplomatic transcription of one subject's written responses to the dictation melody after each of three playings.

Whereas extractive listening is a strategy designed to respond to the limits of short-term musical memory, chunking can increase those very limits themselves. Consider an example of this behavior in action during dictation. Example 3.9(a) shows a thirty-two-note dictation melody. A subject was told to notate the melody in bass clef, with a tonic of D and beat unit of an eighth note. He was given three playings, with a minute for working out his response after each playing. Example 3.9(b) shows the subject's written responses after each of three playings. When questioned about his responses, he reported the following:

[After Playing 1]
SUBJECT This is a I chord [points to mm. 1–2], then we went to a V chord statement—there was a triadic V chord right here [points to space to the right of mm. 1–2] . . . and . . . then we went back and restated this at the end [points toward beginning].

[After Playing 3]
SUBJECT . . . so on the first playing I knew I heard this: just descending through a five [points to m. 1.1], a four [points to m. 1.4], a three [points to m. 2.1], and back up to a five [points to m. 2.4], with a little "skip" on each one of them . . . filled in.

. . .

GSK So then on the second playing, you were able to get . . . just be explicit about it.

SUBJECT Right. Well, I pretty much knew what was coming, so let's see, I knew up to here [points at the end of m. 2], and then all I needed to do was hear where this arpeggiation was happening in the V chord, and then I knew there was an exact restatement [points to mm. 5–6] . . . and then, again . . . hearing where this was arpeggiating on the very end [points to m. 7].

This subject chunked the material in two ways: first, based on extra-opus prototypes, such as his references to the "I chord," the "V chord," "arpeggiation," and several scale degree functions; second, based on intra-opus prototypes, such as his recognition of the parallel phrase structure and the sequence of the opening three notes on descending scale degrees.

Chunking obviously increases listeners' abilities to remember music. It is one of the main factors, along with retroactive interference, that determine acuity level in short-term musical memory. Indeed, it is one of the *goals* of aural training rather than a mere tool useful for achieving better grades in dictation: listeners who chunk are thinking analytically, functionally, and structurally.

CONCLUSION Short-term musical memory is a capricious thing, complicated by the length and complexity of the material to be remembered, disrupted by thwarted expectations, and affected in various ways by a host of other factors. Dictation and the many concomitant activities that can improve and increase short-term musical memory also go a long way toward improving musicianship in general.

Example 3.10. Protonotation, indicating pulses and meter through vertical lines and rhythms through horizontal lines.

Musical Understanding

At any given time during dictation, whatever portion of music has been heard and remembered may be subject to musical understanding. Exactly *which* features of the music are to be understood may be left to individual curricula. Most seem to center on meter and rhythm on the one hand and pitch on the other. The following discussions will focus on those parameters.

Musical understanding differs from musical memory. A sufficient test of musical memory is the ability to repeat what has been heard. In contrast, tests of understanding measure comprehension of relationships such as metric grouping, relative rhythmic proportions, and tonal function.

Musical understanding also differs from notation. It is entirely possible (even desirable) to understand the meter, rhythms, and tonal functions of a musical passage without any regard to its notation in a particular meter, key, and clef. Indeed, by separating musical understanding into a process separate from both memory and notation, we will be able to focus closely on this unique stage of music perception.

In investigating the various facets of musical understanding, we will examine aspects of duration first, then pitch.

METER AND RHYTHM   With the pulse, meter, beat, and measure felt and understood as discussed in chapter 2, we have convenient units for measuring the durations of musical sounds. These measurements will exist relative to an internal standard (the pulse, from which the beat and measure are derived) and—obviously—relative to one another. Thus, returning to our primary temporal case study from chapter 2—the second movement of Beethoven's Seventh Symphony—we can calculate and label several simple durations.

Example 3.10 introduces a new symbol: the horizontal line, which represents the duration of a sound relative to the pulses. A sound that lasts one beat is represented by a line that spans the distance between two successive pulses, as for the first note; a sound that lasts a half-beat is half that width, as during the second beat; a sound that lasts two beats is correspondingly twice as long, drawn right through the intervening pulse. For visual clarity, a small space is left between a horizontal line and a pulse whenever a sound begins or ends at that pulse; only sounds that cross a pulse (syncopations and notes longer than one beat) have lines that actually touch and cross the pulse lines.[19]

Of course, this system of protonotation is capable of representing more complex rhythms than these. In particular, it is well suited to introducing basic syncopations and quadruple divisions of the beat. However, the system does become somewhat imprecise when contrasting more than a handful of beat divisions (say adding triplets to the preceding or including subdivisions in compound meters), but by the point in the learning sequence when such rhythms are being introduced there should no longer be a need to resort to protonotation, as actual music notation will have long since supplanted it.

One important goal at this point is to foster the categorical perception of rhythm patterns. Studies have shown that listeners tend to perceive groups of rhythms as belonging to categories—specific, well-learned patterns.[20] An important part of aural training is the inculcation of such patterns.[21]

Since dictation materials are often relatively brief (made so by the exigencies of short-term memory), the amount of rhythmic material reaching listeners is quite limited. Because of this, there exists the possibility that music excerpted or composed for rhythmic or melodic dictation might be ambiguous with regard to its meter.[22] For example, consider the second rhythmic dictation presented in Ottman and Dworak's *Basic Ear Training Skills*, reproduced in Example 3.11(a) (Ottman and Dworak 1991, 225). Without providing the meter for listeners through printed

---

19. Compare the "graph notation" in Steele and McDowell (1982). Also compare the "cross-modal matching symbols" used by Walker (1981, 33). Walker found that the use of such symbols (as opposed to simple rhythmic solmization) before introducing notation "induced better results, and therefore better understanding of the concepts involved" (p. 38).

20. See Radocy and Boyle (1997, 133–40) for a survey of these studies.

21. For examples of these types of patterns, see the "rhythmic cells" in White (1981, 38–39).

22. Sloboda (1978) commented on listeners' tendency to "mis-hear" when only given small amounts of musical information, "for instance, at the start of a piece, where misperceptions of rhythmic structure are quite common even among musically sophisticated listeners" (p. 5). For illuminating introductory discussions of metric ambiguity, see Cooper and Meyer (1960, 88–92) and Lester (1986, 86–103).

a.

b.

Example 3.11. (a) Ottman and Dworak, *Basic Ear Training Skills*, p. 225, Exercise (2); (b) Rebarred in triple meter.

bar lines and meter signs or counting prior to or during performance, this short excerpt could just as easily be perceived in triple meter, as shown in Example 3.11 (b).[23]

The problems of metric ambiguity are not always confined to short melodic dictations. Longer melodies can be metrically ambiguous as well. In general, it is wise to approach all dictation materials with a critical ear sensitive to the cognitive aspects of how listeners infer meter from merely listening and to save ambiguous materials for points in the curriculum when metric ambiguity is addressed explicitly.

RHYTHM SOLMIZATION FOR UNDERSTANDING   A variety of rhythm solmization systems have been developed over the last two centuries; several are in common use today.[24] Some, the Galin-Paris-Chevé method chief among them, label specific rhythm symbols and not their function in relation to the beat and are therefore inappropriate for modeling rhythmic understanding.[25] Some stand somewhere in between functional and

23. Ottman and Dworak are not alone in this matter; other texts offer similarly ambiguous materials. For instance, in Horacek and Lefkoff (1989, vol. 1), the rhythmic dictations on pp. 113–37 and 197–221 are much too short to be presented without the supplied meter signs; the bar line and meter dictations on pp. 291–322 (note that these come *after* the basic and intermediate rhythmic dictations) are more appropriate, but many of these can be ambiguous without supplying artificial accents or counting aloud. Also see my comments in Karpinski (1993, 244–46).

24. See Gordon (1993): pages 264–65 give a historical overview of various systems; pages 275–86 offer detailed descriptions and critiques of each. See also Hoffman, Pelto, and White (1996, 8–13), which presents a brief but extremely clear survey of other systems.

25. The Galin-Paris-Chevé method, also known as the "French Time-Names" system, was popularized during the nineteenth century in France, Switzerland, the Netherlands, Russia, and England by Pierre Galin, Aimé Paris and his sister Nanine, and her husband, Emile Chevé. See Gordon (1993, 265, 278–79) for a synopsis.

symbol-specific systems. The Kodaly system, for example, labels all beats (e.g., quarters) as "ta" but relabels those beat positions as "ti" when the beat is divided in half (e.g., "ti-ti" for two eighth notes).

Some rhythm solmization systems strive to model duration in relation to metric position, so that all notes that fall in specific metric positions (for example, on the second beat of any measure in $\frac{2}{8}$, $\frac{2}{4}$, $\frac{2}{2}$, etc.) receive the same kind of syllable. Such systems are therefore candidates for modeling rhythmic understanding. Several systems seek to associate unique syllables with at least some of the specific divisions of the multilevel pulse structure. One such system, in common use in U.S. schools, often is referred to simply as "1 ee & a" after the labels given to the four equal divisions of a first beat. In this system, notes that fall on a beat are labeled with the number of that beat within the measure ("1," "2," etc.), duple divisions of the beat are all labeled "&" ("1 & 2 &," etc.), and so on. However, the 1 ee & a system uses some of those same syllables to represent very different divisions in compound meters. McHose and Tibbs (1945) incorporated a similar system in their *Sight-singing Manual*, numbering the beats, but distinguishing between duple divisions ("te") and triple divisions ("lah-lee"). All further divisions are solmized "ta."[26] Edwin Gordon has proposed a system in which each beat is labeled "du," each half-beat in simple meters labeled "de," and the triple divisions that follow "du" in compound meters are "da" and "di," respectively. Further divisions are all labeled "ta." Gordon's system also accommodates complex meters. Although more rigorous and comprehensive than the other systems discussed thus far, this kind of labeling can become overly complex when applied to the kind of extended situations it is meant to encompass.[27] In addition, Gordon's rather narrow focus on "macrobeats" and "microbeats" misses the larger structure of *multiple* levels of pulse. And neither McHose/Tibbs nor Gordon specifies unique labels beyond the first divisions of the beat in simple or compound meters (see the ubiquitous "ta" in both systems).

The most systematic and comprehensive system of rhythmic solmization in use today—and one that is gaining adherents as it gains wider exposure—is known as "Takadimi." This system has been extensively and clearly introduced elsewhere,[28] so it will suffice to discuss its main features here. When one is using Takadimi all notes are labeled in terms of their proportional rhythmic position within the beat, what Hoffman, Pelto, and White (1996) call "discrete one-to-one mapping onto metric attack

26. See McHose and Tibbs (1945, 6, 30, 36, 63–64, 78, 92–93).
27. See, for example, the patterns in $\frac{5}{8}$ in Gordon (1993, 284): "Du Ba Bi Du Be | Du Ta Be Ta Du Ta Ba Ta Bi Tal."
28. Hoffman, Pelto, and White (1996) present the most systematic and comprehensive incarnation of this system. London (1996) examines the bases in human perception and cognition for the features of the Takadimi system.

points" (p. 16). In other words, each unique metric division—down to second-order divisions in both simple and compound meters (e.g., sixteenth notes in $\frac{2}{4}$ or $\frac{6}{8}$)—receives a syllable it does not share with any other division. Syncopations, tuplets, hemiola, and other rhythmic/metric figures all acquire unique solmization on the basis of attack points within measure and beat. Thus—as in movable-*do* solmization—practitioners of Takadimi determine and execute analyses of the structures they sing as they sing them.

Although many of the preceding rhythm solmization systems aspire to represent rhythmic function, in Takadimi we have a functional system of rhythm solmization that most closely models the aural understanding listeners engage in when they apprehend rhythms in relation to pulse and meter. In this sense, it is a verbal analogue to the beat-unit-neutral protonotation used thus far to represent such understanding on paper.

PITCH   By this stage in the process, listeners have heard, remembered, and understood the meter and rhythms of the passage at hand. This provides for them a framework in which to identify pitches.

In order to understand the pitch content of a remembered musical passage, listeners must execute the pitch-understanding skills discussed in chapter 2: inference of tonic, perception of melodic contour, and identification of scale degrees. If necessary, readers should refer back to those discussions; what follows here are brief examinations of how those skills should be implemented during dictation.

All functional tonal pitch evaluations stem from a sense of the tonic. Without an ability to infer the tonic, listeners operate without the very frame of reference at the heart of tonality itself. With tonic inference, listeners can determine scale degrees, harmonic functions, modulations, and a host of other tonal features. This must be an explicit and accurately executed part of the dictation process or all subsequent pitch processing will be for naught.

Although most listeners assess contour intuitively and accurately with consistency, all listeners must be certain that they do indeed correctly assess the contour of whatever melodic fragment they are working on. Accurate interpretation of contour (and by this I refer to contour assessments of accurately remembered melodies) is essential for any subsequent understanding of pitch. A more specific component of contour (by some definitions) is the distinction between step and skip for each note-to-note motion in a melody. This distinction is crucial to the process of scaledegree identification, which follows shortly. Without it, listeners must treat each pitch in a melody as if it were a unique starting pitch, adrift in a diatonic field, to be measured against the tonic. In contrast, listeners who make facile step-versus-skip judgments can concentrate on discerning the scale degree of the first pitch and any pitch after a skip, leaving the stepwise pitches in between to mere enumeration.

As listeners proceed to understanding the individual pitches of a melody, their first task is to identify the scale degree of the first pitch of the remembered portion they are working out. These scale degrees are most easily expressed as numbers or solmization syllables. (Indeed, this and further discussions of scale-degree identification assume an intimate facility with some form of tonally functional solmization.)

The scale degrees of subsequent stepwise pitches can be processed next. As mentioned earlier, listeners who are adept at distinguishing between stepwise motion and motion by skip can rather mechanically apply strings of scale degrees to stepwise passages once an initial pitch has been determined. With attention to contour in the form of simple changes of direction and with facility at solmization, such strings of syllables or numbers fall easily into place.

When the musical material skips, each pitch that follows a skip should be treated as a new starting pitch (q.v., earlier). It may be tempting to calculate the interval from the preceding pitch, but—particularly during the early months of dictation study—this approach neither fosters a sensitivity to tonal function (which is first and foremost calculated in relation to the tonic) nor ensures accuracy, since any mistake made in reaching the pitch *before* the skip will be continued into the pitch that *follows* the skip. For example, a listener who misidentifies the first seven pitches of "London Bridge" as $\hat{2}$, $\hat{3}$, $\hat{2}$, $\hat{1}$, $\hat{7}$, $\hat{1}$, $\hat{2}$, would (using an intervallic approach to leaps) consequently mislabel the following pitch as $\hat{6}$. A listener who stopped on the eighth pitch and compared it to the tonic would stand a much better chance of getting on the right track from that point forward and might even take that new information as an indication to go back and recheck the previous seven pitches. In practice, as listeners become more familiar with the territory of the scale degrees, intervallic strategies become more reliable as a means of quickly calculating the number of scale degrees traversed by a skip.

Incorporating this information into protonotation is a relatively straightforward process. The protonotation provides a metric and rhythmic framework in which to work out the scale degrees. Consider, as an example, the theme from Telemann's Fantasia for Keyboard, Group 1, No. 7, in G, rendered in protonotation in Example 3.12. Note the use of letters that represent movable-*do* syllables with the addition of small superscript or subscript ticks that precede certain letters to indicate the direction of skips.

In the process of taking such a dictation, most beginning listeners (and many advanced ones) will have to employ extractive listening. Because of this, the protonotation will not spring forth full-fledged but will instead be developed in pieces after successive listenings. This occurs as a listener remembers a portion of the melody after one listening, then sketches out the meter and rhythm in protonotation *for that remembered portion* and places syllables (or other symbols) in that framework to represent the

|D̲ ̲|ᴵM̲ ̲|R̲ ̲|ᴵF̲ ̲|M̲ᴵL̲ ̲|S̲ ̲⌐̲|F̲ ̲|M̲ ̲|ᴅ̲ᴅ̲|ᴵF̲ ̲|ᴿR̲ ̲|ᴵS̲M̲|ᴅ̲ ̲⌐̲| |

Example 3.12. Telemann, Fantasia for Keyboard, Group 1, No. 7, in G, mm. 1–4, transcribed in protonotation.

pitches. This process is then repeated for other remembered portions after further listenings.

Just as dictation materials can be ambiguous with regard to meter, they can also exhibit *tonal* ambiguity. Having established the importance of developing listeners' abilities to infer tonics from musical contexts alone, we must examine just how clearly melodies used for dictation imply their tonics. If a melody is not unambiguous in tonicizing a single pitch, it will not be very useful in developing the skill of tonic inference. It is therefore crucial at the beginning stages of the learning sequence for instructors to conscript or create melodies that clearly define a tonic.

One of the factors that impedes the construction of tonally unambiguous melodies for dictation has to do with the length of dictations themselves. Due to constraints of short-term memory, melodic dictations present listeners with a relatively small number of notes (when compared to actual musical compositions): almost always fewer than thirty, usually fewer than twenty. At beginning stages, curricula frequently restrict this number to fewer than ten. Given such a small amount of material, it can occasionally be challenging to excerpt or compose melodies that clearly tonicize a single pitch.

Consider as an example the dictation melody composed by a teaching assistant in 1995 shown in Example 3.13 Despite the good intentions of this teaching assistant (he *notated* two sharps in the key signature and began and ended on the tonic and dominant of D), many students perceived the *second* note as tonic in this melody. Several factors can cause such difficulties. In the case of the melody in Example 3.13, the pitch collection is not actually the two-sharp collection but a five-member subset of the diatonic collection class, known more commonly as "the" pentatonic scale. Its specific members here are D–E–G–A–B. This collection is ambiguous in the context of diatonicism due to its potential member-

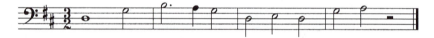

Example 3.13. Dictation melody.

ship in three different diatonic supersets: the no-sharp/no-flat collection (also called the white-key collection) and the one-sharp and two-sharp collections.[29] The letter classes F and C therefore retain the potential to be inferred (but never actually heard) as either F or F♯ and C or C♯, respectively. In addition, the specific temporal context of the pitches D–E–G–A–B in this melody tends to tonicize G more than D: note in particular the immediate proximity of the first two pitches, D and G (implying 5̂–1̂), the D–G–B triad that frames the opening two measures, and the metric placement of D and G on downbeats 3 and 4 (once again implying 5̂–1̂).[30]

This small section of this book doesn't pretend to present a theory of what makes a short melody seem to be "in" a key[31] or to provide exhaustive rules about how to construct tonally unambiguous dictations.[32] But the reader, after reviewing the current section and "Inference of Tonic" in chapter 2, should be well armed enough to carry a sensitive eye and ear into the process of extracting or composing tonally unambiguous dictation materials.

PITCH SOLMIZATION FOR UNDERSTANDING   At this stage, a functional solmization system can serve both to instill and to diagnose tonal function. Once listeners become fluent in a functional solmization system, the

29. Because they include harmonic minor and ascending melodic minor as diatonic collections, Van Egmond and Butler (1997) consider these pitches to be a subset of *four* different diatonic collections, the fourth being D melodic minor.

30. Brown (1985) first investigated the relationships between temporal context and tonicization. A related article is Brown (1988). See Hershman (1995) for further indications of the role rhythmic and metric factors play in tonicization. Vos (1999) summarizes recent research into how aspects of rhythm, meter, and pitch produce the 5̂–1̂ relationship.

31. The scholarly debate on this subject has spanned a century, beginning at least as early as Meyer (1900). Recent literature has attempted to find some common ground. Radocy and Boyle (1997) conclude that "the tonal hierarchy theory and Butler's rare interval theory may be two sides of the same coin" (p. 199). Butler (1998), too, sees room for multiple explanations: "The process of key discovery may result from a mix of evidence" including tonal hierarchy, rare interval information, and "stability" cues. Karpinski (1997) discusses the tonality-implying characteristics of some of these "stability" cues, including the dominant–tonic, leading tone–tonic, and mediant–tonic relationships, with special reference to dictation materials. These are special, culturally bound instances of the Lipps-Meyer effect (see Meyer 1900, esp. pp. 246–47; and Farnsworth 1969, 37–39). Compare Croonen and Kop's (1989) notion of "tonal clarity."

32. Kirnberger ([1771–79] 1982) dealt with this very issue (pp. 348–50). He discusses how to compose a melody so that "the main key of the entire composition [is] felt immediately and without the least ambiguity" (p. 348) and even presents an example of which he writes "no one would know whether it is written in G major or C major" (p. 349).

syllables become self-reinforcing and serve as immediate and facile means of communicating functional understanding. "*Do*" and "1" become more than just shorthand for "tonic"; they become intimately associated with tonic function, resulting in a personal knowledge of the tonic and how it *feels*. As training continues, more and more tonal constructs undergo such close association—the dominant triad (*sol-ti-re* /$\hat{5}$–$\hat{7}$–$\hat{2}$") or a move to the relative minor (*si–la*/ ↑$\hat{5}$–$\hat{6}$) to name but two examples.

Movable-*do* solmization is one such functional system, wherein the syllables *do, re, mi, fa, sol, la,* and *ti* stand for the seven scale degrees in major mode. Upward chromatic inflections of *do, re, fa, sol,* and *la* are effected by inflecting the vowel to the Latinate "i": *di, ri, fi, si,* and *li.* (There is no such thing as a *functional* chromatic raising of *mi* or *ti.*) Downward chromatic inflections of *mi, sol, la,* and *ti* are effected by inflecting the vowel to the Latinate "e": *me, se, le,* and *te.* *Re,* the one exception, is lowered to *ra.* (There is no such thing as a *functional* chromatic lowering of *do* or *fa.*) In this way, the seven unique consonants *d, r, m, f, s, l,* and *t* map directly onto the seven scale degrees in major, and the terminal vowels indicate diatonic or specific chromatic status.

There are, however, two flavors of movable-*do* when it comes to solmizing minor and the other modes. One—often referred to as "*do*-based minor"—always maps *do* onto the tonic, inflecting individual scale degrees as necessary to model specific modes. The other—often referred to as "*la*-based minor"—always maps the two diatonic semitones as *mi-fa* and *ti-do,* letting the tonic or final fall on various syllables in various modes. *Do*-based minor takes a *parallel* approach to the modes: all modal tonics or finals are solmized as *do*; all parallel scale degrees receive the same initial consonant. *La*-based minor takes a *relative* approach to the modes: all modes that share a single diatonic collection also share a single set of syllables that map directly onto the pitches in that collection, regardless of where the tonic or final is positioned within that collection. *Do*-based minor directly models the functional scale degrees within a key or mode. *La*-based minor models the diatonic collection. Although there are advantages to both systems, *do*-based minor is the more appropriate of the two when one is seeking to model tonal function.[33] As Larson (1993b) concluded, after an exhaustive comparison of the *do*- and *la*-based systems, "If our purpose is to vivify scale degree function, *do*-based minor appears to be a better choice" (p. 115).

---

33. For more detailed examinations of the purposes and utility of *la*-based and *do*-based systems, see Larson (1989; 1993b), Smith (1991; 1992; 1994), and Houlahan and Tacka (1992; 1994).

Similar to *do*-based movable-*do*, solmizing scale degrees by singing numbers (i.e., "one, two, three") maps directly onto tonal function.[34] Using scale-degree numbers removes the linguistic separation inherent in movable-*do*: scale-degree numbers as solmization syllables use the exact same labels to represent scale-degree numbers as those used in spoken discourse. However, one must think carefully about choosing to sing on scale-degree numbers. The fact that five of the seven scale-degree numbers end with consonants makes singing with them more awkward, less musical, and somewhat clumsy rhythmically. And the absence of any widely accepted chromatic inflections for scale-degree numbers is even more problematic. For example, singing "four" for both a diatonic and a chromatically raised fourth scale degree maps the same label onto two different functions.

Regardless of what system is chosen to model tonal function, solmization training cannot be undertaken halfheartedly. Developing listeners must cast the syllables across the diatonic collection with constant repetition and learn to associate specific syllables with specific scale degrees—particularly the tonic during early stages—so that a kind of brainwashing in musical functionality takes hold. Frequent sight singing and prepared materials (including melodies, pitch patterns, sequentials, and similar materials) coupled with frequent listening work (including tonic inference and scale-degree identification) all carried out using a functional solmization system help to bring this inculcation about. As Guido ([n.d.] 1998) noted about solmization, it "will be of great use to you either in the competent singing of an unknown melody as soon as you see it written down, or in the accurate transcription of an unwritten melody immediately upon hearing it" (pp. 217–18).[35]

Notation

The last step in melodic dictation is taking what has been heard, remembered, and understood and notating it. This requires sufficient familiarity and facility with the elements, logic, and vagaries of Western music notation.

Familiarity and facility with notation are indeed among the goals of aural skills training. Notation is an essential part of the dictation process, necessary in translating musical sounds into symbols. Whereas de-

---

34. Unless a curious subspecies of this system is adopted wherein "6" maps onto the tonic in minor. See Damrosch (1894, 25) and Winnick (1987, 24) for examples of this usage.

35. Guido was referring to hexachordal solmization, but the principle is very similar.

clarative knowledge about notation has long belonged to the domain of "written-theory" training, facility in notation can be developed through the *procedural* knowledge gained through the frequent use of notation in such activities as composing, arranging, transcribing, and taking dictation. Of these activities, music training (as it is presently conceived at most U.S. universities, colleges, and conservatories) typically requires the vast majority of music students only to take dictation. Thus, in most circumstances, it falls on aural skills training to develop not only musical hearing, memory, and understanding but facility with notation as well.

To augment written-theory training in notation, aural skills instructors can assign readings and exercises from appropriate books on notation.[36] It is also possible to distill the principles of notation necessary for most dictations into several concisely written pages to be studied and consulted while working on practice dictations. In addition, timed drills can be devised that improve speed and accuracy in writing (and reading) specific aspects of the notational system. It is extremely instructive to establish well-defined expectations about notational theory and conventions and to require adherence to these expectations. Musicians who thereby acquire an intimate working knowledge of Western music notation are well prepared to interpret and employ the broad range of meanings the system is capable of communicating.

In one sense, it is a rather straightforward matter to translate what has been heard, remembered, and understood from protonotation into actual music notation. However, research (Taylor and Pembrook 1983, 33) has shown—and many aural skills instructors know quite well—that many errors in dictation can be introduced during the notation stage. In order to improve their notation skills, students can practice the task of translating understanding into notation in isolation—using prefabricated passages of protonotation as templates from which they can practice transcription using various clefs, keys, and beat units (an especially effective means of improving the notational facility and accuracy of listeners who have been diagnosed as wanting for speed or correctness at the notational stage), thereby temporarily eliminating the vagaries of hearing, memory, and understanding while focusing practice time most efficiently on aspects of notation.

But important goals include speed, fluency, and immediacy across the entire spectrum of skills required for dictation. In acquiring these various skills, musicians should strive to bring hearing, understanding, and notation into almost immediate succession, so that they can begin to visu-

---

36. The standard reference on notational practice is Read (1979). For manuscript techniques, see Heussenstamm (1987), Warfield ([1977] 1986), and Donato ([1963] 1977). For popular/commercial manuscript techniques, see Roemer (1985).

Example 3.14. The meter and rhythms of Mozart, Piano Sonata, K. 545, mmt. 2, mm. 1–4, in protonotation and translated into actual notation.

alize the notation for music while they hear it. Therefore, in dictation, the time between playings and after the final playing should be controlled to durations that require listeners to work as quickly as possible from hearing through memory and understanding into notation. An eventual goal of aural skills training is to develop listeners who *shadow* the music they hear: that is, they should eventually be able to hear, understand, and visualize notation for music as it sounds in real time.[37] This is one of the important features of dictation that sets it apart from transcription, in which vast spans of time are allowed for translating sounds into notation.[38]

METER AND RHYTHM   Once listeners have understood the meter and rhythms of a passage, they need only be supplied with a beat unit (e.g., "eighth note") or a bottom numeral for the meter sign (e.g., "8") in order to translate their protonotation (or their internalized protounderstanding) into actual rhythm notation. Primary pulse lines become bar lines, and individual durations calculated proportionally in terms of beat values become specific rhythm symbols, calculated in reference to the prevailing beat unit. Example 3.14 shows a passage represented in protonotation and its subsequent translation into actual meter and rhythm notation.

The use of various beat units is important to develop fluency in notation. It seems that modern musicians, at least first-year music majors, have a prejudice toward certain beat units. In a study of rhythmic dictation, Hofstetter (1981) found "the number on the bottom of the time signature had a significant impact on the percent of correct responses, with students scoring higher when a four was on the bottom in simple meter, and when an eight was on the bottom in compound meter" (p. 272). Thus—for example—students were more fluent in $\frac{4}{4}$ than in $\frac{4}{8}$ and in $\frac{6}{8}$ than in $\frac{6}{4}$. It therefore seems important to spend equal time with these "orphaned" beat units (at least 2 and 8 in simple meters, 4 and 16

37. See Karpinski (1990, 207, 226) for a brief discussion of this process and for further information on shadowing in language and its analogues in music listening.
38. See the discussion of transcription in chapter 5.

in compound meters) so that they will not impede speed and accuracy when encountered during notation *or* reading.

It is possible at this stage to employ one of the solmization systems that associate syllables directly with specific note values. In such systems a quarter note is always labeled identically (e.g., "noir"), regardless of beat unit or metric placement. We hear some English-speaking teachers and students chanting "quarter, eighth-eighth, half . . ." in similar fashion. This directly labels the notation rather than the function or sound of rhythmic relationships and is eminently appropriate for modeling music notation in real time.

PITCH   Once listeners have understood the scale degrees of the pitches of a passage, they need only be supplied with the name of a tonic pitch in order to translate their protonotation (or their internalized protounderstanding) into actual pitch notation. Individual scale degrees calculated relatively to the perceived tonic become specific pitches, calculated in reference to the absolute pitch of the prevailing tonic.

Once listeners are given sufficient familiarity and facility with music notation, it is a rather straightforward process for them to translate their understanding of the pitches of a musical passage into notation. Example 3.15 shows one such translation. Note the correspondences between the prototypical representations of meter, rhythm, and pitch and the actual music notation.

Solmization can serve to facilitate fluency in pitch notation as well. Whereas functional systems such as numbers or movable-*do* (with *do*-based minor) model the scale degrees of pitches—a feature in the realm of musical understanding—fixed systems, such as fixed-*do*, model the letter names that represent those absolute pitches in notation. Thus, systems in this latter category (fixed) are specifically oriented toward the notation stage in the dictation process and their use assumes proper execution of the previous stages: hearing, memory, and understanding. Both types of systems offer much to assist in developing listeners' skills and providing them with means of expressing what they hear succinctly and fluently. It therefore seems wise to adopt and employ one variety of each system.[39]

But practitioners must be extremely careful in choosing two simultaneous systems for pitch solmization, one modeling scale-degree function and another modeling letter names. One should choose two systems that use labels with a high degree of disambiguity. Consider the four possible interactions between pairs of the most common movable and fixed systems.

39. See Riggins (1988), who also calls for such a dual strategy. Also see the discussion of solmization for sight singing in chapter 7.

Example 3.15. Vivaldi, Flute Sonata No. 1 from Six Sonatas "Il Pastor Fido," Aria, mm. 49–52, in protonotation and translated into actual notation.

If one chooses movable-*do* to model scale-degree function and fixed-*do* to model letter names, the meanings of the syllables will not be unique. For example, *do* will mean tonic in movable-*do* (but potentially any letter name) while *do* will mean "C" in fixed-*do* (but potentially any scale degree). In a number of (admittedly undocumented) clinical trials, this has proven to be unworkable for students and instructors alike. Therefore, using the same set of syllables for different purposes must be avoided.

If one is using movable-*do* for scale degrees and English letter names to stand directly for letter names, there is minimal—but not entirely insignificant—overlap. The diatonic syllables *do, re, mi, fa, sol, la,* and *ti* do not intersect at all with the letter names A, B, C, D, E, F, and G. However, the pronunciations (but not the spellings) of two of the chromatic movable-*do* syllables overlap with letter names: *di* with D and *si* with C.[40] Assuming that clarity of communication is an important criterion in choosing solmization systems, one must be careful to distinguish between the members of these homonym pairs during discourse.

Neither pairing between scale-degree numbers and fixed-*do* syllables nor between scale-degree numbers and letter names creates any homonym-pair ambiguities. The latter pairing—between scale-degree numbers and letter names—is particularly attractive since these are the same labels used in spoken English. This pairing tightly integrates the solmization used in music listening and reading with the vocabulary used in discussing, analyzing, and writing music.[41]

40. Compare what Larson (1995, 87) calls "monosyllabic chromatic English letter names," which—like fixed-*do*—model letter names. Pairing these with movable-*do* would yield overlaps at "cee"/"si," "dee"/"di," and "fee"/"fi." In contrast, White (1981) advocates simply using English letter names. He concludes that asking Americans to use fixed-*do* "would be asking us to use a foreign language when we already have a perfectly good set of symbols for pitches [i.e., letter names]" (p. 31).

41. But one must keep in mind the caveats that concern chromatic inflection and singability in considering the adoption of scale-degree numbers. See "Pitch Solmization for Understanding" earlier.

Presenting Melodic Dictations

The means by which melodic dictations are presented can have profound influences on the results listeners achieve, for both any individual dictation and their overall skill development.

Extramusical Cues

It is widespread practice to provide a variety of extramusical cues while giving dictation. Evidence for this can be found in the number of textbooks, audio recordings, and computer applications that provide printed and recorded information (the sound of the tonic, beats counted aloud, etc.) in addition to their dictations.

METER AND RHYTHM   Since recognizing meter is such a fundamental temporal skill, it seems surprising that many dictation materials are presented with extramusical cues designed to provide metric information for listeners. One text (Brooks and Warfield 1978) directs instructors to "count the *first measure aloud* (during the dictation) in order to establish the meter and tempo" (p. vii). The software that accompanies Benward and Kolosick (1996a) sounds a metronome pulse before and during each dictation. Many books and programs supply a meter sign and rhythmic value for the first note of each dictation (for example, the rhythmic dictation exercises in Trubitt and Hines 1979). These practices minimize or eliminate attention to a very important skill that should be focused on and developed from the beginning: *perceiving* meter (as opposed to merely *being told* about it).

Even the practice of supplying the number of measures (either as a mere number or in the form of blank measures printed on a page) can provide information better left to the aural domain. Practically all dictation textbooks, tape/workbook combinations, and computer-assisted instruction materials use this practice. Perhaps most egregiously, this constrains the listening experience within predefined temporal parameters, offering clues about where (when) things happened that ought to be perceived from the music itself. It can even decrease the need to infer meter, making such temporal decisions a product more of "fitting" the notes into the space allotted than of true metric perception.

PITCH   Regardless of how well we understand the mechanisms behind tonic inference, it should be apparent by this point in our discussion that it is a fundamental, important musical skill. However, there seem to be few places in ear-training texts, tapes, and software where this skill is even mentioned, much less developed. Typically, the dictation materials in these sources are presented with one or more noncontextual cues that either hand over the tonic on a silver platter or eliminate the need to infer it in the first place.

The most obvious category of noncontextual cues contains those that actually establish the tonic through sounds other than those within the dictation itself. The simplest merely sounds the tonic pitch before a dictation begins.[42] Others supply the sound of a scale, thereby providing *both* diatonic collection and tonic, the latter through the implication that its terminal pitches should automatically be endowed with the sense of tonic that, in actuality, only the temporalized and rhythmically differentiated pitches can truly impart.[43] Some sound an isolated "tonic" chord before playing scale degrees to identify.[44] Some merely exhort instructors in general terms: "Firmly establish the key center before beginning each exercise" (Kreter 1976, 1: 279). But as Butler (1992) has concluded, "It is not necessary to prepare the listener with complete scales or series of chords" (p. 119). Listeners can and should learn to infer the tonic from the music itself.

Another category provides tonics to listeners by indicating that exercises will begin and/or end on that pitch.[45] Although this might technically seem to be a type of intramusical cue, it can hardly be considered a functional one—particularly of the variety used in everyday listening. We know, on the basis of Brown and Butler's work, that musicians listen to tonal music while in a constant state of determining the tonic based on the interrelations of the pitches heard up to any given point. If students are given the artificial certainty that dictations will begin or end on the tonic (even though many compositions do end there), they can mechanically extract the tonic from such exercises without ever developing their ability to *infer* the tonic through interpreting the interrelations of the pitches.

42. See, for example, Kraft (1999). Each exercise on the recordings that accompany this programmed text is preceded by "the sounding of a preparatory (prep) note, which is always the tonic" (p. 3).

43. Several computer-assisted instruction packages behave this way. See *Explorations* (Mountain View, CA: Mayfield) as one example.

44. For example, *MusicLab* (Redmond, WA: Musicware) has a module called Names that drills students on scale-degree recognition using movable-*do* solmization. The program plays a triad that is meant to be interpreted as tonic, then a scale degree, and users respond by clicking on buttons with movable-*do* syllables.

45. Consider two examples: (1) The first two of the four melodic-dictation sections in Kraft (1999) contain hundreds of melodic dictations—approximately half of those in the book—all of which both begin and end on the tonic pitch. In the later sections, melodies that do not end on the tonic are clearly labeled as such above the answer blanks. (2) Ottman and Dworak (1991, 91–92) present exercises in "recognizing and locating the tonic in a melody," that all begin and end on the tonic. Follow-up exercises on pp. 93–94 include a few melodies that begin and/or end on other pitches as well.

Many aural skills materials provide both key signatures and starting pitches for their dictations.[46] This practice greatly downplays the need to infer the tonic of a passage before notation can begin.[47] For example, if a key signature of two sharps is provided, followed by a starting pitch on D5, then—given the restrictions of most sources to the major and minor modes at this level—listeners would be required to choose between only two possible scale-degree interpretations for the given starting pitch: $\hat{1}$ and $\hat{3}$. An even more generous approach provides both tonic and mode—either through implicit restriction throughout a particular set of dictations (e.g., "in this chapter, we encounter only major-mode melodies") or through simple revelation (e.g., "the following dictation is in E♭ minor")—in addition to providing a starting pitch. Such an approach requires no auditory perception in order to determine the scale degrees of its melodies' given starting pitches.

Providing starting pitches so grossly violates the goal of helping listeners to perceive tonal functions that it warrants a separate discussion here. First, let us recall that memory for melodies is encoded in at least two ways: (1) through contour and (2) as specific pitches (see the discussions of contour earlier in this chapter and in chapter 2). Also recall that memory for specific pitches is a much more accurate, specialized, and narrowly distributed skill. (In other words, it is much easier to remember the shape of a melody than its exact pitches and many more people can perform the former task than can perform the latter.) Listeners provided with tonic, mode, and starting pitch can rely on only their contour perception to arrive at what often seem like convincingly accurate responses to melodic dictations. Refer back to the subject's response shown in Example 3.1(b). He *coincidentally* started on the correct staff position (through, you will recall, a combination of serendipitous errors) and followed his contour memory but understood almost nothing of the scale-degree functions in the melody. If we supply such starting pitches (in the form of

46. This tradition is so ubiquitous that it seems unfair to single out as examples any particular sources that use it. Some notable *exceptions* include Thomson and DeLone (1967) and Steele and McDowell (1982), both of which print some (but not all) dictation blanks without starting pitches; Ottman and Dworak (1991), which includes three types of exercises: (1) those with both key signatures and starting pitches (thereby eliminating the need to infer the tonic), (2) those with only key signatures (requiring tonic inference), and (3) those with only starting pitches (again requiring tonic inference); and McHose (1948), which prescribes a procedure identical to Ottman and Dworak's third type: "From the very beginning of melodic dictation, the student should be given the name of the first note. After hearing the exercise from the given note, the key of the exercise is determined" (p. 22). This procedure does slightly open the door to some problems in contour following (see the following discussion).

47. Rogers (1984) recognized the importance of requiring students "to gather accumulating aural clues and derive a feel for the tonic center of the tune from the *internal evidence* rather than from a given note or chord" (p. 115).

notes printed on answer blanks or through other means), we are obviating the need for listeners to hear in tonally meaningful ways.

As an analogy, consider the kinds of linguistic understanding necessary for vocalists to perform songs in a foreign language. On the one hand, singers must be able to pronounce the phonemes of the text. On the other, they must understand the *meaning* of the text. They must know the definition of each word and its grammatical and syntactic functions. They must read the text for the information it carries, not just for its sounds. Melodic perception is similar. Listeners must not only recall the contour of a melody but also understand the tonal meaning of its pitches.[48] Consider the experience of hearing a vocalist perform a song learned only phonetically, without recourse to the meaning of the text. Such performances are typically devoid of meaning, vacant, and emotionless. Listeners who hear melodies only through contour are similarly impoverished.[49]

What happens to such listeners is that they use coexistent information (contour) as a substitute for more meaningful information (tonal function) in order to arrive—rather unwittingly—at the right answer. Analogies can be found in the field of artificial intelligence, wherein computer programmers train software that "learns." Goodacre, Neal, and Kell (1996) reported the following: Researchers attempted to train an artificially intelligent neural network to recognize the difference between aerial photographs that contained images of tanks and other photographs without tanks. After initial training—feeding in various images with and without tanks—the software began to make accurate assessments of which were which. Heartened by these early results, the researchers initially ventured to conclude that their algorithms could truly "learn" to recognize the presence or absence of man-made vehicles against the background of a complex natural terrain. However, when the software was presented with a new set of images, it failed miserably. Why was the algorithm successful with the first set of images and not with the second? The team

48. Of course, perhaps much more than in language, there are different kinds of meaning in music. Tonal function is but one, but it forms a central, indispensable, and predominant role in Western music training.

49. As are *performances* uninformed by tonal function. A revelatory account came to me from a clarinet studio instructor: As one of his students played an assigned passage he listened while he puzzled over the fact that—although she performed all the pitches and rhythms accurately—there was still something drastically wrong. On a hunch, he asked, "What key is that in?" She replied, "A♭ major." The passage was in fact in F minor. He spent some time reeducating her to hear the passage with its proper tonal functions, to the ultimate benefit of her performance. See Sloboda (1978, 3–9) for a discussion of the perceptual and cognitive processes in *literate* reading music. See "Establishing Collection and Tonic" in chapter 6 for further information on the importance of key awareness.

reexamined the first set and noticed one important detail: all the photographs that contained tanks were taken on sunny days; all those without tanks were taken on cloudy ones. The software had learned well, but it had learned to recognize not tanks but weather conditions. Thus it is with providing starting pitches for listeners who have yet to develop the ability to identify the scale degrees of pitches in relation to the tonic. Such listeners will follow the contour—particularly for stepwise passages at the beginning of a dictation—and mimic correct responses while being unable to perform the very task we ask of them: comprehension of tonal function.

ACCEPTABLE CUES   So, let us come to some conclusions about which extramusical cues to give for dictations. It is possible, even desirable, to give only the following information before playing dictations: tonic and beat unit. For example, one might say, "The following dictation is in E♭, with a quarter-note beat unit," or, "The tonic is E♭, and the number on the bottom of the meter sign is 4," or some similar instructions. Many instructors may also choose to specify a clef, particularly when seeking to foster practice in particular clefs. One further restriction might be desirable at times: to ensure that listeners work in compound meter, an injunction to notate certain dictations in compound meter *if possible* is appropriate. This will prevent responses to dictations conceived in compound meter from being written by listeners in a fast simple triple meter. Such an injunction can be given before a group of dictations, perhaps only some of which may actually be written in compound meter.

The goal behind giving only this minimal amount of information is to cultivate development of certain basic aural skills. Without meter signs, starting pitches and rhythms, preannounced modes, preliminary tonic-orienting pitches, and beat counting, listeners must infer pulse and meter, tonic, starting scale degrees, and other important musical information.

Instructors who announce only clef, tonic, and beat unit must be prepared to accept several notated versions of a single dictation. This manifests itself primarily in metric terms. Without pulses counted before or during a dictation, without a preprinted meter sign, without a prescribed number of measures, and without a rhythmic value for the starting note, listeners are free to choose one of several pulse levels as a beat unit. Instructors might therefore see two or three perfectly correct combinations of rhythm and meter, each of which is completely accurate in and of itself. Example 3.16 shows two such versions listeners might supply if informed only that the half note is the beat unit.

Beethoven's version is the first one, but considering that Beethoven's metronome marking (above m. 362) places the half note at a rate of 224, instructors playing this dictation at the original tempo would be likely to see the second version as well.

Example 3.16. Beethoven, Symphony No. 5, mmt. 4, mm. 390–97, two versions based on different pulse levels.

In addition, since there is no way to audibly distinguish whether anything with three (or more) adjacent levels of duple pulses has been notated in duple or quadruple meter (see chapter 2), the versions in Example 3.17 could be just as acceptable.

Not only must instructors be willing to *accept* such different responses as correct; they must also *discuss* such differences with their students. Through teaching such concepts as the different levels of perceptible pulse and the inherent relationship between duple and quadruple meters, they can develop in their students deeper understanding of the phenomena of meter and rhythm, as well as of our system of metric and rhythmic notation.

The only such difficulty to be encountered in the pitch domain concerns the specific octave in which scale-degree perceptions are to be notated. Listeners who hear a succession of tonal functions relative to a tonic (e.g., $\hat{5}$–$\hat{4}$–$\hat{3}$–$\hat{2}$–$\hat{1}$) and are told the name of that tonic (or the starting pitch) should be capable of easily translating them into specific pitch-name classes (e.g., B♭–A♭–G–F–E♭); it is a small but hardly automatic matter to have perceived and to notate those pitch-name classes in the proper

Example 3.17. Beethoven, Symphony No. 5, mmt. 4, mm. 390–97, two versions based on quadruple interpretation.

octave. Instructors must decide how important this is and how to calculate its value relative to other pitch and rhythm factors.

Tempo

The rate of presentation has a measurable effect on listeners' abilities to process pitch-discrimination tasks. Common sense would dictate that as speed increases, discrimination becomes more difficult. Like many armchair suppositions, this is only partially true. There is not a direct linear relationship between rate of presentation and aural perception. In a test of same/different melodic discrimination, Tunks, Bowers, and Eagle (1993) found that if pitches progress at a rate anywhere between 100 and 240 per minute, perception is uniformly at a maximum.[50] Perception suffers above 240 pitches per minute and falls to near chance levels as a rate of 480 pitches per minute is approached. Interestingly (and quite illuminating for those presenting dictations), perception also deteriorates at *slower* rates (below 100 per minute), although not quite as severely as at the extremely fast rates.

Length and Number of Playings

The length of a dictation and the number of times it is heard affect listeners' use of extractive listening and short-term musical memory. At one end of the scale, were we to offer many playings of a relatively short dictation, we would place limited demands on listeners' needs to extract meaningfully long portions of the music and on their abilities to accurately remember such portions upon initial hearings. Numerous or unlimited playings take dictation into the realm of *transcription*, which—although similar to dictation—does not require listeners to develop musical memory in the same ways or to the same level that dictation does.[51] At the other end of the scale, one or two playings of a relatively long dictation would overtax the limits of most listeners' short-term memories and result in anxiety, frustration, and little opportunity for improvement at the subsequent stages of musical understanding and notation.

As a general rule of thumb, using Miller's limits of short-term memory as modified by Marple, it is prudent to think first of allotting one playing for every six to ten chunks in a dictation.[52] This represents an idealized

---

50. These numbers represent the actual number of isochronous *pitches* per minute, not *beats* per minute (which would not be very meaningful in this context).

51. See the discussion of transcription in chapter 5.

52. With a chunk defined as a single memorable unit. For the purposes of the current discussion, we can assume that—for many beginning aural skills students—one chunk is equal to one note. However, see the section titled "Chunking" earlier.

listening experience, without significant errors, within the limits of short-term musical memory. Obviously, many listeners will endure listening experiences, even within the controlled environs of melodic dictation, that will fall short of this idealized plan. Any one of the various steps in the process of taking dictation affords ample opportunity for difficulties at various stages of aural development. Clinical experience with over a thousand university freshmen has shown that—for dictations with a level of complexity appropriate to listeners' theoretical knowledge and skills level—an additional playing is typically needed to bring accuracy rates within acceptable grading percentages and will still challenge more skilled listeners while giving others more opportunity to develop their skills.

Thus, we can arrive at a very rough formula that describes the relationship between length and number of playings: $P = (Ch/L) + 1$, where P = number of playings, Ch = number of chunks in the dictation (with a chunk defined as a single memorable unit), and L = limit of listener's short-term memory, in chunks (a number typically between 6 and 10, inclusive, as defined by Marple). Rendering the formula in descriptive discourse, we can say the following: "To calculate an appropriate number of playings for a dictation, divide the number of chunks it contains by the limit of the listener's short-term memory (in chunks) and add one extra playing."

The variable L can be assigned an integer value of 6, 7, 8, 9, or 10. This affords rather wide latitude: a twenty-chunk dictation would require three playings while $L = 10$, whereas the same dictation would require more than four playings while L = six. Obviously, pushing L toward its upper limits will require listeners to hone their short-term memory skills. This can often be accomplished through drills that involve singbacks of progressively longer melodic fragments and extractive singbacks from dictation-length melodies.

The variable Ch is even more difficult to pin down. This will vary from listener to listener, from dictation to dictation, depending upon each listener's chunking abilities and how each dictation relates to each listener's prior experience. Certain assumptions can be made within a carefully coordinated curriculum (in which specific musical structures are taught in theory courses and reinforced in aural skills and keyboard courses), but even under such circumstances it is difficult to be certain which listeners will recognize and chunk which specific structures. With these caveats in mind, it is nonetheless possible to broadly structure a learning sequence in which a chunk is simply equal to one note during early weeks or months and dictations are gradually lengthened through the addition of carefully chosen recognizable figures that listeners are expected to chunk into memorable units.

The formula can also be solved for Ch in order to arrive at an appropriate number of chunks for dictations: $Ch = (P - 1) L$. Rendering this formula in descriptive discourse, we can say the following: "To calculate the appropriate length of a dictation (in chunks), subtract 1 from the total number of playings and multiply the result by the limit of the listener's short-term memory (in chunks)."

We can also solve for L to find what demands certain dictations will place on listeners' short-term memories: $L = Ch/(P - 1)$. Rendering this formula in descriptive discourse, we can say the following: "To calculate the limit of the listener's short-term memory (in chunks) necessary to successfully complete a dictation, divide the number of chunks the dictation contains by one fewer than the total number of playings."

As an interesting test of this formula, let us examine the melodic dictation given as representative of those on the GRE Revised Music Test (Educational Testing Service 1993, 68, 86). It contains twenty-two notes and is played four times. Assuming, for the moment, that one note equals one chunk, we find that $L = 22/3$, or 7 1/3—well within the Miller-Marple limit of six to ten chunks of information per playing.

Readers must bear in mind that such formulas are capricious, containing variables that are difficult to quantify and depending upon some decidedly non-numerical factors such as prior experience, education, and even each listener's success at focusing attention during any given playing.[53] Particularly important is the match between listeners' knowledge and skill on the one hand and the types of figures contained in a dictation on the other. For example, listeners unfamiliar with triplets or chromatics would encounter much greater difficulties than the number of notes and number of playings would seem to indicate. In addition, the usefulness of these formulas has been tested on dictations of only typical length— up to about thirty notes long. Nonetheless, these calculations provide us with a point of departure from which we can tailor dictation experiences for individual classes and even specific listeners.

Duration between Playings

The time between playings places demands on all dictation-taking skills, but particularly on listeners' facility with notation. When listeners are working with protonotation only, thirty seconds (or even less) between playings can often be sufficient. Similar durations between playings are appropriate during an intermediary learning stage wherein listeners use

---

53. Compare the more general formula for "memory retention limit" in Lawson (1970), which includes the chunking factors "amount of information previously stored in the memory similar to the stimulus" and "redundancy factor of the stimulus" (p. 8) in addition to other parameters, few of which are quantified by Lawson. Butler and Lochstampfor (1993, 12) offer a "difficulty index" for melodic dictations based on length, number and direction of skips, chromatics, sequences, and phrase structure. Also see Gillespie's (1993) use of "rating systems" (for number of direction changes, range, total interval content, interval difficulty, and "tonal fit") in attempting to determine what makes a melodic pattern difficult to hear.

protonotation *between* playings and translate that protonotation into actual notation only after the final playing. In this case, additional time should be provided after the final playing to allow listeners to complete their notation. This allows for specific control over the time allotted for attention, memory, and understanding on the one hand and for notation on the other.

It is helpful to allow listeners to become relatively adept at musical hearing, memory, and understanding (if only at a basic level of difficulty) through the use of either protonotation or singbacks with solmization before allowing notation to encroach on the time required for these other skills. Once listeners demonstrate competence with hearing, memory, and understanding, they can more easily incorporate notation into their work from the first playing. When listeners use actual notation from the first playing of a dictation, they work out that notation after each playing. This transfers their use of notational skills back into the time between playings, which is also used for memory and understanding. When this occurs, it requires a consequential increase in the amount of time provided between playings. Typically, a minute between playings and two minutes after the final playing will afford listeners just enough time to process their memory and understanding and work out the proper notation. Of course, this depends on many factors, including the degree of match between the complexity of the material and listeners' knowledge and skills, the length of the dictation, the number of playings, and other variables. Some listeners at certain stages may need to practice with more time, progressively shortening these durations toward a specific goal. This is one application for which audio recordings and computer-assisted instruction are extremely appropriate. These resources allow listeners to control the time between playings at their own discretion.

It is interesting to independently vary the *time* between playings and the *number* of playings. Listeners who struggle when the time between playings has been shortened but prosper when the time has been lengthened are almost certainly working correctly but slowly or inefficiently. Since speed is of the essence (music does happen in real time, after all), such listeners can benefit from counseling and drills designed specifically to increase their speed and efficiency. A variety of activities can do just that. Particular attention must be paid to the time taken to carry out such basic tasks as inferring meter and tonic, calculating scale degrees (particularly after skips), and constructing symbols for notation. This last factor can be particularly important. Facility with music notation is one of the goals of aural skills training in general and of dictation in particular. The more rapidly and efficiently musicians can translate their musical understanding into notation, the deeper and more immediate will be their command of the system of music notation. Carefully scrutinizing every move of the pencil can often yield valuable revelations about how musicians understand and use notation. One effective diagnostic activity is videotaping listeners' writing while they take dictation. This allows for close

experiencing difficulties with focused attention, extractive listening, or other aspects of short-term memory.

Summary of the Dictation Process

On the basis of all this, we can devise a simple flowchart (Figure 3.1) for taking melodic dictations whose length and complexity make them appropriate for extraction into two parts (for the sake of discussion, melodies twelve to twenty notes long for listeners with few or no chunking skills).

In practice, as listeners develop more and varied aural skills, they can begin to entertain some significant deviations from such a process. For instance, listeners who immediately hear that a melody begins and ends on $\hat{1}$ might sketch out opening and closing materials, perhaps even working backward from the end. Others who hear a sequence in the middle of a dictation might quickly block out the contour of what they heard there.[55] But beginning listeners—particularly those new to the process of dictation—usually flounder when trying to draw on too many stimuli at once. They find little success at taking dictation and—most seriously—do not develop important skills such as focused and extractive listening and short-term musical memory. All the concomitant skills necessary for taking dictation well are the true goals here, not success at dictation in and of itself, so most beginners find it best to stick rather closely to the process spelled out in the flowchart.

Assessment Tools and Evaluation Rubrics

General Principles

Three primary principles should guide how dictation work is evaluated. First, there should be some absolute standard against which the work is judged—reported, for example, in the form of a percentage or letter grade. Second, feedback should be given with regard to precisely what was correct and what was incorrect in each dictation. Third, when appropriate, suggestions should be made about what to do to correct systemic problems, whenever possible.

Many of the ideas discussed here are extensible with little modification to polyphonic and harmonic dictation and also to transcription, so that

---

55. For some interesting narratives from expert listeners who use such strategies, see Potter (1990).

no separate discussions of assessment and evaluation of those skills will be necessary.[56]

Representative Examples

There are no published investigations of aural skills assessment in general.[57] What we do have are a few published expositions of specific rubrics: one for a textbook, another for a computer program, and two others for standardized music examinations.

KRAFT, *A NEW APPROACH TO EAR TRAINING*   It is rare to find a textbook that prescribes any principles or guidelines for assessing dictation.[58] One exception appears in Kraft (1999), where students are instructed to score their own dictations. Kraft writes: "Score your answer to the first exercise for pitch: mark an x *over* any incorrect added or omitted pitch. Then score the same exercise for rhythm: mark an x *under* any beat that isn't correctly notated" (p. 4). In order to obtain a numerical score, he continues, "count up the total number of pitch x's and write this number on the reverse of the Worksheet in the space marked 'Px.' Count up the total number of rhythm x's and write it in the space marked 'Rx.' Subtract your Px and Rx from the given figures to get your P-score and R-score" (p. 5).

Kraft's procedure yields two raw scores: one for rhythm and one for pitch, which are to be used as criteria for advancement to further levels in the text. Rhythm and pitch are treated separately—with separate percentages representing each—and a minimum score of 90% in each area is considered necessary for advancement.

These are certainly serviceable guidelines. It is particularly helpful to have separate evaluations of rhythm and pitch accuracy. One possible

---

56. For an exposition of a scoring rubric for two-voice dictation, see Educational Testing Service (1993, 97–102). Educational Testing Service (1993, 102–7) presents a rubric for harmonic dictation, although the responses for individual chords are logged only in the form of multiple-choice selections.

57. Gillespie (personal correspondence, 1998) is conducting research on scoring methods for melodic dictation. At present, his research consists of collecting survey responses from over 400 theory instructors across the United States. His results, when published, should provide interesting insight into how this aspect of aural skills assessment is practiced in situ.

58. For example, Benward and Kolosick (1996a; 1996b) offer none. Durham (1994) merely suggests that "students hear the instructor play an example, write out what was played, then compare their answers against the instructor's key. This process eliminates the instructor's time-consuming task of calling out detailed answers and provides for immediate feedback to the student" (p. vii). But what manner of feedback? This process may be of some limited value for drill and practice, but students need informed, judicious evaluations of where, how, and why discrepancies appear between their notation and the correct answer.

drawback, however, is that these two parameters are treated as being quantitatively equal. Anyone wishing to weight pitch or rhythm more heavily would have to proportionally adjust the percentages accordingly.

One factor Kraft's guidelines do not account for is the temporal displacement of correct pitches or rhythms. If any musical figure—a scalar passage, an arpeggiation, a particular rhythmic pattern—does not appear in its proper location, then it is marked as incorrect. Under this rubric a respondent might drop a single beat early in a dictation, transcribe the rest of the pitches and rhythms exactly correctly (but one beat early), and receive no credit for any of that correct but temporally displaced music.

MACGAMUT SOFTWARE   In contrast, the evaluation routines in Ann Blombach's *MacGamut* (Columbus, OH: MacGamut Music Software International) do indeed account for such temporal shifts.[59] *MacGamut* initially checks in a note-for-note fashion similar to Kraft's but checks rhythms first, then pitches. However, *MacGamut* then checks for the following information: double bar, only at end; proper use of anacrusis and incomplete final measure (if applicable); total number of beats in each barred segment; missing bar lines; incorrectly placed bar lines; and correct total number of notes. In addition, *MacGamut* then checks (if necessary) for contour similarities and especially for segments of three or more pitches in a row that have been temporally displaced fewer than four notes in either direction. From all this information, *MacGamut* provides not only a raw score in the form of a percentage but also markings on and above the music as well as messages about the kinds of errors that may have been made.

Blombach's rubric for handling contour similarities is particularly interesting. If the program detects that incorrect pitches follow the correct contour for at least three pitches in a row, then it prints a message that indicates exactly where this contour matching took place. However, Blombach writes, "a correct contour with the wrong pitches does not improve the student's score. If the student has the right contour but the wrong pitches, then the student must have, at the very least, lost the tonal location of a series of pitches" (Blombach, 1990). Of course, no grading rubric—machine or human—can discern from notation alone whether such a loss of tonal location took place at the memory stage or the understanding stage. Nonetheless, *MacGamut* is effective in diagnosing at the very least the kind of error that took place and not giving credit for mere contour tracing.

MacGamut is a truly remarkable program and uniquely sensitive to matters pedagogical, cognitive, and musical in a sea of rather unintelligent

---

59. Blombach (1990) discusses *MacGamut*'s assessment routines in greater detail.

computer-assisted instruction. It does, however, have two features that limit its usefulness. First, the program always provides a notated key signature and either a starting note, the sound of the tonic, or both for each dictation. This supplies users with either the scale-degree function of the first note or the sound of the tonic, things listeners should be perceiving on their own. Second, *MacGamut*'s interface provides music symbols for users, so that they are not required to create the shapes of note heads, stems, and flags; proper stem direction; correct placement of rests (particularly half and whole rests); and construction of key signatures. Users who are fluent with music notation pose no concern here, but users who need to develop their familiarity and skills with the elements and the system of notation (one of the aims of dictation practice) will find little help while clicking and dragging prefabricated music symbols.

Nonetheless, even considering these caveats, *MacGamut* is at present the most sophisticated yet eminently employable commercially available tool for the machine assessment of dictation, due to its pattern-matching routines and pedagogically sound user feedback.

GRE MUSIC TEST   The most formalized and elaborately explicit published evaluation procedures for dictation are those used for the Graduate Record Examination (GRE) Music Test, for which the Educational Testing Service (ETS) has developed grading rubrics for one- and two-voice melodic dictation (among other things) that are of particular interest to this discussion.[60]

Let us examine in some detail the ETS rubric for single-voice melodic dictations. ETS judges these dictations on a scoring range of 0–8 raw points, 6 for pitch and 2 for rhythm. (Obviously, readers wishing to adapt this rubric can alter the proportion between these two figures to suit their own needs or even report two separate scores.) Two principles are established before any grading takes place: (1) any combination of note and rest that totals a beat's full value is acceptable (for example, notating a performed half note as a quarter note followed by a quarter rest), and (2) this being tonal dictation, enharmonic equivalents are not acceptable.

The grading process begins by scanning the music for pitches. Each pitch must appear at its proper attack point within the measure. Incorrect, missing, or added pitches each result in a deduction worth $6/n$ of a point (rounded to the nearest half-point), where n equals the total number of pitches to be notated in the dictation. Groups of adjacent pitches that are either (1) added or (2) in the wrong octave are equivalent to only one pitch error (again, $6/n$ of a point).

60. These procedures are printed in Educational Testing Service (1993, 93–102).

Next, the rhythm is judged. The two rhythm points are spread evenly across a four-measure dictation, one half-point per measure. Any measure not completely correct rhythmically automatically results in a one half-point deduction.

Finally, points can be *added back* if both pitch and rhythm are notated correctly but metrically shifted from their proper position. If three, four, or five beats in a row are so shifted, one half-point is added back; if six beats in a row are so shifted, one full point is added back.

The GRE rubric is similar to Blombach's, with several main differences: (1) it checks pitches before rhythms; (2) it pays less attention to further details of notation, such as the final double bar, total number of notes, and contour similarities;[61] and (3) it provides no feedback to the dictation taker beyond a numerical score.[62]

ADVANCED PLACEMENT EXAMINATION IN MUSIC THEORY   The grading rubric for the Advanced Placement Examination in Music Theory is somewhat less elaborate than that for the GRE.[63] The "regular scoring guide" for the Advanced Placement Examination assigns one point for each half-measure of a four-measure dictation and adds one point to the total, for a highest possible score of 9. Each half-measure must be correct in both rhythm and pitch—even if shifted from its original metric position—to earn a point. Alternate scoring guides allow for awarding partial points if correct pitches appear with mostly or completely incorrect rhythms or if correct rhythms appear with mostly or completely incorrect pitches.

The Advanced Placement Examination—like the GRE—yields a very coarse score and can certainly distinguish broadly between excellent and poor dictation takers. But both tests' rubrics ignore details of notation beyond rhythm and pitch and provide no further feedback to examinees.

---

61. To be fair to the GRE, reading sessions *always* specify more rigorous and detailed guidelines than those published in Educational Testing Service (1993).

62. In a unique and outstanding article, Phillips (in press) details how he has incorporated principles and practices from his experiences as a reader and chief reader for the GRE in music and as chief faculty consultant designate for the Advanced Placement Examination in Music Theory. Phillips makes some excellent observations about the grading rubrics used for these exams and suggests sound practical methods for increasing consistency and efficiency in scoring papers and tests and maximizing the written feedback students receive on their work.

63. The Advanced Placement Examination grading procedures are printed in Educational Testing Service (1998, 52–55).

a.

b.

Example 3.18. (a) A melodic dictation. (b) One student response (in diplomatic transcription) corrected only for rhythm.

Some Proposals

It is possible to mark every detail of pitch and rhythm and still remain quite consistent while yielding meaningful scores *and* providing ample feedback for students. The following suggestions adhere to these principles.

1. *Correct and evaluate the rhythms first.* Although it is possible to evaluate pitches before rhythms, it is more informative to leave the pitches until after the rhythms have been evaluated. This procedure allows us first to examine *when* students thought things occurred and then to examine *what* they thought they heard in the light of our understanding of their perception of the timing of things. This can involve some of what I will refer to as "normalizing" the rhythms of responses to dictations. Simply put, our first job is to straighten out whatever rhythms (or absence thereof) appear on student papers. Blombach (1990) describes checking from the beginning and from the end. These are good places to start, considering the serial-curve response of short-term memory.[64] However, such statistics are valid across populations, not necessarily for any one individual during any particular dictation. So it behooves us to check for segments of correct rhythmic material from all portions of the dictation. The amount of rhythmic displacement an instructor is willing to accept is a personal matter, although such criteria should be clear to students. All corrections and normalizations of the rhythm should be written outside the staff, to allow room for pitch corrections. Example 3.18(a) shows a melodic dictation; Example 3.18(b) shows one student response, with rather liberal rhythm corrections added. It is helpful to join the normal-

---

64. In brief, the serial curve for memory is a graphic representation of the fact that we tend to remember initial and recent elements more than those in the middle.

Example 3.19. The response from Example 3.18, now also corrected for pitch.

ized or corrected rhythms to their incorrect notations through some kind of marking: note the rectangle in Figure 3.18(b).

2. *Correct and evaluate the pitches in light of the corrected rhythms.* Now that the corrected or normalized rhythms have been supplied, treat the pitches as if they were written in those normalized rhythms. As with rhythm, look for correct segments (not individual pitches[65]). How short a segment to accept and how much displacement to allow are, again, personal matters. Incorrect pitches should be crossed out (but left legible to allow students to interpret their own errors). Correct pitches can be written either directly within the staff (if there is room) or on a staff provided above or below explicitly for this purpose. Example 3.19 shows pitch corrections added to the normalized rhythms from Example 3.18(b).

Of course, the level of tolerance exercised during rhythm normalization will affect the number of errors recorded during pitch evaluation. In the preceding case, if none of the pitches beyond m. 3 were adjusted for rhythmic displacement, then far more pitch errors would be recorded.

3. *Evaluate other details of notation.* It is also important to assess notational features that do not stem directly from the meanings of the perceived pitches and rhythms. This includes such features as clefs (proper construction and placement), key signatures (correct number of sharps or flats and proper placement), meter signs (proper placement and notation), construction of note heads, stems (direction, length, straightness, and verticality), flags (proper shape), beams (consistency with beats or measures), accidentals (proper placement), rests (proper shape and placement), and any other aspects of notation deemed important enough to correct.

4. *Look for obvious sources of errors and offer meaningful, usable feedback.* Although notation alone is a rather poor indicator of specific

---

65. A principle adhered to by ETS, much to the consternation of many GRE readers, is that of "intersection with reality," whereby *any* pitch that appears in its proper metric position is counted as correct. Following this principle, it is possible for an incorrect answer of, say, five pitches that ascend stepwise from C to G to intersect the correct answer *descending* stepwise from G to C and where those two intersect (at E) no points are deducted. In actuality, such errors typically occur amid such otherwise abysmal passages that these minor "intersections with reality" do little or nothing to enhance a student's score.

causes for listening problems, dictation responses should nonetheless be scanned for evidence of *sources* for errors. For example, a string of incorrect pitches might be evidence of a clef-reading error or thinking in the wrong key. Even more important, evidence should be sought for the underlying causes of consistent error types. For example, responses that frequently begin on incorrect pitches but follow correct contours generally point to three possible causes: (1) short-term memory difficulties, (2) incorrect tonic inference, and (3) difficulties in identifying scale degrees in relation to the tonic. In contrast, responses that begin mostly incorrectly but end mostly correctly are usually indications of difficulties with extractive listening due to retroactive interference. It is crucial to offer meaningful, usable feedback for listeners' future development. It is one thing to mark all the incorrect rhythms and pitches for dictation but quite another to take broader assessments into account and draw conclusions that can guide listeners toward remedial drills and exercises designed to correct their underlying difficulties.

4

Polyphonic and Harmonic
Dictation

Polyphonic Dictation

Two-voice dictation is a small (but perhaps essential) component of musical training, judging from an examination of the single most popular
ear-training text and the GRE Revised Music Test. Pembrook and Riggins
(1990) noted that "among those instructors who use a commercially published text to teach dictation and error detection, Benward's *Ear Training:
A Technique for Listening* is the dominant text almost to the exclusion
of all others" (p. 239). The fifth edition of *Ear Training* (Benward and
Kolosick 1996a) devotes only a few pages to multipart dictation per se,
and less than 5% overall even if one counts all the transcription activities
that include two and three voices. The GRE Revised Music Test includes
one two-voice dictation worth 2.5% of the entire exam (see Educational
Testing Service 1993, 10–12). Three- (and more-) voice dictation is rare
indeed, at least in U.S. universities, colleges, and conservatories.

Despite its infrequent implementation, polyphonic dictation is important because it involves modes of listening that can remain otherwise
underdeveloped, can function as preparatory skill development that leads
to bass line perception, and models quite closely the kinds of rhythmic
textural differentiation found in most common-practice-period music.[1]
Schenker ([1935] 1979) commented on the importance of polyphonic perception: "It is certain [!] that almost half of mankind is unmusical, even
incapable of singing a folk tune—a sorry ratio, one which would be un-
thinkable in the case of language. How then can the ear be expected to
hear polyphony, which is fundamental to the linear progression? The
musical person, however, is certainly capable of recognizing linear pro-

---

1. Lester (1986) notes that "homorhythmic textures are not all that common outside
of obvious chorales and tutti unisons" (p. 248).

gressions" (p. xxiv). To be a musical person, then, according to Schenker, one must be able to hear polyphony.

Parallel Perception and the "Cocktail Party" Effect

There is nearly universal agreement, among the ear-training texts that address multiple-voice listening at all, that listeners should learn to process multiple voices *at the same time*. Benward and Kolosick (1996b) enjoin instructors to perform two-voice dictations "slowly enough to ensure proper understanding, but do not play either voice separately" (p. 176). McHose (1948) decrees "the instructor should never dictate each voice separately" (p. 171). Trubitt and Hines (1979) warn students: "If you avoid listening to the two parts simultaneously you will delay your mastery of this skill" (p. 116).

Whereas it may be a straightforward matter for instructors to follow Benward/Kolosick and McHose in always playing parts together, it may be quite another matter for listeners to attend to two parts simultaneously. Jeppesen ([1946] 1970) noted this problem with particular clarity in assessing the role of the listener:

> He must assemble all the participating parts mentally and condense them into a total impression; yet he may not always be able to abandon himself freely to this total impression, but sometimes be forced, or enticed, to follow and spiritually to merge himself in single voices or parts. However, the more he is absorbed in the totality of the impression, the less distinctly will he be able to follow the course of the single lines; and the more he concentrates his attention upon the single parts, the more will his conception of the collective effect recede into the background. (p. 27)

Research on speech perception confirmed decades ago what most of us come to intuit in our daily lives: that our minds can focus on and extract the meaning from one of several simultaneous conversations even though the sounds they produce in combination are meaningless. This ability to filter out all but a single meaningful stream of information has been dubbed the "cocktail party" effect.[2] At one time, it was thought that only one channel of access could transmit information into memory.[3] We might be led to the analogy that listeners attend to polyphonic music in

---

2. Follow Butler's (1992, 211) recommendations for a review of the literature on the cocktail party effect.

3. See, for example, Broadbent (1958; 1962), which concluded that competing streams of information do not necessarily mask one another at the sensory level but nonetheless interfere with one another due to a "difficulty . . . within the central nervous system" (Broadbent 1958, 13).

much the same way as they do to competing conversations. Indeed, Levin and Martin (1988b) remark that "it is common practice to bring out the voice the students are writing down. They should try to concentrate on the individual melodic shape of each line as they write it down" (p. 44).

But the analogy between language and music is never a perfect one, and in this instance it breaks down over the word "competing." It may be true that parallel attention to competing conversations inhibits overall comprehension, but listening to two or more voices of a polyphonic texture involves attention to (usually) *cooperating* stimuli. Sloboda and Edworthy (1981) recognized "the intimate relationship of the separate lines one to another. Although in one sense they *are* separate, in another very important sense, they make up a single piece of music" (p. 39). Sloboda and Edworthy found a direct relationship between the circle-of-fifth relatedness of the keys of voices in two-part counterpoint and the ability of listeners to detect errors in either of the voices. As we shall see later, stylistic strictures and principles of voice leading constrain the motion of individual contrapuntal lines and listeners are able to process verticalities as well as lines (unlike the randomness between two competing conversations) so that polyphonic dictation is often a matter of marshaling a variety of listening strategies, including concurrent listening, to component strands of contrapuntal activity.

Other research has shown that listeners *can* perceive and remember two or more simultaneous stimuli. Keele and Neill (1978) concluded that "when messages do not interfere, they can be processed in parallel through at least the memory stage" (p. 41). But they also found that "in many situations, however, parallel access to memory entails costs. When stimuli are complex and in the same modality, they may mask or merge with one another" (p. 41). Gregory (1990) also found that parallel processing takes place and that retention is enhanced when the voices are related in key (see also Sloboda and Edworthy 1981) but distinguished by timbre. Gregory (1994) confirmed and amplified the importance of timbre in distinguishing between contrapuntal voices. In addition, numerous studies have found that it is much more difficult for listeners to segregate two contrapuntal voices when they cross each other than when they are in completely separate tessituras (see, for example, Dowling 1973a).

These findings, particularly those about timbre and register, should cause aural skills instructors to reevaluate the use of closely voiced two-part piano music for introductory polyphonic dictation.[4]

4. See the discussion in Sloboda (1985, 166–174) for a fuller examination of attending to multiple parts simultaneously. Wright and Bregman (1987, 66–73) and Butler (1992, 104–10) summarize various factors that influence polyphonic perception. In a fascinating and illuminating study, Gjerdingen (1994) models auditory stream segregation, Gestalt effects, and other multiple-voice listening behaviors.

Contextual Inference

What kind of information can listeners glean from the cooperative stimuli formed by two or more lines of polyphonic music? Benward and Kolosick (1996a) tell instructors to "encourage class members to think of each voice in relation to the other" (p. 176) and to "make the student more aware of the relationship between two melodies" (p. 195). Levin and Martin (1988b) note that students can "check their work by listening to the intervals between the voices" (p. 44). Trubitt and Hines (1979) conclude that "in addition to the melodic lines themselves, there is the interest of the harmonic intervals, the interaction of the rhythm of the two parts, and the harmonic background" (p. 107).

The metric and rhythmic interaction between the parts is certainly an important aspect of how they work together to form cooperating streams of activity. As Koch ([1787/1793] 1983) noted, "The correct movement of meter does not depend on the main part alone, but on all the voices together" (p. 70).[5] Although such cooperation is typical in common-practice-period music, there does exist the concept of *metric dissonance*, which accounts for conflict between concurrent strands of metric activity. Seeger (1930) first hinted at this concept. The concept reaches a mature stage in Yeston (1976, 89–118, 121–47). Krebs (1987) explores the idea further. Both Yeston and Krebs include some examples simple enough for undergraduate dictation (and a few others so suitable if stripped down to two-voice texture). Earlier music is much more problematic. Jeppesen ([1946] 1970) noted that "in the 16th century, or perhaps even earlier, there was introduced a collective rhythm with regularly recurring accents, between which and the individual rhythm of the single parts there arose mutual strife and contradictions" (p. 27).

Listening to rhythm and meter is often made simpler in polyphonic settings once listeners have learned to attend to certain features. In much common-practice-period music, various textural strata distinguish themselves through rhythmic differentiation. Thus, we find conspicuous rhythmic differences between a fugue subject and its countersubject, between a melody and its accompaniment, and so on.[6] Aggregate rhythmic patterns may be repeated verbatim. Single-voice rhythmic figures may be traded between voices. The rhythmic relationships between the voices may clarify simple structures such as metric divisions or more complex ones such as syncopation and hemiola. Cross-rhythms—if familiar to listeners—can be identified quite rapidly.[7]

5. See Koch's ([1787/1793] 1983) discussion of how voices interact to "preserve the identity of metrical stress" on pp. 70–74.
6. See Lester (1986, 244–59) for a detailed discussion of the role of rhythm in polyphony.
7. In a test of university music majors, Wapnick (1984) found that the "2 against 3" cross-rhythm was identified correctly 81.3 percent of the time. Other, less common

To heighten awareness of these relationships, listeners can explore two types of rhythmic dictation from polyphonic music: (1) dictation of the *aggregate* rhythms resultant from the confluence of the parts, wherein a single rhythmic part is notated to represent the combination of multiple parts; and (2) dictation of two (or more) concurrent rhythmic lines on separate staves to represent each of the individual parts.[8] Such isolated rhythmic drills, if practiced at all, should be integrated as soon as possible into the world of pitches. The interaction between rhythmic and metric features on the one hand and tonal function on the other is so important that it should be instilled continually from the earliest possible point.

It seems that it is most advantageous for listeners to attend to the meter and rhythm of polyphonic dictations first. Beckett (1997) studied the efficacy of rhythm-first, pitch-first, and "nondirected" strategies during two-voice dictation and found that "delaying pitch notation did not adversely affect rhythmic notation . . . [but] delaying rhythmic notation did indeed adversely affect pitch notation" (p. 621). As with melodic dictation (chapter 3), listeners can work out a metric and rhythmic framework for each remembered portion and then fill the pitches into that framework, before moving on to a new portion to remember after the next listening.

It is possible for listeners to attend to the harmonic intervals formed between the voices. Like atomistic melodic interval identification, this has broad ramifications with regard to the relationships between acontextual and contextual listening and in terms of how listeners *ought* to listen to tonal music.[9] In addition, Killam, Lorton, and Schubert (1975) and Wuthrich and Tunks (1989) showed that harmonic intervals are indeed more difficult to identify than melodic ones. Nonetheless, listeners can and should learn to attend to verticalities in the following ways.

Among the most fundamental and important contextual pitch distinctions to be made is that between consonance and dissonance. Listeners should be able to separate contextual verticalities into one of these two categories with relative ease.[10] This is important for at least two reasons:

cross-rhythms were identified correctly less than 50% of the time. For example, "5 against 7" was identified correctly only 7.5% of the time. See his table 1 on p. 63 for a complete list.

8. Jeppesen ([1946] 1970) referred to these as the "Macro" (total) and "Micro" (partial) rhythms, respectively (p. 28).

9. See the discussions in chapter 2 under "Identification of Intervals" and chapter 3 under "Musical Understanding."

10. The labels "consonance" and "dissonance" take on different, more acoustically based meanings in acontextual settings. Note with care that the current discussion is limited to *contextual* verticalities. Cogan and Escot (1976) address this issue; they refer to consonance and dissonance as part of "a *context* that creates a hierarchy of intervals (or interval cells), some of which are *predominant* (consonances), some *subordinate* (dissonances)" (p. 128). They emphasize that "which intervals take on which roles is defined and reconfirmed by the compositional context" (p. 128). Bobbitt (1959) surveys widely used definitions of the terms "consonance" and "dissonance" and advises using

TABLE 4.1. Perceptually based taxonomy for dissonances.

Temporal	Kinetic
suspension	passing tone
anticipation	neighboring tone

(1) the distinction between consonance and dissonance is intrinsically musical, carrying with it information about function, implication and realization, sonority, and texture; and (2) knowing a particular pitch in one part and whether its attendant verticality is a consonance or a dissonance significantly reduces the pitch choices in (and thus simplifies perception of) the other part.

Distinctions can be made within each of these categories as well. Consonances can be broadly perceived as either perfect or imperfect. This is an ideal opportunity for both atomistic and contextual drills that point up this distinction. It is also a good time for coordinated theoretical and historical discussions of their structure and usage.

Dissonances in the form of nonharmonic tones can be categorized in a number of ways,[11] but one simple taxonomy bears particularly close relationships with both aural perception and the structural nature of voice leading. This taxonomy is shown in Table 4.1.[12] Its broadest distinction is between *temporal* and *kinetic* dissonances. Temporal dissonances are those that arise from the delay or acceleration of one voice in relation to the others. A delay results in a *suspension*, including the upwardly resolving retardation and various resolutions by skip, which are surface-level substitutions for deeper linear resolutions. An acceleration results in an *anticipation*. Kinetic dissonances are those that arise from the more rapid melodic motion of one part against another. Kinetic dissonances also fall into two broad categories: the *passing tone* and the *neighboring tone*. Many dissonances that move by skip on the surface are in fact manifestations of deeper stepwise passing or neighboring voice leading.

All nonchord dissonances—even including such phenomena as the *cambiata* and "free tone"—can be perceived as one of these four types. Listeners do well at first to make the simple distinction between temporal

these terms "only when referring to an individual's psychological response to contextual situations" (pp. 177–78). It is in this sense—psychological response as described by Bobbitt and contextuality as described by Cogan and Escot and by Bobbitt—that I seek to shape listeners' aural perception of consonance and dissonance.

11. Kostka and Payne (2000, 178) is typical of many current harmony texts in listing nine different types of "non-chord" tones. See the brief survey in Gauldin (1996, 79).

12. Compare the taxonomy in Gauldin (1996).

and kinetic dissonances; further refinement categorizes temporal dissonances into suspensions and anticipations and kinetic dissonances into
passing and neighboring varieties.

One other important type of contextual clue results from the harmonic
implications of the parts over time. To the extent that listeners develop
a sensitivity to these implications (see the later discussions under "Harmonic Dictation"), they will be able to use their inference of prevailing
harmonies to guide their perception of the individual parts that make up
those harmonies.

Integrated Listening

Perhaps the best approach to polyphonic listening is not one but several—
all at the ready and flexible enough to be brought to bear on various
situations. Trubitt and Hines intertwine approaches in their first "conference" on two-part music:

> While listening . . . be aware of two factors: the harmonic intervals
> formed by the parts, and the motion of each separate part. . . .
> Sing each part melodically. If you cannot hear the parts sepa-
> rately it will be impossible to hear them together.
> Fuse the two parts in the same manner that harmonic intervals
> and chords have been fused. (Trubitt and Hines 1979, 70)

But they also note that "the potentially enormous complexity of part
music must be coupled with some regard for human limitations; our attention cannot be directed simultaneously to melody A, melody B, the
harmonic intervals resulting, *and* the implied harmonic background—not
to mention the variety of rhythmic relationships between the parts" (Trubitt and Hines 1979, 108).

So, rather than expect listeners to employ all of these various modes
of listening at the same time, we might nurture their ability to shift among
them as the need arises. This would correspond to Potter's observations
that "the best dictation-takers have a whole box of tools to work with"
(Potter 1990, 69). Listeners can thus be empowered and guided to apply
the most suitable tools to the appropriate listening job at any given moment.

Harmonic Dictation

Learning to hear harmonically is a crucial part of training in Western
music. Morris and Ferguson (1931) noted that "aural training and harmonic study are to a large extent one and the same. If you want to
develop your sense of harmony, train your ear; if you want to improve

your power of hearing, study harmony and counterpoint—only in the right way. They must be studied as *sound*, not as mathematical equations. It will soon be found that a single inward faculty is involved both in aural and harmonic training" (p. iii). However, as Rogers (1984) notes, "No job in ear training is more difficult than taking harmonic dictation" (p. 120). There are various ways to approach harmonic listening with the goal of improving success at harmonic dictation while improving sensitivity to harmony and voice leading in general. The next section of this chapter examines a few of the more commonly taught methods.

Part Writing

This procedure takes as its fundamental premise the notion that transcribing all the voices in a multivoice texture yields the information necessary to identify the harmonies they produce. This is the second example of what Rahn and McKay (1988) call "reductionist" listening: its practitioners "undertake melodic dictations of all the lines in a texture . . . and on comparing the diverse lines, they might arrive at an overall conclusion concerning the chord progression" (p. 101).

On the surface, this seems absolutely true: notate every heard voice, perform the same kind of "analysis" carried out in so many theory and analysis classes (i.e., look at each verticality; find each root; label the inversions), and the result is harmonic dictation. Or is it? Chittum (1969) concludes that listeners who use this technique are "not actually being trained to recognize harmonic movement but rather to infer this after examining the important melodic lines" (p. 65). Indeed, this is not really harmonic dictation but rather a series of melodic dictations that result in a renotation of the passage, after which not harmonic *listening* but harmonic *looking* takes place. This is in no way intended to denigrate the importance of multivoice dictation, but if our goal is to develop harmonic listening, then harmonic analysis should occur as an integral part of the listening process and not be withheld as an afterthought to operate postmortem on the artifacts of listening.

Arpeggiation

Yet another approach requires listeners to arpeggiate the members of each prevailing harmony as it passes. This is perhaps practical in contexts with slow harmonic rhythms but eminently impractical in faster contexts, such as chorales. This is the first "reductionist" approach referred to by Rahn and McKay (1988): "Students might arrive at a conclusion about the whole (a chord or a chord progression) on the basis of its smallest, most detailed parts. . . . Students might, for example, examine every simultaneity (every set of simultaneously sounding notes), analyze it atomistically (e.g., C3, C4, E4, and G4 . . .), compare these parts with the prevailing tonality (e.g., G major . . .), and arrive at a functional conclusion concerning the chord in question (e.g., 'IV')" (p. 101). White (1981) offers a sample narrative of how this might proceed during chord inversion and quality identification (his example is a G-major chord with B in the bass): "(1) Teacher plays inversion at the piano. (2) Student sings the bass tone. (3) Student sings upward from the bass tone to nearest available pitch-classes found in the triad. (4) Student identifies m3 and P4 sung in step 3. (5) Student identifies first-inversion major triad" (p. 64).

Arpeggiating chords as they are heard can become quite tedious and detail-oriented and rapidly loses its practicality as harmonic rhythm increases. It does, however, have the advantage of linking closely with the kinds of arpeggiation exercises practiced in some sight-singing curricula (see chapter 7 under "Arpeggiating Chord Progressions").

Gestalt

In yet another approach, listeners are asked to learn to identify chords as complete entities—to recognize the "subdominantness" of the subdominant chord, for instance.[13] This goal seems reasonable enough: an integral aspect of many expert listeners' strategies involves a certain amount of raw, whole-harmony recognition. But whereas such Gestalt listening is in the end quite rapid and fluid, it is difficult to develop directly. Listeners at any given stage of development either recognize a particular chord or don't. In the absence of other listening strategies, they can be taught no concrete means for recognizing a "new" chord as a Gestalt. Instead, we might think of Gestalt listening as a by-product or result of other techniques. After weeks, months, or even years of repeatedly recognizing and labeling particular chords, those chords can become instantly recognizable—in the same Gestalt manner we recognize a well-known face, a familiar voice on the telephone, or the taste of a common spice. Over time, individual chords, harmonic groups—indeed, many musical figures—drop out of the class of stimuli that require intellectual scrutiny in order to be perceived and take a place in a personal pantheon of essentially instantaneously recognizable entities.

Research performed by Anderson and Tunks (1992) seems to bear this out. They found that listeners' ratings of chords on a scale from "expected" to "unexpected" correlated strongly with their ability to recognize

---

13. For example, in introducing the subdominant, Trubitt and Hines (1979) write: "It is this triad that is clearly heard in the IV–I (plagal) cadence at the end of numerous hymns, the 'Amen.' Aurally, the I–IV or IV–I progression has a mellower, less intense effect when compared to the I–V or V–I" (p. 104). This is roughly equivalent to Rahn and McKay's (1988) "holistic" approach (pp. 101–2). Also see Rogers's (1984) attention to "the affective and psychological response of certain patterns" (p. 122).

the chords during dictation. Anderson and Tunks's subjects' dictation scores were "significantly higher for high expectancy chords than for medium expectancy chords, which in turn yielded significantly higher scores than low expectancy chords" (p. 8).

The Bass Line as the Basis of Harmonic Function

There are indeed various ways to approach harmonic listening, but underpinning many approaches is a keen perception of the bass line. The bass line plays a central role in a long tradition as a foundation of harmonic function. Over four hundred years ago Zarlino wrote: "As the earth is the foundation of the other elements, the bass has the function of sustaining and stabilizing, fortifying and giving growth to the other parts. It is the foundation of the harmony and for this reason is called bass, as if to say the base and sustenance of the other parts" (Zarlino [1558] 1968, 179 [chapter 58]).[14] Obviously, the importance of the bass voice to thoroughbass musicians is suffusive. Rameau and his successors—despite their attention to the *fundamental* bass—also paid respect to the power of the bass *voice* to control things. Rameau's title to chapter 11 from book 3 of the *Traité* begins: "On the progression of the Bass, which simultaneously determines the progression of the chords" (Rameau [1722] 1971, 226). More recently, Schoenberg wrote that "the bass should participate in every change of the harmony. . . . The ear is trained to pay much attention to the bass" (Schoenberg 1967, 86). And at the heart of Schenker's theories is the notion that the *Bassbrechung* forms a support for and counterpoint to the *Urlinie* to form the *Ursatz*: "The bass participates in the formation of all unified configurations of the upper voice, of whatever nature they may be, and decisively determines their beginnings and endings. The value of a masterwork rests to no small degree upon a purposeful and ingenious construction of the bass" (Schenker [1935] 1979, 102 [§257]).

In order to perceive bass lines, listeners must be able to focus their attention on the lowest voice in whatever textures they encounter. For some, this is an entirely new mode of perception—at first puzzling and seemingly inscrutable. For others, it seems to pose little additional difficulty. Many, but not all, of those to whom this comes easily have already had experience in attention to bass lines: jazz and pop musicians, keyboard (or keyboard percussion) players, and (perhaps obviously) bass players and bass vocalists. In any case, it is important at this stage in the

---

14. Granted, Zarlino was not thinking about *functional* harmony here, but the importance of the bass as support for the other parts is not lost across the gulf between modality and tonality.

learning sequence to enable listeners to attend to bass lines and process what they encounter there.

Polyphonic dictation—particularly making the leap from single-voice melodic dictation to two-voice dictation—can often serve as an intermediary step and an extremely controlled environment within which to hone lower-voice attention skills. Two-voice study allows listeners to practice shifting attention between streams of melodic activity, using clues such as timbre (where applicable), tessitura, and functional continuity. Listeners can learn to attend to the differences between voices *and* the cooperation between them. Perception studies have shown that subjects can take in a group of stimuli and learn to shift their perception of those stimuli into one of two or more competing modalities. The psychological literature on *visual* perception and mental representation contains numerous examples of figures that may be interpreted in at least two different ways. The "duck/rabbit" is one such example.[15] One can take in the duck/rabbit as a whole and—through only shifting modes of perception, not through looking at one side or the other, or covering portions of the figure—shift easily between seeing it as a duck on the one hand and a rabbit on the other. In a somewhat similar vein, subjects can take in two voices and learn to shift between hearing them as a melody with bass accompaniment and a bass line with accompanying melody.

In some senses, then, bass line dictation is simply another form of melodic dictation. Listeners capable of focusing attention on bass voices can apply their dictation-taking skills to whatever bass lines they perceive. Much of the following discussions is predicated on the assumption that listeners are adept at perceiving bass lines and that any harmonic investigations will take place after (or in lockstep with) perception of the bass voice.

Inversion

One approach to harmonic listening couples bass line information with listeners' perceptions of chord inversions. Listeners who learn to identify the inversion of atomistically isolated chord structures proceed to apply this skill in the context of harmonic dictation (and, presumably, real listening situations). As an example, consider the excerpt shown in Example 4.1, which might serve for purposes of harmonic dictation.

After determining the pitches of the bass line, listeners can move on to identifying the inversions of individual chords. Coupling bass line scale

15. See the work of Chambers and Reisberg (1985; 1992) for good illustrations of the duck/rabbit and other ambiguous figures, as well as some interesting conclusions about ambiguity in the visual domain.

Example 4.1. Beethoven, Piano Sonata, Op. 2, No. 3, mmt. 3, Trio, mm. 17–21.

degrees with inversions yields root identification and Roman-numeral labels. Through deductive reasoning, the conjunction of bass scale degree and chord inversion leads logically to a single chord root. Each of the verticalities in Example 4.1, when subject to this kind of processing, results in each of the columns in Figure 4.1.

Like interval identification, atomistic inversion identification is not uncommon in textbooks and curricula.[16] And as in interval identification, there is no hard evidence that listeners are able to carry this skill directly into context. I have observed many developing listeners who, for example, identify a I^6 in context as a root position chord (perhaps because the strong tonic functionality of this chord imparts a sense of "rootedness" that can easily be confused with "root position"; see the confusion matrices in Hofstetter [1980, 88] and Killam, Lorton, and Schubert [1976, 8] for similar misidentifications *out* of context). In addition, some skilled listeners, upon hearing a I^6 chord, first track $\hat{3}$ in the bass and then either perceive the chord's tonic Gestalt or hear the strategic upper voice on $\hat{1}$ and *deduce* the inversion therefrom. However, other listeners make frequent, productive use of the juncture between bass voice and inversion. Whether this anecdotal evidence warrants extra drill and practice in chord inversions is unclear; no controlled studies have examined the carryover from atomistic to contextual inversion identification. And without some

Scale Degree of Bass	$\hat{1}$	$\hat{2}$	$\hat{3}$	$\hat{4}$	$\hat{5}$
Inversion of Chord	root position	second inversion	first inversion	third inversion	first inversion
Root	i	V	i	V	i

Figure 4.1. Roots as a product of bass scale degree and inversion in Beethoven, Piano Sonata, Op. 2, No. 3, mmt. 3, Trio, mm. 17–21.

16. See, for example, Horacek and Lefkoff (1989, vol. 2), Ottman and Dworak (1991, 134–42), and Benward and Kolosick (1996a, 11–12, 26). Many computer-assisted instruction applications, such as *MacGamut* and the *GUIDO* system (see Hofstetter 1980), drill this as well.

acknowledgment of chord quality, this system becomes ineffective when chromatic harmony is introduced.

Chord Quality

Another approach hinges on the intersection between the contents of the bass line and the qualities of the chords above. As with inversion identification, the functional label of a harmony is to be arrived at as a by-product of the bass scale degree and a separate, atomistic piece of knowledge—this time, the quality of the chord.[17] For instance, if restricted to diatonic possibilities, a minor triad supported by $\hat{4}$ in major mode can only be a first-inversion supertonic chord (the other diatonic possibilities being a major triad in root position and a diminished triad in second inversion). When considering all scale degrees as potential bass pitches, one can readily see that certain of them potentially support root position and second-inversion chords of identical quality. For example, $\hat{5}$ in major can support two different major triads: V and I$_4^6$.

When chromatic harmonies are introduced, this system becomes entirely unworkable. Consider the quandary in which listeners would find themselves if armed only with having heard that a particular $\hat{3}$ in major mode supported a major-minor seventh chord. Unfortunately, this pairing of bass note and quality occurs in three different circumstances: a secondary dominant seventh of the submediant, a secondary dominant $_5^6$ of the subdominant, and a secondary dominant $_3^4$ of the supertonic.

Therefore, the combination of bass pitch and chord quality alone is insufficient to take listeners very far beyond the most limited listening situations. Thus, we must arrive at a hybrid approach, one that incorporates both inversion and chord quality with bass scale degree in order to achieve an assessment of harmonic function. Consider as one example the possibilities that conjoin various inversions with some sample chord qualities over $\hat{3}$ in major as shown in Table 4.2.

The third scale degree in major can support three different root position triads, two different first-inversion triads, two different second-inversion triads, and three different inversions of seventh chords. In terms of chord quality, it can support three different major triads, two minor triads, two diminished triads, and three major-minor seventh chords. Only through the confluence of these two factors—inversion and quality—can one deduce the specific harmonic function of any verticality.

To achieve this end, listeners must become skilled in the rapid identification of isolated chord qualities and inversions. In typical drills of this

17. As with inversion identification, there are many examples of texts and computer programs that focus on this acontextual skill.

TABLE 4.2 Combinations of chord inversion and quality over $\hat{3}$ in the major mode.

Inversion	Quality	Roman numeral and figured bass
$\frac{5}{3}$	major	V/vi
$\frac{5}{3}$	minor	iii
$\frac{5}{3}$	diminished	vii°/IV
$\frac{6}{3}$	major	I^6
$\frac{6}{3}$	diminished	vii°^{6}/ii
$\frac{6}{4}$	major	V$^6_4$/ii
$\frac{6}{4}$	minor	vi$^{\cdot 6}_4$
7	major-minor	V^7/vi
$\frac{6}{5}$	major-minor	V$^6_5$/IV
$\frac{4}{3}$	major-minor	V$^4_3$/ii

sort, listeners are asked to identify the quality, inversion, or both of chords sounded—in principle—in isolation from one another.[18] Perhaps the skills learned through such atomistic drills as interval identification and chord quality and inversion are important ones. We must assess— perhaps individually for each learner—whether these skills are worth earning at the expense of the time and effort necessary to acquire them or that time and effort can be better spent on more contextual work.

Voice Leading and Harmony

In a technique that seeks to develop perception of voice leading and its relationships with harmonic function,[19] listeners can learn to (1) follow, remember, understand, and notate a bass line; and (2) trace certain voices at specific crucial locations in order to make conclusions about the functions of chord progressions.[20] This (or any) technique is best intertwined with Gestalt listening, as will be seen in the following discussion.

18. See, for example, Ottman and Dworak (1991, 127–47) and the "Chord Dictation" and "Chord-Type Identification" lessons in Horacek and Lefkoff (1989, vol. 2).

19. These relationships are of primal importance in music. Salzer and Schachter ([1969] 1989) remarked that "harmony and counterpoint assert their roles in cooperation, on a prolonging as well as on a structural level" (p. 289).

20. Compare this approach to the "guide-tone" method described in Rahn and McKay (1988), which begins with simple binary voice identifications (such as *do* or *ti*) and includes the process of chord arpeggiation as a means of making further distinctions. A study by Alvarez (1980) demonstrated the efficacy of a rudimentary version of this approach with untrained listeners.

Example 4.2. J. S. Bach, chorale No. 26, "O Ewigkeit, du Donnerwort," mm. 1–2.

As an example of how this technique works, consider the opening to J. S. Bach's chorale No. 26, "O Ewigkeit, du Donnerwort," shown in Example 4.2. Let us assume that we are currently training listeners to grasp diatonic triadic materials. Let us further assume as a prerequisite for harmonic listening that all listeners should be able to write down the bass line after hearing it (given one or several playings). Beyond that, there are many listeners with various degrees of Gestalt listening abilities. For the sake of discussion, let us consider listeners with a modicum of such abilities—to recognize without calculation the two tonic chords on the anacrusis and first downbeat and the authentic cadence at the end of the excerpt.[21]

That leaves four verticalities for these listeners to deal with (mm. 1.2, 1.3, 1.4, and 2.1). A good starting point—remembering that we are dealing with only diatonic triadic verticalities at this time—is for listeners to consider that the vast majority of such verticalities are in either $\frac{5}{3}$ or $\frac{6}{3}$ position. (We can deal with $\frac{6}{4}$ figures and seventh chords as special cases a bit later.) The verticality at m. 1.2 would present the first set of options. With $\hat{2}$ in the bass, $\frac{5}{3}$ position would yield a supertonic chord, whereas $\frac{6}{3}$ position would yield a leading-tone chord. The difference—in terms of voice—is between the fifth and sixth above the bass: in this case, D and E, respectively. Listeners unable to hear these as holistically different chords can listen for the presence or absence of each of these pitches.

This is particularly musical and effective if the pitches are arrived at as a product of *voice leading* (not by following parts). The distinction

---

21. Of course, many beginning listeners lack even these Gestalt listening skills. In the absence of other cognitive difficulties, training listeners to recognize holistically such basics as tonic openings and authentic cadences is often (although not always) a matter of frequent exposure that uses one or more of the systems described here, resulting in gradual familiarization.

between *part* and *voice* is an important one.[22] A *part* is a feature of the musical surface, a line performed as a continuity. In ensemble music, a *part* is just that—the notes played or sung from a single printed part (e.g., "Bassoon I"; "Altos"). In keyboard music, parts are those lines separated from one another by the musical texture (often pointed up by composers or editors through the use of markings such as stem direction, slurs, and dotted lines). A *voice*, however, is a theoretical construct. Upper voices are the abstract lines formed by the smoothest possible voice leading from one prevailing harmony to the next.[23]

To a certain extent, attending to voice leading must be an active process for listeners. It is often not possible for them merely to wait to hear these pitches; they must actively sing the voice they are following (being mindful not to sing too loudly and overshadow the music itself). Thus, in the case of m. 1.2 in Figure 4.5, listeners might try to follow a voice that begins C–C in the first two verticalities (note the difference between this simple *voice* that joins common tones and the inner *parts*, which trade performance of them) and then attempt to move to D on m. 1.2. (At this juncture, one could diagnose which listeners have a well-developed sensitivity for chord membership.) However, they might try to follow a voice that proceeds F–F–E, in which case they should experience the chord membership quality of the harmonic tone E and deduce its participation as the sixth in a $^6_3$ position chord—vii°⁶. Other comparable tests can lead to similar conclusions about the remaining verticalities. For instance, the essential question at m. 2.1 would be "is there an F or a G above the bass?" If the former, the chord is IV; if the latter, it is ii⁶.

As listeners become more adept at this technique and as they relegate more verticalities to Gestalt listening, more complex materials can be introduced. For example, the cadential $^6_4$ can be approached as a dominant-function fifth scale degree in the bass over which listeners trace the parallel voices $\hat{6}$–$\hat{5}$ and $\hat{4}$–$\hat{3}$. Chromatic harmonies derive their special status under this approach precisely because of their chromatic members: for example, the characteristic pitch in a secondary dominant of the su-

---

22. Along these same lines, Salzer and Schachter ([1969] 1989) refer to "the elements of voice leading" in contrast to "the fabric of living music" (p. xvi); they also speak of voice leading as being "divested of the individual rhythmic and textural features of the actual composition" (pp. 117–19). This contrast is at the heart of Schenker's distinction between *free composition* and *voice leading* (see, for example, his discussions in Schenker [1910/1922] 1987, 1, vol. 10, 200). See also Cadwallader and Gagné's (1998) distinction between the "musical surface" and the slightly deeper "level of melodic coherence" (p. 19).

23. The bass voice is a product of the series of pitches that support each of those prevailing harmonies. Although appreciation of this concept is important in taking dictation and transcription—particularly from music with elaborate bass parts—it does not bear directly on our current discussion, which is focused on perception of upper voices.

pertonic would be the raised tonic; the important linear motion in the progression I–V/ii–ii would be $\hat{1}$– $\uparrow\hat{1}$–$\hat{2}$.

Listeners who learn to trace strategic aspects of voice leading not only find success in taking harmonic dictation but also develop an approach to hearing that paves the way toward an experientially based understanding of such concepts as prolongation, diminution, structural levels, and compound melody. Another important connection made through this approach is among voice leading, figured bass, and harmony. Tracing the motions of voices above the bass is precisely what figured bass theory is about. Indeed, one text even recommends exercises specifically focused on using figured bass as a means of responding to harmonic dictation (Edlund [1967] 1974, 180–92). And as Rothgeb (1981) noted, figured bass "provides an optimal connecting link between the world of pure voice leading . . . and the study of tonal music in all of its dimensions. . . . Through figured bass, the student can be introduced to the sound and behavior of the basic chords of tonal music" (p. 147).

It may seem that this approach requires a great amount of theoretical thinking in a short amount of time, and indeed it does. But that is one of its virtues, as well as one of its challenges: as part of a larger curriculum in dictation, sight singing, theory, harmony, and keyboard skills—as part of the broadest kind of integrated musical training, in which music listening, reading, improvising, and thinking are all connected—listeners learn to think rapidly, efficiently, and instinctively about harmonic potential and voice leading above supporting bass lines.

$$5$$

Other Listening Skills

Although many of the activities and skills discussed in the preceding chapters—particularly dictation—can be rather comprehensive and musically important, there are other activities listeners can engage in that enhance their listening skills and contextualize them in various ways.

Transcription

In contrast to dictation, transcription involves notating music from in situ performances of compositions through recordings (or, rarely, through live performances). The bulk of the following discussion addresses transcription from recordings.

Some of the chief differences between transcription and dictation are that transcription is usually carried out without limitations on the number of listenings and the durations between listenings are under control of the listeners. In addition—since the object of transcription is often to notate entire sections, movements, or even complete works—the music is divided into memorable sections by listeners, who proceed to subsequent sections under their own control.

Given these conditions, it is therefore possible for listeners to engage in transcription—even over long periods of time—without necessarily developing the following listening skills: (1) improved short-term memory, (2) extractive listening, and (3) speed and fluency (an ultimate goal of which is to compress the time it takes to hear, remember, understand, and notate so that listening and notational imagery can begin to occur simultaneously). This is not to say that transcription *cannot* develop these skills. Indeed, for listeners to work more efficiently at taking transcription, they often learn to listen to longer excerpts, to extract longer segments, and to internalize the understanding phase so that heard events seem to flow directly into notation. But the parameters of transcription do not demand that listeners proceed this way. It is entirely possible (and not uncommon) for listeners to transcribe recordings by repeatedly listening to extremely small segments while taking enormous amounts of time between listenings.

Nonetheless, transcription offers a number of benefits that make it a worthwhile addition to any course of study in aural skills. Among these benefits is the more pragmatic application of skills learned in other aural-training settings. Listeners who have learned to perform various tasks such as pulse and meter inference, tonic finding, and scale-degree identification can begin to apply them in an even more realistic and contextual environment through transcription. Another benefit involves exposure to and indoctrination with a body of literature, be it common-practice-period warhorses, jazz standards, or whatever canon a curriculum deems appropriate. Yet another is the fact that those adept at transcription have developed a practical tool for translating into notation music for which notation does not exist or is not readily available.

In one sense, it is appropriate to reserve large transcription projects for late in an aural skills curriculum, lest such often counterproductive habits as hunting-and-pecking on a piano take hold. However, it is advisable to begin to include at least some transcription-like activities early in a course of study. Transcribing short excerpts from recordings of real literature performed on various instruments can help students realize the practical importance of aural skills much more than listening to dozens of contrived dictations played on a piano by a theory instructor or hours of lecturing on the subject might.

Instrumental Playback

In taking dictation or transcription, listeners hear an aural stimulus, remember all or part of it, understand it, and respond by translating it into notation. It is possible and at times desirable to ask listeners to respond not with notation but rather by repeating the musical stimulus on an instrument.[1]

There is much to be said in favor of this activity. It connects aural skills training more directly to musicians' personal musical experiences, allows individual listeners to use their most highly developed "voice," with its attendant levels of technique and musicality, and becomes a practical application in such activities as studio teaching and improvisation.

---

1. Some computer-assisted instruction programs allow or require this type of input. See, for example, *Listen* (Albany, CA: Imaja), which uses piano-keyboard and guitar-fretboard input windows instead of staff notation. MIDI input allows for more realistic-feeling playback from a variety of controllers (for example, keyboards, woodwind and brass controllers, etc.), as in *Practica Musica* (Kirkland, WA: Ars Nova).

However, instrumental playback should not be considered a substitute for dictation. Playing back a melody on an instrument requires a complete spectrum of skills in the pitch domain: hearing, memory, understanding, and "notation" (in this case, labeling translation into specific pitches on an instrument). But in the rhythm domain, practitioners are required only to hear and remember what they have heard. No rhythmic understanding and no equivalent to notation are necessary to repeat rhythms on an instrument. As yet, no studies have been undertaken to test the effects (if any) of instrumental playback on rhythmic understanding and notation. The results of such studies would be very interesting and have important consequences in curricular planning.

Properly applied to hearing and memory for complete musical ideas and to understanding and labeling pitches (but not rhythms), instrumental playback can take its place in the panoply of activities for developing aural skills. But to ensure that listeners can understand and label rhythms, dictation or transcription must be used as well.

Error Detection and Correction

The importance of error detection and correction skills to most musicians is indisputable. Yet, among the major aural-skills texts, only Benward and Kolosick (1996a) and Kraft (1999) include error detection of any kind. Error detection is similarly rare among computer-assisted instruction programs. And in their survey of aural skills instruction in the United States, Pembrook and Riggins (1990) found that "error detection is the least practiced activity in aural-skills classes. Considering the frequency that students will use this skill (e.g., as conductors, classroom and studio instructors, adjudicators, etc.), it is reasonable to suggest that more time should be devoted to developing this vital skill" (pp. 239–40).

Error detection and correction are indeed indispensable skills that all musicians should possess to a useful degree. Ideally, every time musicians sing or play from notation a constant process of self-correction takes place between their eyes and ears. The more adept musicians are at detecting and correcting discrepancies between sound and notation, the more often such errors can be corrected and even avoided in their own performances. Ottman (1956) found a strong correlation between error detection skills (which he called "music literacy") and achievement in sight singing: "The ability to recognize errors in printed music symbols when those symbols are sounded and the ability to reproduce vocally these same printed symbols seem to be very closely allied" (p. 223).[2]

---

2. This correlation is likely a product of the effect of sight singing on error detection skills. A recent study by Sheldon (1998) found that general training in "sight singing and aural skills" (solmization, tonal pattern repetition, music reading, and singing) seems to have a direct, positive effect on error detection skills. It may be that musicians'

There are other equally important applications of these skills. Conductors and ensemble coaches depend on error detection and correction as significant tools of their trade, relying on their ears to identify exactly *what* was performed incorrectly *where* by *whom* and on their abilities to communicate information about how to correct such errors. Teachers of private lessons, studio classes, and master classes are equally dependent on these skills. Even members of ensembles, particularly section leaders, make use of error detection and correction skills.

Instructors should be aware of various factors that affect listeners' accuracy at error detection.[3] These factors include the number of parts, texture, and error type. Listeners tend to be more accurate when listening to fewer parts, when listening to homorhythmic (as opposed to polyrhythmic) textures, and when identifying rhythm errors (as opposed to pitch errors).

It is possible to integrate instruction in error correction into the earliest phases of aural skills training. As soon as some form of music notation—even if only protonotation—has been presented, students can begin to correlate that notation with musical sound in real time, in the form of identifying and "correcting" discrepancies between the two.

Although errors of pitch and rhythm are most commonly used,[4] other parameters are also available and appropriate for study, including tempo, intonation, articulation, dynamics, timbre, harmony, and chord inversion. Listeners' responses to error detection drills should be specific with regard to the precise kind of error and identify the exact nature of the error itself in comparison with the correct printed notation. To further bring these drills as close as possible to practical experiences, listeners should not be informed about which kinds of errors are to take place or how many errors will occur, nor should they be certain that any errors at all might occur (therefore, "There were no errors" should be a possible response).[5]

Error detection affords ample opportunities to practice using language to communicate musical ideas. It is important for musicians to learn to speak and write clearly about music in general and especially to convey information about errors in performance.

---

error detection skills improve as they study sight singing and dictation, but explicit instruction in the process of detecting and identifying discrepancies between notation and sound can nonetheless help to further develop, formalize, and apply these skills to a variety of circumstances. After surveying nine separate studies of error detection, Byo (1997) concluded that "subjects' ability to detect performance errors improves with practice" (p. 53).

3. An excellent survey and some new empirical evidence appear in Byo (1997).

4. For example, Benward and Kolosick (1996a) include errors of only pitch or rhythm, never both, and always specify which type of error will occur in each group of exercises. Bailey (1992) is a notable exception in including errors of tempo, intonation, dynamics, and articulation, as well as pitch and rhythm.

5. A few guidelines and suggestions about designing tests of error detection skills are given in Boyle and Radocy (1987, 160–61).

To begin with, musicians must be specific and clear about *where* these errors occur. It is unfortunately not uncommon to hear or read something like the following to describe the location of a musical event: "The 'and' of beat 4, bass voice, third measure of the second system." Listeners and readers who encounter such descriptions wait anxiously until the end of these instructions to begin looking for this spot, wasting time and—when listening—not infrequently forgetting some of the details along the way. The solution here is the implementation of guidelines to be adhered to without fail: give the broadest reference first, then move progressively through more and more narrow directions.[6] In this way, the preceding directions could be rendered as follows: "Second system, third measure, beat 4, second half, bass voice."

Listeners should then specify the exact nature of the error, indicating what was performed in comparison with the printed notation. Once again, precision of language is important. It is also important for such responses to be phrased using vocabulary that is as standard and common as possible, so that these corrections can be communicated to musicians in a wide variety of settings. Thus, for example, errors in pitch should be expressed in terms of letter names (D, B♭) rather than in some form of solmization; similarly, rhythms should be expressed as specific note values (quarter note, dotted eighth) rather than through rhythmic solmization.

Although it is expedient and tempting to allow listeners simply to mark a score to indicate the location and nature of errors, this is neither close to most practical applications nor generally helpful in developing language skills for music. Conductors, coaches, teachers, and ensemble members rarely circle a note or cross it out and replace it with a "correction"; indeed, in these circumstances it is the notation that is correct whereas the performance is to be corrected—through words.[7] In general, then, it is best to prescribe the use of words and only words to make error corrections. This is also a good time to implement some aspects of "writing across the curriculum," developing the use of good grammar, mechanics, and construction for the sake of clarity, concision, and cogency.

Advanced Hypermeter

Listeners can be trained to develop rather sophisticated skills for making hypermetric analyses aurally. In chapter 2, we found that most listeners can readily discern musical pulses on several levels. We used that fact to

---

6. These guidelines have been suggested by John Buccheri in numerous College Music Society workshops.

7. If such musicians do mark up a score while detecting errors, it is almost always as a quick self-reminder that must still then be translated into words.

Example 5.1. Schubert, *Moment Musical* in A♭, Op. 94, No. 6, D. 780, mm. 1–8, with hypermetric analysis.

enable listeners to determine meters through hearing how adjacent levels of pulse interact. Hypermetric perception involves taking this process to progressively broader levels.

Schubert's *Moment Musical* in A♭, Op. 94, No. 6, D. 780, will serve as a demonstration case (see Example 5.1). In "strict use" of hypermetric analysis, wherein pulses at one level may be grouped into the next broader level only by twos or threes, we find that the quarter-note pulse (level (a)) groups consistently into threes—the dotted half (level (b))—represented in the notated meter sign $\frac{3}{4}$. The (b) level—the measure level—groups initially into duple hypermeasures. We can represent this feature as a (c) level (which could be indicated by a hypermeter sign of $\frac{6}{4}$). All this can be ascertained entirely aurally and represented with pulse lines as in Example 5.1.

Listeners can use their skills at inferring pulses and grouping pulses to investigate how this hypermetric structure behaves throughout the piece. (For the balance of this discussion, readers must have the score—or, more appropriately for aural analysis, only a recording—of Schubert's Op. 94, No. 6, at hand.) Level (c) continues its duple pattern through the first thirty-two measures, but this pattern clearly changes in the following measures. It is aurally apparent that mm. 37–39 are an exact repetition of mm. 34–36. This sets up a feeling of triple hypermeter for these six measures.

But, beyond this, it is possible to hear and interpret these groups in two different ways. On the one hand, one can hear m. 33 as a hypermetric downbeat—not only as a consequence of the odd-numbered-measure downbeats that continue from the preceding duple hypermeter, but also as the beginning of two three-measure groups: mm. 33–35 and mm. 36–38. This would necessitate placing two successive hypermetric downbeats on mm. 39 and 40 in a hypermetric elision. However, one can hear mm. 33 and 34 as two successive hypermetric downbeats, thereby reinterpreting m. 34 as an elision (or m. 33 as a one-measure extension) so that the triple hypermeasures are formed by mm. 34–36 and mm. 37–39. Although both views have their merits, the latter seems at least somewhat more attuned to several surface-level cues in the music, such as the upbeat figure to mm. 34 and 37 that parallels the similar figure as an upbeat to m. 5 and the *fp* marking on the downbeats that follow it.

In either case, duple hypermeter—by now musically established as internally normative—returns in m. 40 and continues through m. 65. However, mm. 66–77 present yet another deviation from the normative pattern. The music in mm. 66–70 is repeated in mm. 71–75, creating two five-measure groups. Once again, we may choose to hear the strict duple/triple grouping within these measures in different ways. One might interpret them as 3+2 and 3+2 on purely rhythmic grounds (separating quarter-note motion from dotted-half motion) and on harmonic grounds (focusing on the arrival on the $^6_4$ verticality) or interpret them as 2+3 and 2+3 on dynamic grounds (hearing the climax of the crescendi in mm. 68 and 73 as downbeats). Either way, this marks the second departure from the duple-hypermeter norm, with mm. 76–77 serving as a two-measure internal cadence.

The Trio marks yet another return to duple hypermeter. In fact, it is quite regular in its pairing of measures, leading without aberration to the hypermetric downbeat at the return of m. 1 in the Allegretto.

Thus far, we have aurally investigated three levels of pulse in *Moment Musical* No. 6: the beat unit, the measure level, and one level of hypermeter. Although there is more to say about deeper levels of hypermeter, we can stop at this stage and make some observations about the interactions between hypermeter and tonal structure and between hypermeter and form. We can note, for example, the fact that the areas of normative duple hypermeter generally coincide with areas of stable tonicization. The opening measures tonicize A♭ (in major and parallel minor mode) and move smoothly in duple hypermeter. Then mm. 29–32, still normative in terms of hypermeter, begin to imply a larger tonal motion. The arrival on E as local tonic in m. 33 is coupled directly with a concomitant change in hypermeter. With the return to A♭ in mm. 40ff. comes a return to duple hypermeter. The next area of hypermetric instability is spelled by mm. 66ff., this time coupled with the surprising E^4_2 chord, which functions enharmonically as an inverted Gr⁶ harmony. Only as this harmony resolves—first incompletely in mm. 69–70, then completely in mm. 74–77—does duple hypermeter return. The Trio is tonally stable in the local tonic of D♭ and hypermetrically stable in duple throughout. As far as form is concerned, the Trio is set apart from the Allegretto through its locally stable tonality and through its entirely consistent hypermeter.

Deeper levels of hypermeter may be explored aurally as well. As listeners progress to subsequent levels—to groups of groups of measures, and so on—hypermetric analysis tends to become more subjective and occasionally vague.[8] Nonetheless, it should be apparent that continuing with *Moment Musical* No. 6—or many other works—can yield further insights garnered through listening to interactions between hypermeter and other musical parameters.

There are, of course, more difficult aspects of meter and hypermeter—the concepts of ambiguity or metric and hypermetric dissonance,[9] for example—that extend well beyond the introductory scope discussed thus far and that challenge the ear and mind in new ways. These aspects can be addressed aurally as well but would best be reserved for late in a core curriculum or for an advanced course in aural skills or analysis.

Large-Scale Features

Form

In order for listeners to experience the most expansive musical features—form and key relations—they must be able to remember certain important musical components within a work and recognize them when they return. Dahlhaus (1982) noted that "insofar as music is form, it attains its real existence, paradoxically expressed, in the very moment when it is past. Still held firm in the memory, it emerges into a condition that it never entered during its immediate presence; and at a distance it constitutes itself as a surveyable plastic form" (p. 12).[10]

But exactly how much of such valuable musical information do listeners actually attend to and remember? In a series of informal tests, Nich-

---

8. And, some would say, insignificant or imperceptible. See for example, Lester (1986, 161–63) and Lerdahl and Jackendoff (1983, 22–25). Note that I distinguish between vagueness and ambiguity in hypermeter (and elsewhere): The earlier discussion of mm. 66–75 allowed for two valid yet mutually exclusive hypermetric hearings, in contradistinction to what some claim to be imperceptible at deep levels of hypermeter due to extracognitive periodicity (or lack thereof). As Smyth (1990) remarked, "At a certain level—varying from work to work, as well as from one hearing to the next—we suspend our counting" (p. 237).

9. For information on metric and hypermetric ambiguity and dissonance, see the literature surveys and discussions in Grave (1995), Lester (1986, 86–126), and Cohn (1992, 2–4). Also see the discussion of metric dissonance in chapter 4, under "Contextual Inference."

10. In contrast to this view, consider Levinson's (1997) aim "to combat the notion, often only implicit in the writing of many music commentators and theoreticians, that keeping music's form—in particular, large-scale structural relationships, or spatialized representations of a musical composition's shape—before the mind is somehow central to, or even essential for, basic musical understanding" (p. ix). The current discussion views perception of form not as central or essential but simply as valuable. See Repp et al. (1999) for the reactions of four music theorists and one music psychologist to Levinson's position, along with a reply by Levinson.

olas Cook played the first movement of Beethoven's Op. 49, No. 2, for musically trained subjects, a majority of whom *did not even notice the repetition of the exposition* (Cook 1987a; Cook 1990, 45). In other words, more often than not listeners' musical memories fail them in what many music theorists and pedagogues feel are fundamentally important ways and at musically crucial moments. In another experiment, Mitchell Karno and Vladimir Konečni drastically reordered sections of the first movement of Mozart's G-minor Symphony, K. 550, to create four "doctored" versions of the work. Listeners as a whole—even college music students—who listened to the original and to these doctored versions did not prefer any version of the work, even the original, over any other on the bases of pleasingness, interestingness, or desire to own a recording of the version (Karno and Konečni 1992).

However, Cook's follow-up and some studies by Alan Smith show that listeners *can* remember and compare features of a work for the purposes of orienting themselves within a formal structure. Smith found that even musically unsophisticated seventh-graders can be taught to do so. But what Smith also discovered, though, is that listeners—even upper-level and graduate music students—attend to the form of a work *only if specifically instructed to do so beforehand* (Smith 1973, 212–213). It seems that remembering formal cues is not a normal part of listening behavior (at least among upper-level and graduate music students!). Finally, two studies—one by Pollard-Gott (1983) and another by Berz and Kelly (1998)—found that trained listeners significantly outperformed novice listeners in tasks that involved listening for aspects of musical form.

In an effort to develop listeners' skills in attending to form and to help make such attention habitual, two broad types of activities are useful. In the first category is the time-honored tradition of providing listening guidelines or questions to be answered *in prose* about various features of a work that will lead to a clearer understanding of a work's form through repeated listenings.[11] The second category involves some kind of graphic representation of the work as a whole within which listeners can sketch various significant form-signaling events.[12] This graphic representation can take the form of a blank score (with which listeners are supplied or which they create through listening), which they can follow through counting beats and measures; it can also take the form of a hypermetric grid (which listeners construct through listening). In either case, the types

11. Alldahl (1974) referred to several approaches to "formal analysis by ear" at the Stockholm Conservatory of Music and noted that this also "offers the opportunity to approach types of music that are hard to tackle in regular ear training, such as avant-garde, electronic, or music from non-Western cultures" (p. 122).

12. Wittlich and Humphries (1974) include excellent exercises of both types for fourteen different compositions. For excerpts shorter than Wittlich and Humphries's, see the six units labeled "Aural Analysis" in Benward and Kolosick (1996a), which contain a variety of macrolistening exercises.

of cues listeners should be guided toward following include the recurrence of motivic and thematic materials, textural changes (see Levy 1982), harmonic stability versus instability, and key areas. For a psychological investigation of listeners' use of cues in form perception, see Deliège and Mèlen (1997).

To develop the skills needed to attend to these various parameters and use them in drawing conclusions about musical form, the need for *repeated* listening is crucial. Listeners cannot gain much sense of a work's form from one or even a few listenings. They must become intimately familiar with how the piece "goes" as they answer questions, create graphs, make lists of themes, and so on. In gaining this kind of intimacy with even only a handful of works, listeners can begin to learn to attend to salient formal details in unfamiliar works as well.

Key Areas

Cook found that listeners' memories for large-scale tonality may be as capricious as for form. He played subjects two versions of pieces: one original—which began and ended in the same key—and one altered so that it ended up in some key other than its opening. He found that "the influence of tonal closure over listeners' responses is restricted to a maximum time scale, possibly on the order of 1 min" (Cook 1987b, 203). He concluded that "despite the fundamental importance that musicians customarily attach to it, tonal closure lacks psychological reality for the listener—at least when . . . it extends over a duration of several minutes" (Cook 1990, 54–55).

However, Cook asked listeners a series of *aesthetic* questions (about pleasure, expressiveness, coherence, and sense of completion), not technical tonal ones. Marvin and Brinkman (1999) performed two experiments designed more specifically to determine if listeners can perceive large-scale tonal closure. They found that "expert listeners can discriminate between musical passages that begin and end in the tonic key and those that do not" (p. 395). And in their first experiment they found no significant effects due to the lengths of their twelve musical excerpts, which ranged in length from 1' 27" to 3' 02". Significant differences did occur in relation to subjects' major discipline: theory and musicology majors performed best, followed by performers, then composers.[13]

The experiments by Cook and by Marvin and Brinkman asked yes/no questions about tonal closure, which merely provide information about

13. It is still unclear whether better performance on this task is a *product* of such training or students' choice of college major is somehow affected by preexisting tonal-structure listening skills (Marvin and Brinkman 1999, 404).

listeners' abilities to make same/different discriminations about key areas. This is certainly a sensible place to begin training, but it seems reasonable to suggest that any college-level curriculum in theory and aural skills should develop listeners' abilities to hear specific modulations to various keys. In fact, Ottman (1956) asked just such questions in his "Test of Melodic Modulation" (pp. 184–90, 255–58). In addition to testing whether listeners simply heard a modulation or not, he also asked them (after supplying the name of the initial key) to name the key to which each excerpt modulated. His listeners generally made up their minds as to their answers after two playings, and although scores varied widely, some listeners were able to do quite well. This is a simple-enough task, one for which listeners can train.

Listeners can begin attempting to aurally identify large-scale tonal areas in short pieces, although tonal moves in such contexts are often somewhat open to interpretation as mere local "tonicizations" and are rather fleeting in comparison to, say, the modulation to the exposition's second key area in sonata form. With this caveat in mind, training in hearing modulations should begin with short materials, perhaps melodic and harmonic dictations just long enough to establish an initial key and move convincingly to another. Next, short excerpts or complete binary works with moves to the dominant or mediant are useful. They can be followed by slightly longer excerpts or complete short ternary forms, in which a contrasting middle section stands as a more stable key area of its own. Beyond this, larger forms, such as compound ternary, rondo, and sonata can be undertaken. As with the aural analysis of form, practice activities for developing the ability to hear large-scale tonal motion can take the form of answering questions or filling in pitches on blank scores or graphs, in addition to offering Ottman-style fill-in-the-blank responses.[14]

In addition to the more traditional types of score-study and listening assignments, computer technology can offer a great deal of assistance in developing listeners' larger scale formal and tonal perceptual acuity. In particular, hypermedia environments afford a perceptual laboratory within which listeners can explore the sensations, formulations, and implications of formal delineation and tonal structure.[15] In such applications, users can follow a pointer across a graphic representation of a work while listening to a CD-quality recording of that work. Users can also control their motion, making dragonflylike visits to various sections of a

14. Also see the suggestions for "more generalized aural training" in Jones (1949, 60–61).

15. Although this now comes in many varieties, the best software that takes advantage of such control is to be found in Jacobson and Koozin (1996). In particular, consult the "Listening Guides" for Beethoven's Fifth Symphony and Schubert's "Erlking" as exemplars of the comprehension and control with which they empower the user.

work: a kind of noncontiguous version of Schenker's (1923) "flying ear" (p. 55).[16] Intentionally discontinuous listening can be particularly helpful in developing listeners' sensitivity to motivic, thematic, formal, and large-scale tonal relationships.

Identification of Various Other Compositional Devices

There is a host of musical features and compositional devices that musicians ought to be able to identify aurally. Some of these are discussed in detail in chapter 1. It is often a matter of personal choice whether certain features are investigated before, after, or concurrently with the more technical skills discussed in chapters 2 through 4. Other features (for instance, the differences between tonal and real imitation) are better delayed in the learning sequence until listeners have developed skills appropriate to the task.

Many pages of theory and analysis textbooks are devoted to identifying these features by sight from music notation. Much time is spent in classrooms teaching and testing this as a reading skill. But—since music is at heart an aural art form—we should concentrate equally emphatically on the ability to recognize and identify these features through listening.[17] This aural identification can range from a simple "I heard it" to specific placement of individual features along a hypermetric grid or within a blank-measure template.

One of the most basic compositional features available for aural identification is repetition.[18] The simple task of describing *what* is being repeated *where* and *how* can lead to some very illuminating investigations. Listeners should learn to recognize the repetition of rhythms, melodic material, formal sections—any musical material. More specifically, listeners can attend to the subcategory of repetition known as *sequence*, even identifying the interval of sequence and whether it is tonal or real. The use of motives, another form of repetition, can also be investigated aurally. Listeners should learn to identify which parameters (for example, contour or rhythm) are repeated and which are varied among different statements of a motive. The special uses of leitmotives are also worthy

---

16. "Ich zeige als erster . . . der deutschen Meister fliegend ohr, ihr Stegreifschaffen, ihre Sythese [I am the first to show . . . the German masters' flying ear, their extemporaneous output, their synthesis]" (Schenker 1923, 55).

17. One notably exceptional textbook (Wittlich and Humphries 1974) asks listeners to attend to some of these features. The GRE Music Test contains questions based on listening for such features as well (Educational Testing Service 1993, 10, 51–67).

18. For some interesting interpretations of repetition in music and other arts, see Kivy (1993, 327–59) and Harris (1931).

of being recognized by ear. One might also pursue aural analysis of iso-rhythm, ascertaining the *talea* and *color* in a passage.

Imitation is another compositional device appropriate for aural iden-tification. Musicians should be able to recognize the presence of imitation in general and identify various specific types. These specific types include real versus tonal imitation and the more exceptional imitations by inver-sion (both real and tonal), retrograde, and rhythmic augmentation and diminution. Imitation also plays a role in certain compositional genres that musicians should learn to identify aurally, most commonly canon, round, invention/sinfonia, and fugue.

Fugue itself introduces an entire subset of features ripe for aural iden-tification. Listeners can learn to identify a subject and its various returns. They can listen for the subject–answer alternations and identify which voices state what and in what order. They can also aurally identify the differences between real and tonal answers. Other fugal components to listen for include the presence or absence of a countersubject and the appearances of any stretti and episodes.

There are also various accompanimental patterns that should be iden-tified through listening. These include the general use of ostinati and, more specifically, the Alberti bass and the walking bass. Certain accom-paniment schemes should also be identified by ear, including the ground bass, the passacaglia, and the chaconne. Listeners should also be able to recognize the presence of any pedal points and to discern their tonal function.

While taking harmonic dictation, listeners can be acclimated to hearing various cadence types. But aural identification of cadences can be carried out without all the strictures and trappings of harmonic dictation; this can even be done in melodic, as well as harmonic and polyphonic, con-texts. Listeners can simply answer questions or fill in information along a hypermetric grid or blank score, identifying the cadential distinctions "full" versus "half" and "metrically accented" versus "metrically unac-cented," as well as making specific Gestalt identifications with the terms "authentic," "plagal," "deceptive," "Phrygian," and even "Landini."

A few text-setting devices are appropriate for aural analysis. Listeners can attend to the differences between strophic and through-composed songs. In addition, as mentioned in chapter 1, listeners can distinguish between melismatic and syllabic settings.

A few rhythmic devices can be identified aurally without recourse to full-fledged rhythmic dictation. These devices include hemiola, syncopa-tion (as a general condition), and perhaps even hocket. Listeners might even wish to develop the ability to discriminate among the rhythmic modes.

Instructors can add to this list of features in many ways. Many addi-tional compositional devices—for example, the use of *fauxbourdon* or horn fifths—can serve as fodder for the listener.

Finally, such listening can become the basis for the aural analysis of style. It is one thing for listeners to express a vague sense that what they hear is in one style or another. It is much more significant that they be able to arrive at conclusions about the style of an excerpt based on their explicit understandings of many of the various compositional features discussed previously.

Identification of Pitch Collections

It is useful for listeners to be able to make a quick assessment of the pitch collection that governs any particular passage—a Gestalt approach to identifying prevailing pitch collections through listening. This takes place not through carefully calculating intervals but through holistic judgment.

For many this kind of Gestalt approach to pitch-collection identification can occur only after rigorous training in pitch perception through developing tonal memory and understanding, as detailed in chapters 2 through 4. If this training is introduced too early in the learning sequence, some listeners will have neither the general exposure nor the specific tools necessary for making such judgments. Ask such listeners what mode a particular passage is in, and the responses are likely to be little more than guesses.[19] And without such prior training, there is little one can do to develop this skill: listeners need to draw on more atomistic skills (Where's the tonic? What's the interval structure of the scale?) to sense how the components of a pitch collection result in its overall quality.

For those listeners who show an intuitive knack for this ability early in their studies and for all listeners sufficiently advanced along the learning sequence, listening activities can include identifying excerpts rapidly and holistically with regard to mode or collection. Perhaps the broadest categorical distinction to be made aurally is between tonal and atonal. Tonal materials can be divided immediately into either major or minor mode. If desired, certain minor-mode excerpts can be categorized as mostly "natural," "harmonic," or "melodic." In addition, instances of major/minor mixture can be introduced for such Gestalt identification. Pentatonic materials might be included here as subsets of the diatonic major and minor modes or later as part of modal materials. In addition, general assessments of "diatonic" versus "chromatic" can be made.

Modal materials require listeners to judge among many more categories. This process can be simplified somewhat by grouping the modes into

19. Indeed, even for listeners with over ten years of musical training, musical materials that differ only with regard to mode (major or minor) were rated as *most* similar when compared to differences of rhythm and melodic contour in a study by Halpern, Bartlett, and Dowling (1998).

two broad perceptual categories: major-type (Ionian/major, Lydian, Mix-olydian) and minor-type (Aeolian/minor, Dorian, Phrygian). Other quasi-diatonic scale forms (for example, the so-called Gypsy scale and the acoustic scale) can also be included in these activities.

For those who wish to extend this process further, certain post-tonal pitch structures can be included in the mix. A few structures that have become referential on an extra-opus basis in twentieth-century music—whole-tone and octatonic collections, quartal and quintal harmonies—can be recognized through listening. Ultimately, for listeners to identify the prevailing collection of a passage rapidly from among various tonal, modal, and post-tonal choices is a laudable goal.

Aesthetics

All of the audible musical features discussed in the first half of this book—and certainly others as well—can evoke various aesthetic responses in listeners.[20] Sensitive aural skills training can guide listeners in examining such aesthetic responses and some of their causes.

Listeners can begin to investigate and articulate their various reactions, including a sense of mood, the feeling ebb and flow, and the sensation of tension and release. They can attempt to document which musical features seem to bring about these reactions, discussing such topics as the effect of tempo on mood and the role harmony plays in the sensation of tension and release. Discussions of this sort can even range to such personal and subjective issues as which passages give individual listeners the "chills," leading to examinations of *how* and *why* such reactions are elicited.

Listeners' aesthetic responses can be assessed—and even developed through self-examination—in a variety of ways. Perhaps one of the most fruitful is through personal narratives—the documentation of individual responses in writing. The form of such writing can range from brief comments jotted in the margin of a score, through a personal "listening journal," to a formal essay.[21] Other means include the use of multiple-choice questions and brief responses to pointed questions. Adventurous instructors and listeners might even attempt to paint or dance responses to particular musical passages or compose yet another piece in response to a first one.

20. Some might call these psychological responses. See Pratt's (1998) discussion of "effectors" and "effects" (pp. 31–45).

21. See the assessment essay suggested in Pratt (1998, 150–51).

PART II

READING AND PERFORMING SKILLS

I desire no more in you than
to sing your part sure
and at the first sight
      —Henry Peacham
      ([1634] 1906, 100)

6

Fundamental Reading and
Performing Skills

Music-reading skills comprise the other broad component in most aural skills curricula. By far, the most ubiquitous means through which music-reading skills are developed and assessed is by sight singing. As Ottman (1956) noted, sight singing is broadly justified as a "musical aid in development of mental imagery of the symbols of printed music which in turn leads to higher levels of musicianship and artistic achievement" (p. 37). Therefore, a preponderance of the discussions of reading and performing in the rest of this book will focus on sight singing. This chapter examines the skills that are fundamental and beneficial to good sight singing, and good music reading in general, which are most efficiently learned before the introduction of music notation.

Vocal Production

The singing voice is a tool that all musicians should learn to use. For many college-level musicians, however, a class in aural skills might present the first time in their musical training that they are called upon to sing. Hindemith (1949) noted this problem: "It is quite common to find excellent instrumentalists (not to mention composers) who have gone through six or more years of practical and theoretical studies without ever having opened their mouths for the most natural of all musical utterances!" (p. xi). Such musicians may require some introductory instruction in basic vocal production. This book does not address the techniques of vocal production in great detail; those are matters best left for more appropriate venues.[1] Nonetheless, a few simple guidelines are well worth mentioning here:

1. For some good introductory sources, see Christy and Paton (1997), particularly chapters 1–5, 10, and 11; and Ware (1998), particularly chapters 2–8 and 10. For detailed investigations of vocal mechanisms as they relate to singing, see Vennard

- Posture—singers should sit or stand comfortably upright in order to breathe properly.
- Abdominal support—singers should support their sound from the muscles of the epigastrium (often referred to as support from the "diaphragm," which—although contributing directly to the process of breathing—can neither be sensed nor be consciously controlled).
- Breathing—singers should breathe adequately and musically: they must take in sufficient air to sing each phrase, and they must breathe at musically logical places.
- Range—singers should learn to produce pitches at the extremes of their ranges, particularly high notes, without unduly tightening their throat muscles.

With appropriate attention to these principles, students of aural skills can learn to use their voices without difficulty. In this way, the voice becomes a tool, not an obstacle.

Fundamental Solmization for Reading

Having made certain decisions about which solmization systems are most appropriate to assist in listening training, we now come to the question of solmization for sight singing. The use of solmization in teaching music reading has a long, venerable history. Ten centuries ago, Guido ([n.d.] 1998) introduced the idea of solmization by saying: "We do not need to have constant recourse to the voice of a singer or to the sound of some instrument to become acquainted with an unknown melody" (p. 217). Indeed, one of the powers of solmization is its ability to unlock the meanings and sounds of music notation.

Although there have been various armchair pronouncements that solmization is useless or harmful,[2] only one study (Lorek et al. 1991) has looked at this question in anything that approaches an extensive, scientific manner. Its conclusion: in a content-neutral sight singing curriculum, students' efficacy at sight singing seems unaffected by any particular solmization system (fixed-*do* versus movable-*do*) or the complete absence of any such system (singing all pitches on "lah"). But this study did not test for several important variables about which we ought to know before passing further judgment on solmization. First, the experiment did not

(1967) and Bunch (1997). An integrated examination of vocal mechanisms and pedagogy appears in Miller (1986).

2. For example, Fletcher (1957): "American teaching procedures in the present day, attempting to utilize a syllable (or number) code thus as a way-station to notation-reading, succeed in great degree only in creating further confusion in the minds of many would be readers" (p. 83). Fletcher—like all such critics—fails to present any evidence for this claim.

track students for very long or in a variety of settings. To measure more accurately the effect of solmization on sight singing, we should track an entire two- or three-year curriculum of study and follow students in other settings, such as lessons, ensembles, and theory classes. Second, in order to control a number of variables, identical curricula were used for each subject group (fixed-*do*, movable-*do*, and "lah"). However, the very point of each solmization system is that it be infused into the content and approach of the lectures, drills, and singing materials of its respective course. Thus, fixed-*do* instruction would focus more closely on such skills as pitch reading, clefs, and transposition, whereas movable-*do* would focus more on tonic inference, scale-degree function, and the like. These solmization systems would be used to label and illuminate, to represent and *become*, these important features and conditions. Therefore, it seems that the content-neutral instruction employed by Lorek et al—while it may reflect the instruction in some aural skills classrooms—does little to isolate and clarify the importance of each solmization system. Finally, as Butler and Lochstampfor (1993) noted, "An intrinsic problem with this strategy is that students in *both* groups practiced their *dictation* skills steadily throughout the training period [emphasis added]" (p. 15). It is likely that many listeners in the fixed-*do* group developed scale-degree listening strategies through dictation that they then applied tacitly to sight singing.

In a much narrower study, MacKnight (1975) found strong experimental evidence that "tonal pattern instruction is superior to the note identification teaching techniques and materials in the development of both sight reading skills and auditory-visual discrimination skills" (p. 34). Her tonal pattern instruction included singing with movable-*do* syllables, resulting in a simple comparison of fixed versus movable systems.[3]

So, we are left with little experimental evidence at present. Philosophical studies of solmization systems are more numerous. The merits of fixed and movable systems are discussed in Harris (1918), Multer (1978), Martin (1978), Surace (1978), and Smith (1991), among others. Larson (1989; 1993b) examined the broader pedagogical implications of the differences between *do*-based and *la*-based minor solmization, as did the exchanges between Smith (1991; 1992; 1994) and Houlahan and Tacka (1992; 1994). Regardless of their mixed outcomes, the experiments by Lorek et al. and MacKnight were only looking at accuracy in sight singing. But as Rogers (1996) declared, "The real goal of tonal sightsinging is not just accuracy; it is to hear the music in a particular way—a way that is musically nuanced, that is shaped and directed by goals, and a way that respects the encoded tensions and internal-movement proclivities of the specific environment. The job of sightsinging is context sensitivity and the enculturation of *tonal bearings*" (p. 149).

---

3. Readers should note, however, that her subjects were fourth-grade students and not adults.

We have already seen that, achievement in sight singing aside, instruction in music *listening* can benefit from solmization used as a tool for labeling scale-degree function. In particular, it affords an expeditious means through which instructor and student can communicate such functions (e.g., "sing *do*"). It also offers benefits when coordinated with training in written theory, keyboard skills, and other related disciplines (e.g., discussing *le* and *fi* as tendency tones in augmented sixth-chords). In the final analysis, these may be the strongest arguments in favor of using a functional solmization system such as scale-degree numbers or *do*-based major/minor movable-*do*.[4] Certainly for our purposes in this chapter—establishing collection *and* tonic, and using protonotation to read scale-degree functions—such a functional system is most appropriate. Accordingly, the rest of these discussions will employ *do*-based major/minor movable-*do* wherever appropriate.

Inculcating Scale and Solmization

Where, then, to begin training? As we have seen in previous chapters, it is helpful to consider certain musical skills as axiomatic. For instance, some listening skills, such as the abilities to discern various levels of pulse and infer a tonic, are most easily treated as givens. Instilling such skills in developing musicians is often a difficult and time-consuming task. In the realm of music reading and performance, one such skill is the ability to auralize and sing basic tonal structures.

One convenient structure to begin with is the major scale, both because it covers all members of the diatonic collection in scale-degree form and because it is nearly ubiquitously familiar to university, college, and conservatory students. Nonetheless, instructors might find a few students who are at first unable to sing a scale. Such students might also exhibit difficulties in matching pitches (see chapter 2), or they might display problems only when moving beyond individual pitches. By far, the most common types of difficulties in scale singing involve some kind of contour-appropriate but pitch-inappropriate responses—often resulting in a narrowing of range during the ascending portion of the scale. Such errors are rarely a result of vocal problems; a quick test asks the singer to match the lowest and highest notes in the scale, and most can do this. More often, the difficulties lie in the mental conception of the scale pitches before they are produced and in the auto-correction mechanism among voice, ear, and brain. For some, practicing scales while sustaining the tonic pitch on a piano (or other instrument) is a great remedy. For others,

---

4. Also note that a recent textbook (Gottschalk and Kloeckner 1997)—in order to develop *functional* hearing and sight singing—uses movable-*do* (with *do*-based minor) exclusively.

Do Ti La Sol La Ti La Sol Fa Mi Re Do Ti Do Re Mi Fa Mi Re Do Re Mi Fa Sol La Sol Fa Mi Fa Sol La Ti Do Re Do

Example 6.1. One possible result of a direction-changing drill designed to acclimate musicians to the diatonic collection and solmization.

a similar drone on both tonic and dominant is helpful. Still others may need these pitches (and occasionally others) played as aim points along the way. All of these crutches are temporary measures aimed at instilling a referential sense of tonic against which all the tones in a scale must be calibrated. In any case, such difficulties are quite fundamental and should lie generally before the scope of this study.

The developing musician's task at this point should be to attach solmization syllables to the pitches of the scale in such a way that those syllables become intimately associated with particular scale-degree functions. Musicians must become fluent in singing syllables in both ascending and descending scalar contexts. To this end, it is useful to practice scales in at least two ways: (1) beginning (in the traditional fashion) with the lowest pitch, ascending to the highest, and returning to the lowest; and (2) beginning with the *highest* pitch, descending to the lowest, and returning to the highest. In this way, the descending segment of the scale receives equal treatment and need not always follow the ascending segment in a Pavlovian fashion. At this stage, it is most productive to learn to sing scales without reference to any notation whatsoever, neither regular notation nor protonotation. This facilitates the most intimate acquaintance between syllables and pitches and encourages living directly in the world of the syllables with as little distraction as possible.

An additional kind of drill involves the use of scale segments. For example, students can begin to sing a scale (either ascending or descending) and be instructed to change direction at a specific cue (the easiest is perhaps a conducted upbeat and downbeat). The hypothetical results of one such session are shown in Example 6.1.[5] This exercise is also best practiced without reference to notation of any kind.

Another type of exercise that is very effective in developing fluency in solmization is the sequential. Sequential exercises take a small contour and rhythm pattern and move it to successive scale degrees. One of the simplest is shown in Example 6.2

Any sequential can be represented by the rhythm and pitches of its initial pattern for each direction, ascending and descending. In this manner, the sequential shown in Example 6.2 would be written as the first

5. I would like to thank Eileen Ruby, one of my teaching assistants during 1995–97, for suggesting this valuable exercise.

Example 6.2. A simple sequential exercise.

line in Example 6.3; the remaining lines in that figure show some other representative sequentials.

Once again, as with scales, sequentials are most beneficial when practiced without notation. In this case, that also means without reference even to their abbreviated notation: they should be memorized.

Another set of exercises designed to develop functional reading and sight singing was constructed by the Danish composer and pedagogue Jorgen Jersild (see Jersild 1966 and Rogers 1996). Jersild's "functional progressions" are basic note-pair resolutions: $\hat{7}–\hat{1}$, $\hat{5}–\hat{1}$, $\hat{6}–\hat{1}$, $\hat{4}–\hat{3}$, $\hat{6}–\hat{5}$, $\hat{2}–\hat{1}$, $\hat{5}–\hat{3}$, $\uparrow\hat{5}–\hat{6}$, $\uparrow\hat{4}–\hat{5}$, and $\downarrow\hat{7}–\hat{6}$. Singing these note pairs in various keys (as on Jersild's text insert "Diagram of Functional Progressions") offers what Rogers (1996) called "a vigorous, multifaceted, concentrated, and extended workout for hearing melodic function and for acquiring tonal bearings" (p. 155). Although originally intended to be read from

Example 6.3. Some representative sequentials, written in abbreviated form.

notation, these note pairs—like scalar materials and sequentials—make excellent prototypes to be learned through functional solmization without notation.[6]

With the conscientious practice and execution of these scalar exercises, sequentials, and resolution and tendency-tone patterns, musicians can gain some fluency at singing with syllables and will begin to associate specific syllables with particular scale degree functions.

Establishing Collection and Tonic

Many difficulties in sight singing can be avoided if readers first make certain that they have the appropriate diatonic pitch collection and tonic in mind. It is not uncommon for readers to make egregious errors—often too simply diagnosed as "improper interval reading"—if they haven't properly established these two parameters.

It is helpful and illuminating to separate the establishment of collection and tonic into two separate processes. On one hand, we have the diatonic pitch collection—represented in notation by the "key" signature.[7] On the other hand, we have the tonic—which is determined by the particular structural relationships among the pitches of that collection in any given musical passage. Musicians must be able to establish and manipulate these two parameters independently.

Before beginning to sing, it is instructive to be given only one sound: the *starting* pitch. The reasons behind this are several. First, as we shall see, it helps place an emphasis on the idea of collection—the pitches that make up the scale, chords, and other patterns within a key—more than merely the tonic and scale. Second, there are performance situations (auditions, rehearsals, etc.) in which similar cues are all that are given (for example, the single note on a pitch pipe in some choral performances), so a familiarity with that experience is wisely offered here. Third, as a preparation for future work in the aural skills sequence when music modulates, readers must become adept at adjusting to a new collection around a pitch.

Establishing a collection is one task for which the acontextual production of intervals is appropriate. Since the point of this exercise is to *create* a context, we must begin somewhere without one. A single given pitch and the name of its scale-degree function are the only information needed when combined with the reader's ability to produce whole and half steps above and below given pitches at will. This is significantly

---

6. Jersild (1966, 31) does introduce his seven basic functional progressions through generic scale-degree numbers but progresses into notation before the page is through.

7. A "key" signature does not actually designate a key but merely a diatonic collection.

Example 6.4. Whole and half steps above and below a given pitch.

different from the simple injunction merely to sing a major scale. For that task, one can always begin with the tonic at any feasible pitch level. In contrast, to establish a collection one must begin with a preselected scale degree from a given pitch.

In order to facilitate this process, musicians must develop the ability to sing both whole and half steps above and below any given pitch. In fact, a millennium ago the *Enchiridion musices* warned that "mediocre singers often fall into the greatest error because they scarcely consider the qualities of tone and semitone" (Pseudo-Odo of Cluny [n.d.] 1998, 205). Various preliminary exercises may be employed to develop this skill. One particularly useful type of such exercises involves singing three-pitch turn-around patterns that produce both whole and half steps above and below a single pitch, then gradually progressing to produce these patterns singly from various pitches. For example, the pitch G can be used as a common-tone link among the four patterns shown in Example 6.4. (Although these figures are written here in music notation, note that they can all be pre-scribed entirely aurally.) Subsequently, different starting pitches can be paired or grouped so as to obfuscate the more obvious diatonic implications of the initial pattern. See Example 6.5 for some examples (the first pitch of each three-note group is to be supplied aurally).

Example 6.5. Groups of whole and half steps designed to obfuscate diatonic implications.

With the ability to produce whole and half steps above and below any pitch, readers are ready to establish a diatonic collection from a starting pitch. To do so, they should perform the following steps:

- Listen to the starting pitch.
- If necessary, sing by whole steps to reach the nearest half step within the collection.
- Sing the nearest half step to fix its position.
- Sing by whole steps to reach the other half step in the collection.
- Sing that half step to fix its position as well.
- (optional) Sing the entire scale.

For most, placing the two half steps and whatever whole steps they traversed to get to them will be sufficient to imply the entire diatonic collection. Should this prove insufficient, the final option of singing the entire scale will eliminate any further problems.

But this has only served to fix a collection of pitches in mind, not to establish any one of them as a tonic. Therefore, the following steps should be added to the procedure:

- If necessary, sing by steps to reach the tonic.
- Sing the tonic and dominant pitches.
- (optional) Sing tonic and dominant chords.

There may be some who wish to add further collection- and key-orienting patterns *after* this procedure. These are fine, but they should be carried out only after following the preceeding procedure. Most important, upon being given a starting pitch, one should not try to jump immediately to the tonic. Readers should use the stepwise procedure outlined here and pay particular attention to the separate aspects they are establishing—collection and tonic.

This procedure can be learned and assessed *out loud*, but after a certain period of time (perhaps a few weeks) it should become an auralized process, taking place entirely in the practitioner's mind, so that readers can mentally hear the half and whole steps and tonic and dominant pitches before beginning to sing.

For those who learn most easily in a procedural way, the preceding instructions will be sufficient. However, for those who prefer to deduce procedures from specific examples, lists of what to sing in certain cases are helpful. For example, Table 6.1 lists the patterns to sing when establishing collection and tonic from each of the three members of the tonic triad in the major mode (pitches are given in scale-degree numbers; appropriate solmization syllables may be substituted).

Obviously, the procedure yields other sequences when working in other modes or from other scale degrees, but the essential process remains the same. In addition, certain individuals who use these procedures may

TABLE 6.1. Patterns for establishing collection and tonic in major mode from $\hat{1}$, $\hat{3}$, and $\hat{5}$.

$\hat{1}$	$\hat{3}$	$\hat{5}$
$\hat{1}$–$\hat{7}$–$\hat{1}$	$\hat{3}$–$\hat{4}$–$\hat{3}$	$\hat{5}$–$\hat{4}$–$\hat{3}$
$\hat{1}$–$\hat{2}$–$\hat{3}$	$\hat{3}$–$\hat{2}$–$\hat{1}$	$\hat{3}$–$\hat{4}$–$\hat{3}$
$\hat{3}$–$\hat{4}$–$\hat{3}$	$\hat{1}$–$\hat{7}$–$\hat{1}$	$\hat{3}$–$\hat{2}$–$\hat{1}$
$\hat{3}$–$\hat{2}$–$\hat{1}$		$\hat{1}$–$\hat{7}$–$\hat{1}$
	$\hat{1}$–$\hat{5}$–$\hat{1}$	
$\hat{1}$–$\hat{5}$–$\hat{1}$		$\hat{1}$–$\hat{5}$–$\hat{1}$

find that small alterations facilitate execution. For instance, a common alternative for establishing the major mode from $\hat{5}$ involves *ascending* immediately from $\hat{5}$ to $\hat{1}$ and then proceeding as if establishing the key from $\hat{1}$. As long as they do not alter the basic principles at work here (separately establishing collection and tonic; stepwise establishment of whole and half steps), such small changes may be welcomed with little comment.

As the learning sequence progresses into notation in various keys, the ability to establish collection and tonic becomes a useful, powerful tool. At this stage, for example, individuals given a starting pitch of B♭ in the key of G♭ major will be able to establish the six-flat collection around B♭ and a sense of tonic on G♭ quickly and effectively. At later stages of study, they will find that modulations (particularly those that use common tones) are often easily executed using similar techniques.

Establishing Pulse, Tempo, and Meter

A sense of steady pulse is as important to music reading and performance as it is to listening. Accurate rhythms, a feeling of tempo, and musical phrasing depend on a steady, energetic pulse. For performing familiar music (a well-rehearsed composition, a well-known folk tune, etc.), establishing a pulse at an appropriate tempo usually involves auralizing a passage of the music in tempo before beginning to perform. But for true sight reading, for performing unfamiliar music for the first time, other factors come into play. In some circumstances, sight readers may not have enough time to auralize any passage of the music in real time before performing. As we shall see in chapter 7, sight reading from music notation requires a number of steps even before pitch and rhythm orientation can be established. Auralizing any passage of the music within the proper diatonic and tonal frameworks at a serviceable tempo must occur after various aspects of the notation have been deciphered and incorporated in preperformance orientation. In these circumstances, a steady, slow (but musical) tempo is advisable. But even in circumstances that allow enough time to auralize some of the music, unfamiliarity with the music requires that sight readers take certain more abstract factors into account—particularly the limitations of executing any especially difficult passages. When scanning music before sight reading, musicians should take note of any particularly challenging spots and gauge their tempo accordingly.

Musicians must be able to control the tempo they establish for themselves. The following exchange is all too typical in our universities, colleges, and conservatories:

> STUDENT   [performs at ♩=120; makes many mistakes]
> INSTRUCTOR   Please try that again, much more slowly.
> STUDENT   [performs at ♩=120; makes many mistakes]

Of course, this exchange repeats itself in many venues (aural skills classes, studio lessons, and ensembles) with various initial tempi, various wordings of the request to slow down, and occasional (usually insignificant) alterations to the tempo of the second performance. But the underlying cause remains the same: some students are either frustratingly unable or merely reluctant to control the tempo they establish for themselves. Any musician with this deficit needs to prepare exercises specifically designed to address tempo control. Such exercises include (1) listening to recordings of pieces at specific tempi, (2) learning to establish tempi from memory according to M.M. marking without recourse to any external reference such as a metronome or clock,[8] (3) preparing individual melodies at several different tempi, and (4) learning to maintain a reasonably steady average tempo while exercising musically expressive deviations therefrom.[9]

It is important that there remain a continuity—both mental and physical—between the pulse and tempo established before performing and the one used during performance. Musicians must be able to carry the tempo they establish for themselves directly and unaltered into the music for which it was established. Toward this end, it is useful to encourage students to use physical motions to embody the pulse they establish. Suggestions for such motions include foot tapping, head or torso motions, and conducting.[10]

---

8. (1) and (2) are particularly important. Levitin and Cook (1996) showed that most musicians and non-musicians are able to recall *well-learned* tempi very accurately.

9. Chapter 7 discusses specific remedies for this difficulty in greater detail. For an interesting examination of tempo behaviors in general, see Brown (1979).

10. Much maligned at present, foot tapping boasts a long tradition of service in developing a sense of pulse: Quantz remarked that a beginner "must always mark the beat—that is, the quaver in slow pieces and the crotchet in quick ones—with his foot" (Quantz [1752] 1985, 110). Boyle (1968) found that students who used foot tapping

Meter is another significant parameter to be established before performance. Among the most musical and practical means to aid in this process and express it physically is conducting. In conjunction with sight singing, the act of conducting brings with it the benefits of establishing and communicating a sense of pulse, tempo, and meter in a single activity. Benefits can be achieved through accompanying most or all performing activities from the earliest stages and throughout the aural skills curriculum with conducting.[11] Integrating conducting at the earliest stages of music reading also lays the foundation for its further use in supporting other musical parameters, such as dynamics and articulation, and fosters an intimate understanding of the conductor's motions performers see from within an ensemble.

Aural Imagery prior to Sound Production

The five basic procedures discussed thus far in this chapter—establishment of collection, tonic, pulse, tempo, and meter—must all be performed in some external fashion (that is, via singing, tapping, clapping, or conducting) if they are to be assessed by teachers or peers. However, it is important for these procedures to be internalized as soon as possible. Before performing, musicians should be able to establish a key or set a tempo without making a sound. The ability to auralize these procedures is valuable not only in actual performing situations but also for everyday music-reading tasks. Anyone reading metric tonal music must be able to auralize key and meter before beginning to interpret and understand the individual notes.

And the ability to auralize the sounds of the individual notes is equally important. Proficient readers scan ahead, taking in musically meaningful groups of notes and hearing them internally before producing their sounds. The next chapter will deal with this skill at greater length.

Reading from Protonotation

All of the skills discussed in this chapter can be introduced and developed without the added complexities presented by the systems of rhythm and pitch notation. Using the same system of protonotation proposed in chapters 2 and 3, sight singers can learn to read and perform meter, rhythm,

---

made significantly better increases in music reading than those who used no such movements. Rohwer (1998) concluded that "using bodily movement and participating in musical activities in a variety of tempos appear to have a positive effect on performance ability" (p. 422).

11. Indeed, Kelly (1993) found that training in conducting had a strong, positive effect on beginners' abilities to read rhythms.

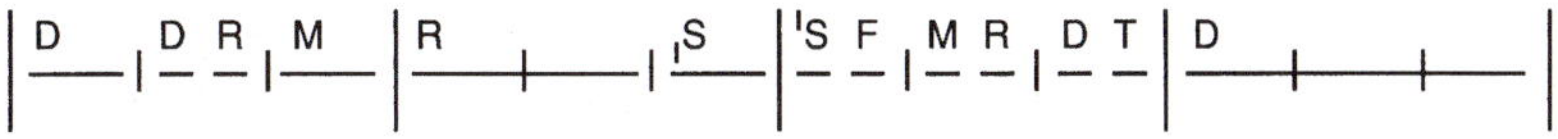

Figure 6.1. Protonotation for sight singing.

and pitch as skills separate from the ability to read and understand music written in various meter signs and keys. Those skills, once learned, can be projected onto various rhythmic values and tonics, thereby focusing on the skills involved in reading in specific beat units and keys after other skills (vocal production; familiarity with solmization; establishing collection and tonic; establishing pulse, meter, and tempo; and aural imagery) are more firmly under control.

Individual preferences may vary with regard to how long the introduction of actual music notation should be delayed. In any case, it is possible and quite practical for readers to develop their fundamental reading skills through preparing and reading at sight melodies presented in protonotation as in Figure 6.1.

7

Sight Reading

All of the skills discussed in the preceding chapter are just as easily (and in some ways better) introduced and practiced *before* notation has been employed in the aural skills sequence. It is much easier to identify and remedy difficulties with these skills in the absence of the variables introduced by reading and interpreting notation.

But now it is time to address the issues involved in sight reading from actual music notation. Let us begin with some basic procedures that have proven to be extremely helpful in orienting sight readers before they utter a sound.

Scanning Music before Sight Reading

Global Parameters

It is wise to develop the habit of starting by orienting oneself to the global information that appears at the beginning of the musical staff. One can scan this information roughly in the order in which it appears, from left to right: instrument or voice and transposition (if applicable), clef, key signature, meter, and tempo.

If a passage is labeled with the name of an instrument, readers must be cognizant of whether it is a transposing instrument. A transposition might also be indicated beside or above the staff (for example, "in E"). In either case, readers must make adjustments accordingly (primarily if reading on fixed-*do* or letter names).

Although it may seem rather pedestrian, it is just as important to make note of the printed clef before beginning to sing. It is certainly not unheard of for students to begin reading in the wrong clef, even if their current studies are restricted to only treble and bass clefs. When further clefs are encountered, it is all the more important to scrutinize the clef

with explicit comprehension (perhaps even to speak its name aloud—
"tenor clef"). In this manner, one can avoid the time and effort wasted
in becoming oriented to the music in the wrong clef and eliminate the
need to unlearn that incorrect orientation and learn the proper one.

The next global symbol—the key signature—is a more complex entity.
What we commonly refer to as a "key" signature does not represent a
key at all. Instead, it represents a specific diatonic collection—the two-
sharp collection, for example. Put another way, a key signature tells only
which letter classes are to be played natural, sharp, or flat. No key signature alone can represent a key, because "key" is a result of the confluence of two factors: (1) diatonic collection and (2) tonic. Whereas a diatonic collection can be determined by a "key" signature, a tonic is the
result of the temporal and structural ordering of the pitches in that collection.[1] In this way, a single "key" signature may precede any of two
keys (major and minor) or five other modes, which are similarly products
of the confluence of diatonic collection and tonic or final.[2] With this in
mind it is possible to note the key signature at the opening of a piece and
know the diatonic collection (barring functional chromatic alterations of
that collection), but determining the tonic (and therefore the key) involves
more sophisticated interpretation of the pitches, meter, and rhythm of the
music. Structural connections between pitches that form dominant and
leading-tone relationships to another pitch are particularly indicative of
tonic function.[3]

Once the tonic has been determined, an important step is locating the
tonic on the staff as a point of reference. As Fletcher (1957) observed,
"The tonal center, identified with a specific staff-location at the beginning,
held in mind during the entire decoding [reading] procedure . . . , is the
point of reference by which the ambiguities in the visual code [notation]
are resolved" (p. 82). Readers use the location of the tonic as a fundamental point of reference from which to decipher the tonal meanings of
pitch structures in the notation.

Having identified the diatonic collection and tonic, readers should explicitly carry out the procedures necessary to *establish* each of these parameters in their minds (see the outline of these procedures in the section
of chapter 6 titled "Establishing Collection and Tonic").

Similar preparatory attention must be paid to the meter sign. It must
be immediately assessed as to whether it represents a simple or compound

1. See the discussions in chapter 2 under "Memory of Pitch Collections" and "Inference of Tonic."

2. The totals of two keys and five modes within any given diatonic collection account for the inclusion of Locrian mode. If you do not admit Locrian into your store
of modes, reduce the total number of modes to four.

3. Readers should be aware of old saws such as "look at the last note—it'll be the
tonic" or "if there are chromatics, it's probably in minor." For obvious reasons, such
instructions are of limited use.

meter. Subsequent to that, the number of beats per measure must be registered. Finally, the reader must consider whether the beat should be subdivided. If applicable, the appropriate conducting pattern must be chosen.

The two modern abbreviated symbols for meter signs that have survived from the mensural system, ℂ and ₵, must be interpreted properly. Many inexperienced readers harbor the notion that ₵ indicates a $\frac{4}{4}$ measure performed twice as fast, so that half notes, rather than quarters, become beat units. Although ₵ finds its origins in the mensural system of proportions, its common-practice-period meaning is much more diverse.

First, according to George Houle's well-documented study, *Meter in Music: 1600–1800*, the precise meanings of the mensuration signs that survived into the eighteenth century "varied depending on the signs' relations to one another. In some cases ₵, in contrast to ℂ, meant a 2:1 change of tempo, in others, merely a faster tempo not necessarily in the ratio of 2:1." Some theorists—notably French writers—did not interpret the signs as representing a time relationship at all (Houle 1987, 57). And as meter signs and tempo indications took on completely independent roles during the subsequent centuries, the signs ℂ and ₵ lost their ability to indicate relative speed. Because of this, modern readers should think of ₵ (when it represents $\frac{2}{2}$) in a family with $\frac{2}{4}$, $\frac{2}{8}$, and other simple duple meters, not as some halved, double-speed version of $\frac{4}{4}$.

Second, although some writers at some points held that ₵ indicated a two-beat measure and ℂ a four-beat measure, the symbol ₵ has never exclusively represented duple meter. Many twentieth-century transcriptions of mensural notation use ₵ to represent $\frac{4}{2}$. Common-practice-period notation uses it this way as well. For example, the symbol represents $\frac{4}{2}$ in the E-major Fugue from book 2 of Bach's *Well-Tempered Clavier* and in "Der Gerechten Seelen sind in Gottes Hand" and "Herr, du bist würdig" in Brahms's *German Requiem* (to pick one representative composition from each of two different centuries). Finally, some editions and transcriptions that use the symbol ₵ forgo bar lines altogether or use them only to indicate phrase divisions. Examples of this type often fall into the hands of students: see the chorale settings by Christoph Peter and Hans Leo Hassler in Burkhart (1994, 555–56, 557–59) and Michael Praetorius's setting of "Es ist ein' Ros' entsprungen" in DeVoto (1992, 3).

The only thing a modern reader can depend on when facing the vast body of Western music is that ₵ indicates that the half note will be worth one beat; the specific meter must be inferred from the musical context. Modern music readers who wish to be prepared for such a variety of interpretations for ₵ must come to understand its various meanings, learn its one certainty (that the half note is the beat unit), and practice many musical excerpts that showcase ₵ in its various meanings.

Considering the variety of beat units of which composers have availed themselves, it is important for music readers to have much experience with beat units that range at least from the half note through the sixteenth note,[4] and with a variety of tempi that vary independently of these beat units. A word about the interaction between beat unit and tempo is warranted here. For some time, a convention was held over from mensural notation into modern metric notation "that smaller notes were performed faster and larger notes were performed slower" (Houle 1987, 2). Notational practice over subsequent centuries made that notion archaic, through a separation of functions: meter signs to represent meter and beat unit; tempo indications or metronome markings to represent speed. One need only compare the relative speeds of whole notes in the finale of Beethoven's Fifth Symphony, mm. 362ff (*Presto*; o=*112*) and dotted eighth notes in the arietta from Beethoven's Piano Sonata, Op. 111 (*Adagio molto*; $\flat$. = ca. *36*) to see the modern dissociation of note values from speed.

The skills involved in executing rhythms depend upon the values of the notes relative to the prevailing beat unit. Consider the eighth note, for example. It is one-half of a beat long in $\frac{4}{4}$ meter, two beats long in $\frac{4}{16}$ meter, two-thirds of a beat long in $\frac{6}{8}$ meter, and so on. The skills required to read and perform these different meanings are quite distinct from one another and should be learned separately—grouped by function relative to beat durations rather than by specific rhythm symbols[5]—so that they may be dealt with separately when sight-reading.

The final global symbol at the opening of a composition is the tempo. This can take one or both of two forms: a verbal indication of tempo, or a metronome marking. In the first case, it is incumbent on readers to interpret the tempo implied by the printed words. As discussed in chapter 1, some of these indications are more specific than others. Such imprecision notwithstanding, readers should choose an appropriate speed based on the tempo indication (taking into account historical stylistic considerations and the character of the music to which it applies). In the second case, readers must be able to recall or synthesize specific tempi within a relatively small margin of tolerance. For example, if the tempo indication reads "$\flat$=100," then readers must be able to establish a tempo roughly

---

4. Meter signs with 2, 4, 8, and 16 as beat units are quite common. Instructors might also consider exposing students to those meters in which the whole note serves as tactus (even if notated in $\frac{2}{2}$ or $\frac{4}{4}$) and those in which 32d, 64th, and perhaps even 128th notes are counted (see especially the music of George Crumb). For helpful lists of compositions in various meters, see Read (1979, 159–63).

5. Many aural skills texts (e.g., Ottman 1996 and Benward and Kolosick 1996a) do indeed organize their rhythmic materials by beat function. Others use specific rhythm symbols as organizing factors. For example, Friedman (1981) devotes an entire chapter to introducing the sixteenth note (pp. 136–56) in both simple and compound meters, which create very different skill contexts; Berkowitz, Fontrier, and Kraft (1997) introduce the rhythm $\downarrow\flat$ immediately in meters with both the quarter note and half note as beat unit (pp. 6–7), commingling beat-extending and beat-dividing skills.

in the region between about 92 and 108 beats per minute. For this, it is helpful to memorize several representative compositions at tempo, each of which embodies a specific metronome marking;[6] from these, one can also obtain other tempi through doubling and halving speeds. No matter whether tempo is indicated verbally or through M.M. marking, readers must firmly establish a *steady* tempo in their minds before beginning to sing and maintain that tempo as they actually begin to sing, making changes in tempo only for musically expressive reasons or in response to tempo indications in the notation.

Obviously, any changes to these global parameters (for example, a change of clef or meter) must be accounted for in advance of encountering them in real time. Readers should scan the music for such changes and make note of their location and function before beginning to sight sing.

Placement of Scale Degrees on Staff; Starting Pitch

Once the clef and key signature have been ascertained, readers should orient themselves tonally by mentally locating the scale degrees on the staff in that clef. This process can begin with locating the tonic in its position(s) on the staff. A prudent next step involves placement of the members of the tonic triad on the staff. With these positions firmly fixed in mind, readers can use them as reference points while singing—they account for three of the seven diatonic pitches, and none of the other scale degrees will ever be more than a single step away from one of them. Perhaps it should go without saying, but they are also important points of tonal arrival and departure in most music.

An extra moment should be taken at this time to locate the starting pitch within the scale-degree structure thus established. A vast majority of excerpts begin on a member of the tonic triad. There are a few that begin elsewhere. Some begin on *embellishments* of members of the tonic triads (for example, Mozart, Symphony No. 40, mmt. 1, first theme [6̂–5̂–5̂] and Haydn, Symphony No. 99, mmt. 1, second theme [↑ 4̂–5̂–3̂–1̂]), whereas others begin entirely off-tonic (for example, the opening of the violin part in the first movement of Franck's Sonata in a major for Violin and Piano [4̂–6̂–4̂–2̂–7̂–6̂–2̂–4̂] as shown in Example 2.15). In any case, readers should be able to auralize a starting pitch in relation to the tonic before singing.

---

6. Levitin and Cook (1996) showed that most listeners are quite capable of remembering a repeatedly heard composition within 8% of the tempo at which it has been heard.

Range and Tessitura

A quick scan of the pitches should also yield the highest and lowest pitches. Readers should be aware of their own vocal ranges and request a transposition, if necessary. More important, the general tessitura of the passage should be assessed, particularly with an eye toward the lines and spaces on which the members of the tonic triad will lie within that tessitura. Of particular interest is how those tonic-triad reference tones are deployed within the tessitura: Does î form the lower boundary, or does 5̂ or perhaps 3̂? Does the music span the octave above this lower demarcation, or does it only traverse a fourth or fifth or perhaps extend even beyond the octave? The answers to such questions have profound implications for how one goes about framing the tonality and scale degrees within the actual tessitura of any particular passage.[7]

Repetition Signs

Before singing, readers must take note of any repetition signs in the music. Students must be taught the meanings of various signs, including slashes for repeating single beats, slashes with dots for repeating entire measures, repeat bars at the ends (and beginnings) of passages, first and second endings, and the various incarnations of *da capo*, *dal segno*, *fine*, and *coda* indications.[8] Instructors should think twice before directing students to "skip the repeats": correct observation of repetition signs is an important aspect of good music reading and should be integrated into prepared aural skills singing and singing at sight.

"Mumbling"

A very useful next step involves "mumbling" through the music.[9] "Mumbling," in this context, refers to a kind of rapid reading that stands somewhere between freely scanning out of sequence on the one hand and reading actively in real time on the other. Its main goal is to point up salient aspects of pitch that will provide anchor points along the way and help to keep the actual sight singing moving as smoothly as possible.

7. Similarly, Thomson and DeLone (1967) refers to the "tonality frame . . . the *structural* pitch boundaries of a melody" (p. 29); see pp. 29–31.

8. See the concise yet comprehensive discussion of repetition signs in Read (1979, 223–31).

9. I would like to thank Steve Larson for suggesting this valuable routine.

Example 7.1. Ottman, *Music for Sight Singing*, 4th ed., #370.

Above all, when mumbling one should pay particular attention to structural pitches such as those at beginnings and endings of phrases, high and low points, and any special figures such as sequences, turnarounds, arpeggiations, and the like. Especially striking or challenging aspects of rhythm should also be noted, although mumbling seems to be most particularly suited to aspects of pitch.

At first, mumbling can be practiced on simple excerpts that maintain a single clef, key, and meter. Later, it may incorporate such features as modulations, meter changes, clef changes, and so on.

An Example

As an example of the kinds of things presented in this chapter thus far, consider the sight-singing excerpt from Robert Ottman's *Music for Sight Singing* (Ottman 1996) shown in Example 7.1. Preliminary observations of the global symbols in this excerpt might proceed as follows:

> Treble clef; one sharp . . . in this case representing E minor; ȼ standing for ⁴⁄₄ meter; no tempo indication.

Tonal and registral observations would include these:

> Tonic on the first line and fourth space; tonic triad on the first three lines; begins on $\hat{1}$; lies mostly in the E4–E5 ($\hat{1}$–$\hat{1}$) octave; dips down to $\hat{5}$ below at the end.

A brief mumbling session for this tune might go something like this:

> Start on $\hat{1}$; skip to $\hat{6}$; descend to $\hat{3}$; skip to $\hat{1}$ above; start next phrase on $\hat{1}$ and end it on $\hat{2}$; start next phrase on $\hat{3}$; end on $\hat{4}$ to $\hat{5}$.

A more detailed mumbling session for this tune might include the following:

> Scale $\hat{1}$ to $\hat{3}$; skip $\hat{1}$ to $\hat{6}$ [N.B.: not $\hat{5}$]; scale down to $\hat{3}$; skip to $\hat{1}$ above; lower neighbor and back to $\hat{1}$ skip to $\hat{5}$; scale down to $\hat{2}$; skip $\hat{3}$ to $\hat{1}$; skip down to low $\hat{4}$ [N.B.: not $\hat{5}$]; end on $\hat{5}$.

This more detailed mumbling might seem at first like nothing more than a simple "performance" of the music. However, in practice this kind of educated mumbling can be carried out quite rapidly and with exceptional benefits.[10]

Eye Movements

Although eye movements *during* sight reading are discussed at length later in this chapter (see the section titled "Visual Tracking"), it is important at this juncture to note the kinds of eye movements expert readers use while scanning music without performing it. Waters and Underwood (1998) found that expert readers use more and quicker eye fixations for one specific type of nonperforming music-reading task (pattern matching between two successively presented melodic fragments). There are at least two reasonable explanations for this difference: (1) experts understand more about the musical structures they see in notation and comprehend those structures more quickly, and (2) experts have developed more rapid eye movements as a successful skill in and of itself. These explanations point to two strategies that should improve silent music reading: (1) become more knowledgeable about musical structures and more efficient at recognizing them rapidly and (2) develop the skill of scanning music as rapidly as possible.[11]

Interval and Scale-Degree Strategies

Sight-singing training that uses intervals has existed for at least a century. Dannhäuser (1891) includes "exercises for intoning the intervals" (e.g, vol. 1, pp. 5–7). Cole and Lewis (1909) progresses from stepwise melodies through those that contain skips of increasingly larger intervals. Adler

---

10. A competent "mumbler" can mumble through an excerpt like Ottman's #370 in about fifteen seconds and come away with much useful information that will often result in superior first readings.

11. No research has been published that compares eye movements while reading various music typefaces. Valuable information could be gained through learning how readers scan, say, an old Breitkopf edition versus a new Peters score, a page from Durand versus one from a handwritten manuscript, and so on.

(1997) contains "specially composed melodies for the practice of particular intervals."[12]

There are many proponents of focusing on scale-degree approaches to sight singing. Fletcher (1957) discussed the use of both intervallic and scale-degree information: "Each successive tone sung must be referred not only to the previous tone but to a total order of tones, a patterning of tones according to usage in the present-day common experience around a tonal center," and, "It is only when the staff-code representation of an interval is referred to something beyond the staff-code—the tonic-location and all its implications of traditional usage—that the ambiguity [of notation] may be resolved" (p. 82). Jersild (1966) railed against "music reading systems that begin with a more or less abstract study of *intervals*. These rarely provide efficient results. There are two reasons for this. First, the character of the interval changes according to its place in the tonal context. Second, the interval constitutes a subordinated detail in any musical sequence. While reading music, such 'atomistic' detail will rarely be perceived" (p. 5). Rogers (1984) noted that "most students—especially those reading by interval—perform a score with their noses too close to the notes, thereby losing sight of the forest for the trees" (p. 129) and "the functional method in singing tonal melodies offers a corrective to over-reliance on intervals. Sensitivity to scale-degree tendencies, internal tensions, and development of tonal bearings provides a more musical sense of phrase and the long line. One problem with the interval approach to hearing is that it views sightsinging as a skill to be acquired (i.e., becoming accurate at reproducing notated pitches and rhythms) rather than as a means of gathering valuable information about how music itself works" (p. 131).

Much of this correlates with the findings in chapters 2 and 3 about intervallic and functional approaches to listening and with those in chapter 6 about tonal orientation. Therefore, the remainder of this chapter takes a tonally functional approach to reading pitch.

Solmization Systems for Sight Reading

Translating Pitches into Syllables

For readers using a solmization system, one of the tasks to be carried out in real time is translating pitches into syllables. I shall address this process in each of two broad categories of solmization: fixed pitch-naming systems and movable scale-degree systems.

---

12. The first edition of *Sight Singing: Pitch, Interval, Rhythm* focused almost exclusively on an intervallic approach to sight singing. This new edition is well balanced between intervallic and functional approaches.

When using a fixed system—for example, letter names or fixed-*do*—
the task at hand is reading the pitches of the lines and spaces within the
operative clef and assigning the appropriate labels on the basis of that
reading. This requires readers to think in the clef, continually reading the
lines and spaces as individual note names. When readers are using letter
names, there follows the simple matter of articulating the pitches on those
names; other fixed systems (most notably fixed-*do*) require readers to
translate the note names into their corresponding syllables, at least until
readers become fluent at naming pitches directly through these syllables.
The exigencies of fixed systems are therefore quite appropriate for developing and assessing such skills as clef reading and transposition (as
discussed in chapter 8).

Movable systems—*do*-tonic movable-*do* and numbers—require readers to read scale degrees relative to the tonic on the staff. This can take
one of two basic forms: (1) reading the pitches on the staff within the
prevailing clef and then translating them into scale degree syllables by
relating them to the tonic and (2) seeking patterns of functional shapes
on an essentially generically conceived staff. The former procedure is perhaps more cumbersome, since it involves a two-stage translation process.[13] The latter is less complex, but it has the disadvantage of circum-
venting the valuable task of reading fixed pitch names in specific clefs. In
actuality, most practitioners of movable systems employ a combination
of these approaches, shifting between the two systems on the fly depending upon the musical structure of specific passages and how that jibes
with their own musical knowledge. In either case, movable scale-degree
systems involve the mind in reading and thinking in scale degrees and
tonal function.

Both approaches—fixed pitch-naming and movable scale-degrees—are
extremely valuable. Both have been shown to be useful and productive
over centuries of use. There has, however, been a long and sometimes
acrimonious debate between practitioner/advocates of these two approaches to solmization.[14] Without rehashing the entire debate yet again,
it is important to note the following fact: *both sides make some valid
arguments in favor of using their respective systems.* Advocates of the
fixed pitch naming approach often point to improvements in clef reading
and transposition;[15] advocates of the scale-degree approach frequently

13. Indeed, this is one of the main points detractors use in decrying movable systems: that it requires note reading *and* a kind of on-the-fly analysis (see, for example,
Hindemith 1949, vii; and Martin 1978, 24). However, this is precisely the kind of
musical understanding—comprehending both absolute pitches and tonal functions—
we seek to foster in musicians.

14. See, for example, Harris (1918), Multer (1978), Martin (1978), Surace (1978),
Smith (1991), and Larson (1993b).

15. Note, however, that certain arguments—particularly those that claim adult
study of fixed-*do* can develop AP—are not supported by persuasive empirical evidence.

invoke the inculcation of functional hearing and reading and other attendant benefits. The list of potential benefits from each type of system is in
fact quite long. The logical conclusion from all this is to use *both* kinds
of systems.[16]

Several pairings of various specific fixed and movable systems are
possible. For example, one might design a curriculum using movable-*do*
for functional hearing and reading concurrently with letter names for
reading and naming actual pitches. In another sample pairing, scale-
degree numbers can be used to represent functions while French-style
solfège stands in for pitch naming. But as discussed in chapter 3, one
general caveat is in order: similar labels should not be used for the two
approaches.

The choice of solmization systems for pitch is an important one,
with far-reaching ramifications. Most important, the choice should be
well informed, based on empirical criteria that regard the specific musical features modeled and instilled by each system.[17] Above all, all pedagogues—aural skills instructors, studio teachers, conductors, et al.—
should avoid invoking rationalizations such as "*I* was trained that way"
and instead make rational decisions about solmization on the basis of
what we know about how musicians learn and specifically what we
want them to learn.

Regardless of which systems are used, it is crucial that students receive
adequate amounts of drill and practice in their use. In a loose analogy to
the letters of the alphabet, in order to *learn* solmization (not merely be
exposed to it) one must invest the equivalent of the hours, days, weeks,
months, and years young children spend on learning the alphabet—reciting it, singing the "Alphabet Song," recognizing letters, writing letters,
associating their various phonic incarnations, and practicing reading,
writing, and spelling constantly. So, too, must students of solmization be
indoctrinated, through repetition and memorization of pitch patterns,
scales, sequentials, melodies, chord arpeggiations, and other activities designed to ingrain various mental associations between solmization syllables and their musical meanings. A halfhearted "exposure" to solmization
(whether halfhearted on the part of students *or* instructors) is probably
worse than no solmization at all. For sight singers who are not fluent
with solmization, syllables are an impediment, not an aid. It is advisable
to buy into solmization wholeheartedly or not at all.

16. Riggins (1988) also advocates pairing fixed and movable solmization. This approach has been tested and proven in a number of clinical settings. For example,
courses at the Eastman School of Music, Ithaca College, the University of Massachusetts, and the University of Oregon (among others) have all included elements of both
systems. Instructors at all these institutions report positive results.

17. For such discussions, see Smith (1991) and Larson (1989; 1993b).

Translating Rhythms into Syllables

Rhythmic solmization can be just as beneficial as pitch systems. Please refer to the discussions of rhythm solmization in chapter 3 for an introduction to these systems.

Functional systems, chief among them Takadimi, model the metric positions of attack points. They require that readers understand the proportional metric values of the notes and rests as they read. Functional systems are particularly attractive since they use uniform labels for specific rhythmic patterns (and thus for identically performed music) regardless of their different notational incarnations within various meter signs.

Notation-oriented rhythm solmization systems attach specific labels to individual rhythmic symbols, regardless of their function within any given meter sign. Such direct symbol naming has some usefulness in the reading of actual note symbols but no direct relationship to the rhythmic and metric proportions those symbols represent.

Regardless of the kind of rhythmic solmization employed, practitioners must work to become as fluent in it as in pitch solmization. As before, a halfhearted effort will only result in annoyance and hindered performances. But those fluent in rhythm syllables will find that they unlock the door to a level of rhythmic understanding and facility of great power.

Conclusion

Finally, it should be noted that solmization systems all compete for egress through the same verbal channel. It is obvious (but no less a problem for it) that only one system may be performed by any one musician at any given time. Thus, teachers who wish to explicitly develop, say, a specific clef-reading skill, a sense of a particular harmonic function, and attention to a certain rhythmic pattern, all through a single exercise, might consider assigning that exercise three times using three different solmization systems: (1) a fixed pitch naming system, (2) a movable scale-degree system, and (3) a system of rhythmic solmization. Equally effective, and perhaps at times more manageable, is the assignment of separate exercises that use individual solmization systems chosen to highlight and illuminate particular features under study at the time.

Intonation

Chapter 2 examined intonation in great detail as manifested in matching individual pitches. Much of what is covered there is generally applicable to intonation in melodies, but there are some further considerations when intonation operates in tonal contexts.[18]

There are (at least) two kinds of tonal intonation problems: (1) those that involve the key itself, wherein the tonal center shifts or is entirely lost; and (2) those that involve individual pitches within a key while the key remains unaffected. Let us address each of these in turn.

The Key

Doubtless the more severe of the two broad varieties of intonation difficulties, losing the key is a serious musical transgression. Infractions of this variety often result in a complete breakdown of pitch reading (although readers so afflicted occasionally do manage to establish some new tonal center seemingly out of thin air). Often the temptation is to focus on the very spot where the trouble began and attempt to correct specific pitches there. This is typically done hoping that, if one gets over that rough spot the catastrophe will not recur. Unfortunately, it usually does. Musicians afflicted with this type of intonational malady have a much deeper, more general deficiency to remedy.

A quick and obvious test to determine if readers have indeed lost the tonic involves asking that they sing the tonic pitch after such an infraction has occurred. It will be immediately apparent whether they have retained that all-important reference pitch.

Readers who lose the tonic can reap great benefits from the following exercise. Whatever the musical material—scales, sequentials, excerpts from the literature—they should be instructed to pause at regular intervals of time and sing the tonic pitch. At first, these intervals should be on the order of a few pitches (perhaps every measure or every half-measure); later, the readers can progress to pausing at longer intervals (perhaps at the beginning of every phrase). Musicians who practice using this procedure usually see vast improvements in relatively short periods of time.

Those who cannot execute this skill often require a preliminary exercise: spending half their aural skills practice time playing a tonic drone on the piano (or other suitable instrument) while singing exercises and excerpts, stopping often to listen to the drone and to sing its pitch. Occasionally some find that a tonic-dominant drone is even more helpful. In either case, readers must progress at some point from drone playing,

18. Intonation judgments are typically more accurate in tonal contexts than in isolation (see Wapnick, Bourassa, and Sampson 1982 for experimental evidence of this). Tonality provides a more general frame of reference against which intonation can be judged.

to the tonic-repetition exercise described previously, and finally to a new musical life of tonal orientation. Indeed, these exercises serve to infuse readers with a sense of the tonic so that they can refer to it throughout every measure of every performance.

Pitches within a Key

The second variety of intonation problem is perhaps less severe but just as important to diagnose and remedy. This variety involves inaccurate production of pitches within a key without losing the tonic.[19] This may take the form of a few isolated pitches mistuned at a specific spot in a passage, or it may manifest itself as certain scale degrees that are consistently performed out of tune. In the former case, merely calling attention to the spot and comparing it with identical scale degrees elsewhere is often sufficient remedy, since such readers have shown that they can produce those scale degrees in tune in those other locations. In the latter case, it is useful to return to scales and sequences—singing them slowly and carefully while tuning each scale degree to the tonic, if necessary also singing or playing a tonic drone as described in the previous section. Singing with others and singing with harmonic accompaniment can also foster better sensitivity to intonation. After achieving some success in these activities, such readers should return to the passages in which their original errors occurred, approaching them with the same care and accuracy for intonation learned in the drills.[20]

Good intonation depends on performers' abilities to auralize pitches first so that they may zero in on accurate rendering of those pitches. Without a specific pitch in mind to aim for, a performer cannot possibly auralize proper intonation. No target, no bull's-eye. To this end, we must realize that the appropriate kinds of aural training can pave the way for good intonation. This does not mean that such training will automatically result in good intonation. But without the kind of aural skills that enable musicians to auralize pitches before they perform them, good intonation is an impossibility.

19. On the basis of isolated-interval tests, Siegel and Siegel (1977) concluded that there seemed to be a trade-off between categorical (size) perception of intervals and intonation. But Wapnick, Bourassa, and Sampson (1982) found that musicians are more accurate at *both* categorical perception and intonation judgments when materials are presented in a melodic context—that is, when they are listening to music in a key.

20. For a brief survey of the experimental literature on intonation and some interesting data on musicians' intonation adjustments *during* individual pitches within a scale, see Geringer and Sogin (1988).

Example 7.2. J. S. Bach, Brandenburg Concerto No. 4, BWV 1049, mmt. 3, mm. 154–61.

Visual Tracking

Eye Movements

Instructors and students spend a great amount of time and effort developing, teaching, studying, and employing systematic approaches to pitch and rhythm. They use solmization systems, pitch patterns, rhythmic figures, conducting patterns, and various other techniques under the assumption that familiarity and understanding will breed a certain amount of competence. And there is ample evidence, both empirical and anecdotal, both qualitative and quantitative, that this is true.

Nonetheless, it is also true that many individuals become quite competent at these systematic approaches and yet remain disturbingly incompetent at sight singing. Such music readers may exhibit fluency with tonal function and patterns, rhythmic understanding and accuracy, and a generally high level of proficiency in reading prepared materials. But when they are confronted with reading unfamiliar music at sight, they hesitate frequently and make numerous mistakes.

A significant cause of such results is rooted in the eye movements of these readers. In clinical settings, I have noticed that more competent readers often move their gaze across the page with much fluidity, whereas less competent readers often focus in fits and starts. In a particularly strong indication of these kinds of difficulties, I have excerpted and devised certain melodies for sight-singing exams that contain a trap for inefficient readers: a line of music that ends on a long note, followed by the next measure on a new line that begins with more rapid rhythms (see Example 7.2 for an example).

The number and kinds of mistakes this pairing causes are much more severe when split between two lines than when these same measures appear next to each other in the middle of a line. Why? Because certain readers have a habit of staring at whatever note they are singing at the moment, never reading ahead until the next beat comes around. Thus, these readers stare at the long note at the end of the line, only to be overwhelmed by the more rapid pitches when they encounter them—as if by surprise—at the beginning of the next line. I have observed this behavior for many years, even setting up music stands for sight-singing exams in such a way that I can closely observe students' eyes while they sing. In general, it seems that better readers read ahead. Indeed, Sloboda (1976) found that music reading involves "dual coding mechanisms," one visual and one abstract, the latter of which allows musicians to see, understand, and remember more (up to six notes in his study) from a single brief (two-second) glance at music notation than nonmusicians do. From this we can conclude, with C. P. E. Bach ([1753/1762] 1949), that performers should "always look ahead to the approaching notes" (p. 174).[21]

This and other ocular behaviors have been documented empirically in a pair of important reports by Goolsby (1994a; 1994b). Some of his findings: (1) "music reading (i.e., sightreading) is indeed music perception, because music notation is processed before performance" (1994b, 97); (2) "skilled music readers look farther ahead in the notation, and then back to the point of performance, when sightreading" (1994a, 77); (3) "unlike the less-skilled sightreader, the skilled subject does not process the melody 'note by note'" (1994b, 105–6); (4) a skilled subject "used long note values (half notes or longer) to scan about the notation" (1994b, 115), whereas "less-skilled readers fixate on as much of the notation as time allows (i.e., looking at notes/rests in proportion to rhythmic values)" (1994b, 121); and (5) for skilled readers, "some system of 'chunking' is used to grasp more than one note, or item of visual detail, during a single fixation" of the eyes on the page (1994b, 121). Polanka (1995) found similar results, noting that "better readers tended to read in larger units than poorer ones" (p. 182).[22]

Visual and Mental Chunking

Goolsby's conclusion about chunking is an important one. Sophisticated visual tracking is not merely a matter of reading some abstract distance ahead. It is in fact intimately bound up with the kinds of mental chunking of which individual readers are capable. Eye movements during sight reading both determine and depend upon readers' abilities to see and understand musically meaningful chunks: metric groupings, rhythmic patterns, scalar passages, arpeggiations, harmonic implications, and the like.[23] Nearly a century ago, Alchin (1904) remarked: "One must cultivate

21. Bach is speaking here specifically to accompanists, but his words are applicable to all musicians. Also note that Bach applies this aphorism to both prepared performance and "reading at sight."

22. Ottman (1956, 63–74) surveys early research on eye movements during music reading in great detail. Sloboda (1985, 69–73) interprets more recent studies. Two literature reviews by Goolsby (1989, 111–15; 1994a, 77–80) offer the most recent comprehensive surveys.

23. The interplay between eye movements and mental grouping in music is discussed at length in Ray (1964, 17–45).

the habit of thinking in groups, not in unrelated, isolated tones. Playing or singing note by note as some pupils do, is really pitiful" (p. 18). Ray (1964) concluded that "the musical meaning of a pattern is one of the chief factors determining its difficulty" (p. 32) and that individuals' abilities not only to take in groups of notes visually but also to understand those groups as patterns is crucial to good sight reading: "Something more than skill in interval reading is involved in the reading of pitch notation . . . the ability to recognize and perform patterns in larger groups than single intervals" (p. 74).

Perhaps the most fundamental types of chunks are metric and rhythmic groupings. Readers must be able to cast their eyes on metric units— individual beats, half-measures, or entire measures, for example—and grasp them as meaningful entities to be performed as integral components. Closely related to this are individual rhythmic patterns, which also must be apprehended as singular components of musical activity. Equally important are the various pitch-related groupings. Scalewise passages, chordal arpeggiations, sequences, harmonic implications, and modulations are all fodder for the gaze of the sophisticated reader. The more quickly musicians can see and understand such figures, the more fluent their sight reading can be.

Reading Ahead

Unfortunately, there is no paper-and-pencil test for the kind of eye movements characteristic of skilled music readers.[24] Nor is there any single drill to develop the specific kinds of reading ahead and chunking necessary for skilled reading. Nonetheless, there is a simple drill that—in a very unspecific way—does help to foster the habit of looking ahead while reading music: (1) choose a basic unit of metric duration (one beat, one half-measure, etc.); (2) look at the first unit; (3) cover the first unit (with a thumb, a three-by-five card, or whatever), and sing the first unit while looking at the second unit; (4) cover the second unit and sing the second unit while looking at the third unit; and so on, always singing the unit that has just been covered up.

This kind of drill cannot, in and of itself, make readers scan and chunk meaningful musical units, but at least it forces the eyes to read ahead and take in *something* before performing it. And as readers' theoretical knowledge and speed of comprehension grow, so, too, can their abilities to parse meaningful chunks within this advance field of vision. In addition,

24. Indeed, Goolsby used a Stanford Research Institute Dual Purkinje Eyetracker, which "directs a small beam of infrared light (invisible to the human eye) into the subject's right eye" in order to track ocular behavior (Goolsby 1994a, 81–82). His data were collected and analyzed by a DEC PDP-11/40 computer. All the hardware involved in tracking eye movements is described in detail in Goolsby (1989).

the simple kind of "mumbling" described earlier in this chapter can be elevated to a new level of sophistication wherein readers mumble through the music describing such chunks as rhythmic patterns, scales, arpeggiations, and so on. Although too time-consuming to execute before every sight-reading opportunity, this kind of mumbling is useful both as a drill to develop chunking while actually sight reading and as a means of testing readers' abilities to perform this kind of chunking effectively in real time. And long before modern eye-movement studies were carried out, Ray (1964) had already suggested a drill designed to improve visual and mental chunking: "The presentation of note groups at short exposure, with a gradual increase in the number of notes presented in a group, should be an excellent means of developing the perception span and should lead to more efficient music reading" (p. 22).

Metric and Rhythmic Thinking

Every performance of metric music should embody a sense of meter. To that end, readers must be cognizant of metric structure and any deviations therefrom. There are various ways to instill a sense of meter in performers. Gross body motions, foot tapping, and counting all have their advantages, but no method is as universal, extensible, and musical as conducting. It is very profitable for developing readers to perform all their music reading while conducting. Conducting gives hierarchical structure to two levels of pulse, expressing both beats and the downbeats that organize them. Conducting continually provides kinesthetic feedback about relative placement within measures, individual beats being demarcated by unique motions within the pattern. Conducting helps to shape duple performances into duple structures, triple performances into triple structures, and so on, so that performances can clearly manifest the meters they contain. An additional benefit is that aural skills students trained in conducting develop an intimate knowledge and understanding of the motions of the conductors they will sing and play under. It is hard to imagine recommending a course of study in sight singing that does not incorporate conducting into every possible performing activity.

Metric thinking is also aided by stimulating awareness about types of rhythmic grouping. For example, the "tyranny of the bar line" does in fact have its place—where musical grouping falls *within* bar lines. However, many musical passages begin their groups after downbeats and conclude them across bar lines. As an example, see the rhythmic gestures (indicated by brackets) that group across metric boundaries in Example 7.3.[25] Rhythmic grouping can also become a dynamic condition, capable

25. Compare the various groupings of this passage in Lerdahl and Jackendoff (1983).

Example 7.3. Mozart, Symphony No. 40, K. 550, mmt. 1, mm 1–5.

of changing several times even during the course of a relatively short melody.

Thus, in addition to metric grouping, the reader's eye must learn to take in and process rhythmic groups. Common rhythmic patterns should be learned *as patterns*, to be recognized and performed integrally as entities on the fly. This is one skill for which rhythmic solmization is particularly well suited, especially those systems that attach unique syllable groups to specific patterns. For example, readers skilled in Takadimi learn to recognize quadruple division of the beat (in any meter) as *"ta–ka–di–mi"* and reproduce the corresponding rhythm pattern they have learned to associate with that syllable string.

The distinction between metric grouping and rhythmic groups is an important one. Meter and hypermeter are mostly regular phenomena, whereas rhythm is plastic, fluid, and variable. As Kramer (1988) noted, "Rhythmic groups are of flexible size . . . , while (hyper)measures usually have but a few possible lengths (at a particular level). Rhythmic groups move toward their primary accent or away from it; metric units do not move, even though their constituent music may be pushing away from the preceding or toward the upcoming rhythmic accent" (p. 96). Readers must be prepared and alert to recognize rhythmic groups and patterns in their various distributions across the metric framework.

Recognizing rhythmic patterns is often facilitated in notation wherein beams visually group metric divisions. For example, in meters with the quarter note as beat unit, all rhythmic values smaller than a quarter note can be beamed together when they fall within one beat. Composers and editors break beams between beats (or sometimes at the half-measure in $\frac{4}{4}$) and even break secondary beams within beats, so that beat-dividing patterns are usually clearly delineated on the printed page. For example, the divisions of each beat in Example 7.4 are telegraphed through the judicious use of beaming.

However, several notational practices can result in obfuscation of beat patterns. First, the conventions of traditional vocal notation demand that beams be used to delineate syllabification rather than metric divisions. Older vocal scores reflect this practice, which can significantly obscure the beat-unit divisions of the meter. Example 7.5 shows one such score. Some modern composers and publishers still maintain this convention.

Example 7.4. J. S. Bach, Suite in B Minor, BWV 1067, Polonaise/Double, mm. 1–4.

However, as Read (1979) noted, "Practically all progressive vocal publications now print the voice parts with beams [indicating beat units] instead of individual flags, a much-needed revision in notational practice" (pp. 293–95). Similarly, Stone (1980) wrote that "the traditional system of beaming and flagging vocal music according to text syllables has been replaced almost universally with instrumental beaming, i.e., beaming according to beat-units or other metric divisions, with slurs indicating whenever more notes than one are to be sung on one syllable" (p. 293). Readers must be ready to interpret whichever kind of vocal notation they encounter.

Second, meters in which beat units are greater than a quarter note (for example, $\frac{4}{2}$ and $\frac{6}{4}$) hinder the use of beams to show beat groupings. For example, the ungrouped stems and flags in Example 7.6 make real-time beat segmentation a difficult task for many readers. Although I am not for a moment suggesting that such music should be renotated,[26] look at the clarity of beat placement in the odd-numbered measures when the passage is written in $\frac{9}{8}$ to allow beats to be beamed together (Example 7.7).

Third, there are cases when composers wish to point up certain musical groupings—phrasing, motivic figures, and cross-meters, to name the

the   horse and his   ri-der, the horse and his ri-der hath He thrown   in   to the   sea,_____

Example 7.5. Handel, *Israel in Egypt*, "I will sing unto the Lord," mm. 31–33.

26. Indeed, there are composers whose intentions are seemingly deliberately tied up in their use of particular beat units (see, for example, Beethoven's use of half- and whole-note units and Crumb's use of thirty-second-note and smaller units). In addition, the entire sense of motion in Renaissance music is often best reflected in transcriptions that avoid beams and even bar lines.

Example 7.6. Bernstein, *Candide*, "My Love" (Governor's Serenade), mm. 11–18.

most common—for which beaming takes on the responsibility of showing those groupings rather than remaining aligned with beats. Example 7.8 shows one of each of these: (a) shows a beam broken to indicate the beginning of a new half-phrase in m. 2; (b) shows a motivic figure on the downbeat of m. 2 set off as a half-beat beamed together (to separate the two types of clucking by the hen); (c) shows beams used to group eighth notes to show the displacement of metric accent. (There are, of course many similar examples; these are merely three representative excerpts.)

Example 7.7. Bernstein, *Candide*, "My Love" (Governor's Serenade), mm. 11–18, renotated in $\frac{9}{8}$.

a.

b.

c.

Example 7.8. Three examples of beams used to show grouping other than by meter and beat: (a) Mozart, *The Magic Flute*, K. 620 "Der Vogelfänger bin ich ja," mm. 1–4; (b) Rameau, *Pièces de Clavecin*, Book of 1731, "La Poule," mm. 1–3; (c) Brahms, Sonata in F minor for Clarinet and Piano, Op. 120, No. 1, mmt. 1, mm. 147–48.

Once a rhythmic pattern is recognized, it must be performed accurately. This can be the product of one of two processes: (1) matching the pattern against a mental inventory of previously learned patterns and (2) working out an unfamiliar pattern in real time. It should be self-evident that the more patterns readers have experience with, the less computationally intensive and error-prone their sight reading will be.

One final word is necessary regarding rhythmic accuracy. Even good performances deviate from absolute rhythmic precision; in fact, this is generally a characteristic of expressive performance. Gabrielsson (1982) showed that on a note-by-note basis, performers deviate from rendering rhythmic values exactly proportionally to one another. He concluded that "rhythm training solely concentrated on structural aspects in patterns isolated from any musical context is highly inefficient, especially if it happens to be combined with the belief that the symbols used in musical notation should be understood in a very exact, mechanical way" (p. 45). This is yet another reason to contextualize the materials used in aural skills training as much as possible.

Example 7.9. Simple chord arpeggiation with movable-*do* solmization.

Harmonic Thinking

The ability to see and understand the harmonic implications in music is important for performers in at least two ways: (1) readers who quickly grasp the harmonies implied in a passage can use that information to facilitate their performance (for example, knowing that m. 2 outlines a dominant seventh chord can make singing that measure much easier), and (2) readers who take harmonic implications into account can produce more musically meaningful performances.

In fact, musically convincing and satisfying performances of tonal music depend heavily on performers' abilities to think and act harmonically. Performances without a sense of harmonic motion are lifeless and uninteresting, devoid of one of the most essential elements of tonality itself. Performances that incorporate the logic and emotions of harmonic change and progression are cohesive and compelling. To that end, let us examine a few activities that help to develop this kind of musicianship.

Arpeggiating Chord Progressions

It is very profitable for musicians to develop the skills involved in arpeggiating series of chords. This can be done in a variety of ways; two will be discussed here.

One chord-arpeggiating activity involves reading from a series of chord symbols, such as the hybrid Roman numeral/figured-bass symbols used in most schools and colleges in the United States. Using this approach, readers look at a chord progression written in such symbology and sing arpeggiations of the chords those symbols represent. Example 7.9 shows one such chord progression and the arpeggiations and attendant movable-*do* solmization that could be performed to realize it.

Any set of chord symbols appropriate to a reader's theory knowledge and skill level can be used in this manner. For instance, while a pupil is studying augmented-sixth chords, the following progression could be assigned to be arpeggiated at sight or prepared:

i–V–i–iv⁶–VI–Gr⁶–V–i.

Example 7.10. J. S. Bach, Partita No. 2 for Unaccompanied Violin, BWV 1004, Gigue, mm. 1–3.

These kinds of activities serve to ingrain the sounds of chords in the ears and mind, constantly reinforce the links between symbology and sound, increase fluency in the meanings of the symbols, and provide opportunities for discussions of topics such as chord origins, voice leading, and resolution.

A slightly different approach asks readers to arpeggiate the chords implied in a passage of music. Readers must scan the music for its harmonic rhythm and the specific chords implied therein and arpeggiate through those chords. In this case, chord inversion is often much less clearly defined. There is also the possibility that ambiguity exists even with regard to individual harmonies being implied. Therefore, accommodations should be made for appropriate but differing interpretations.

It should be noted that any activity of this kind serves to link the eye, the ear, and the mind in a deeper and more sophisticated understanding and fluency in music. This kind of training flourishes best as part of a larger curriculum that involves the broadest kind of integrated musical training, wherein literate musicians learn to *think* about harmony as rapidly as they can perform it.[27]

Visual and Mental Chunking of Harmony

To read musically, one must see and understand the harmonic implications of the music being read. This skill depends in part on readers' abilities to execute the kind of visual chunking discussed previously under "Visual Tracking." This kind of reading involves taking in groups of pitches with a single fixation of the eyes and making sense of those groups *as groups*. With respect to harmonic thinking, this means scanning ahead in the music and taking in—with a glance—the explicit or implicit harmonic result of the upcoming pitches.

To bring this into distinct relief, let us compare two passages from the solo literature of J. S. Bach. Example 7.10 shows the opening of the Gigue from Partita No. 2 for Unaccompanied Violin, BWV 1004.

27. Compare the discussion of harmonic listening in chapter 4.

Courante.

Example 7.11. J. S. Bach, Suite No. 4 for Unaccompanied Cello, BWV 1010, Courante, mm. 1–3.

Even upon sight reading such a passage, the sensitive musician's eye must grasp the harmonic change at the midpoint of each measure. The first two beats of m. 1 must be seen and performed as tonic harmony. The eye and the heart must accommodate the change to dominant harmony on beat 3, extend that feeling across the bar line through the first two beats of m. 2, and return to the tonic on beat 3 of the second measure. The most sensitive readers will account for even the subtlest of harmonic nuances: the dominant harmony implied in the anacrusis, the reaching over implied in the last note of beat 2 in each measure, and its consequence—the important resolutions F5 to E5 and G5 to F5—for example.

This passage is relatively straightforward with regard to its harmonic motion. Arpeggiations and clear scalar implications divided across clear metric boundaries make the harmonies comparatively easy to see and incorporate in performance.

But even the moderate level of harmonic complexity in the passage shown in Example 7.11 can make such visual chunking much more difficult to execute. In this short passage, readers are confronted with more complicated and subtle harmonic implications, which do not necessarily stand out clearly to the developing musician's eye. The first three pitches are simple enough—they imply tonic harmony—but the following few pitches call for more than a cursory glance from most undergraduates. Do the pitches C3-Ab2-F2 form a supertonic chord (as they seem to on the page), or do C3 and Ab2 suggest a subdominant/supertonic harmony on beat 2, whereas F2 and D3 imply dominant on beat 3? The latter interpretation seems to make more musical sense—especially considering the propensity of harmonic rhythm to be regular—but which readers will take in this measure and make such decisions in real time? Even more demanding is the harmonic motion at the end of m. 2, enabling the fuguelike answer in the dominant in m. 3. Which readers will shift their tonal focus to Bb and repeat in that tonal area the local functionality they expressed in Eb in m. 1?

This kind of skill depends greatly upon each reader's theoretical knowledge *and* ability to read and interpret harmonic implications in real time.

a.

b.

Example 7.12. (a) The American folk tune "Streets of Laredo"; (b) Structural simplification by eliminating passing and neighboring notes.

Structural Singing

Structural and Embellishing Pitches

Sight readers who possess and apply a fundamental knowledge of harmonic structure and of passing and neighboring tones can often navigate through a great many seemingly difficult passages with greater ease than those who employ simple scale-degree or intervallic strategies.[28]

Whether an awareness of passing and neighboring notes, as classically defined by their surface-level melodic motion, can facilitate accuracy in sight singing depends upon the skills possessed by individual readers and the specific content of the melody at hand.

Consider, as an example, the folk tune shown in Example 7.12(a). Viewing the middle pitches in mm. 1, 2, 3, 6, and 7 as passing and neighboring notes, one might simplify these eight measures to the first-order reduction shown in Example 7.12(b). This reduction turns what was an essentially stepwise melody into one with many more skips, making it—for some—more difficult to sing. However, knowledge of the passing and neighboring diminutions and the harmonically consonant skips they prolong can lead readers to a better understanding of the inherent harmonic implications in melodies and foster more musical, harmonically informed performances. In addition, it is possible for this kind of harmonic understanding to guide the ear and voice in such a way as to head off mistakes before they can arise.

---

28. Of the many textbooks devoted to sight singing, only a few incorporate this approach. Some of the "models for interval singing" in Benward and Carr (1999) are structural models of actual excerpts printed elsewhere in the text. Henry (1997) discusses surface-level structural versus embellishing pitches. One entire text (Bland 1984) is structured around the very premise of facilitating sight singing through structural analysis.

a.

b.

c.

d.

Example 7.13. (a) Mozart, Clarinet Concerto, K. 622, mmt. 1, mm. 1–2; (b) Reduced to structural pitches; (c) With passing notes reintroduced; (d) With prefix neighboring note reintroduced.

But where such understanding offers the most assistance to sight singers is in the realm of prefix and suffix neighboring notes. A simple example of a prefix neighbor appears in the opening measures of the first movement of Mozart's Clarinet Concerto, K. 622 (see Example 7.13(a)). Once readers are oriented with respect to diatonic collection, tonic, and starting scale degree, the pitch that is most likely to cause difficulties is the first note in the second measure. Readers who have had some initial training in scale-degree and harmonic reading have most likely been introduced to skips to $\hat{6}$ as part of subdominant, submediant, and perhaps supertonic chords. But the skip to $\hat{6}$ in Example 7.13(a) is part of a prevailing tonic harmony and must be heard and performed as such (de-

a.

b.

Example 7.14. (a) Grofé, *Grand Canyon Suite*, "Sunrise," mm. 53–55; (b) with suffix neighbors removed.

spite the 4̂–6̂ interval that precedes it). Example 7.13(b) reduces these two measures to their structural tonic pitches. The passing tones *between* these structural pitches can be reintroduced, as shown in Example 7.13(c). One can now clearly see that 6̂ at the downbeat of the second bar is a prefix neighboring note (an appoggiatura, in more traditional terms). The aim point is therefore 5̂, with 6̂ as a nonstructural prefix (see Example 7.13(d)). Finally, the temporal dissonance—the C♯ anticipation in m. 2, beat 2, second half—can also be added. Readers who learn to read and hear structural pitches as points of reference and who learn to execute prefix neighbors to these structural pitches will not only find such music easier to sight read but produce much more musical readings as well.

Awareness of suffix neighbors can provide similar assistance. Example 7.14(a) shows a short passage from the opening of Ferde Grofé's *Grand Canyon Suite*. Readers who learn to see and hear the second, fourth, sixth, and eighth pitches (the off-beat C♯, B, A, and G♯) as suffix neighbors will easily hear and perform the scalar underpinnings of this passage, as shown in Example 7.14(b).

Voice Leading

Musicians who read music in a note-to-note fashion will always remain musically stunted to a certain degree. As we discovered in examining ocular behavior and visual chunking earlier, the best sight readers look ahead in the music and grasp musically meaningful combinations of rhythm and pitch to be performed as integral entities. Similar behavior—looking ahead and grasping musical figures—can be employed to detect slightly more abstract but nonetheless extremely important connections

a.

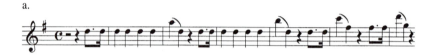

b.

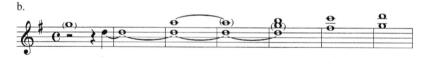

Example 7.15. (a) Mozart, *Marriage of Figaro*, K. 492, Act I, Scene I, No. 1, mm. 1–7; (b) Voice leading for sight singing.

among notes: linear relationships between temporally nonadjacent pitches.

Much single-part music, even much of that used for sight singing, contains inherent implications of more than one voice.[29] We tend to think about such matters in the context of blatantly obvious "compound melody" (sometimes called polyphonic melody), but a sensitivity to the voices lying just below the surface of *most* music can often serve as a great aid in sight singing. Indeed, research performed by Serafine (1983) shows that even untrained listeners distill an "underlying structure that embodies two or more simplified or more basic melodies" from certain single-part melodies (p. 9).

A simple example appears in the first duet between Figaro and Susanna in Mozart's *Marriage of Figaro*, K. 492. The opening seven bars are reproduced in Example 7.15(a). Many beginning sight readers would approach this passage as a series of monotonous repeated pitches broken occasionally by startling leaps that become more frightening as the music progresses. Slightly more astute readers might notice the rising line A–B–C–D and realize that the "leaps" to B, C, and D on the fifth, sixth, and seventh downbeats may be executed as part of a larger linear motion from A. The most astute readers will view this passage as a product of *three* voices as shown in Example 7.15(b): (1) the pedal on D; (2) an upper voice that begins on an implied G (the tonic to which they should orient themselves before beginning) and moves *to* A in m. 3 and subsequently to B, C, and D; and (3) an inner voice that begins on the same G, is regained in m. 5, then moves to F♯ in m. 6 and back to G in m. 7. Hearing the F♯ in relation to G is an extremely practical and musical approach, regardless of whether one

---

29. See the discussion of "voice" and "part" in "Voice Leading and Harmony" in chapter 4.

auralizes it as coming from an imagined G in earlier measures or as a prefix neighbor to the subsequent G in m. 7.

A slightly more sophisticated example also comes from the music of Mozart. The first four measures of the first theme from the first movement of his Piano Sonata in C Major, K. 545, are shown in Example 7.16(a). With regard to voice leading and structural singing, we must address two important pitches: the B on the downbeat of m. 2 and the A on the downbeat of m. 3. Each of these pitches can be heard and sung as a product of the linear voices that begins on C and G, respectively. The lower voice prolongs C for the entire first measure, moves down by half step to B for the first half of m. 2, and resolves back to C on the third beat of that measure. The upper voice prolongs G for two entire measures (as the common tone between the tonic and dominant harmonies), moves up by step to a neighbor note on A for the first half of m. 3, and resolves back to G on the third beat of that measure. These two voices are shown in Example 7.16(b). Even without being presented with such dogmatic Schenkerian concepts and graphics, readers should at least be guided to hear the B as "coming from" the C in m. 1 and the A as "coming from" the G in m. 1.

The literature abounds with such figures. Readers who calculate pitches on a note-by-note basis—regardless of whether they take an in- tervallic or scale-degree approach—will forever struggle with the variety of "leaps" music has to offer. Readers who learn to see, hear, and execute the connections between temporally separate but linearly adjacent pitches will reap many benefits in terms of accuracy, facility, and musicality.

Performance Indications and Musical Expression

So much aural skills training is focused solely on rhythm and pitch that it seems to stand across a wide abyss from the actual world of musical performance. In order to bridge this distance and to make aural skills training as *musical* as possible, instructors must integrate such important musical features as tempo, dynamics, articulation, accent, and phrasing into their curricula.

Sight-singing curricula should include materials with tempo indications as early as possible in the learning sequence. It is important at times (particularly in early training) to allow students to work out particular problems of rhythm and pitch at whatever tempo is comfortable for them. However, students must learn (1) to integrate the skills they learn into predetermined tempi and (2) to read, understand, and execute tempo in- dications. They must learn to interpret simple metronome markings (for example, "♩=110") as static conditions. They must also learn to interpret the many *tempo* indications in various languages (*Allegro, Langsam*). In- structors do well to define a "core" set of such indications that students

a.

b.

Example 7.16. (a) Mozart, Piano Sonata in C Major, K. 545, mmt. 1, mm. 1–4; (b) Voice leading for sight singing.

must know by heart; students must also demonstrate an ability to look up the meanings of other such terms. They must learn to respond appropriately to quantum changes of tempo and to gradual changes (such as *accelerando* and *ritardando*). In addition, they should learn to make their own changes of tempo as part of interpreting phrasing (see the following discussion).[30]

Dynamics, too, should be included as early as possible. Once again, there are static indications (*p*, *mf*) and indications of gradual change (*cresc.*, *dim.*). Students must learn to heed such markings and incorporate their meanings convincingly in performance. In addition, frequent efforts should be made to employ additional dynamics in the service of general musicality—adding interest to repeated figures and shaping phrases, for instance.

Similar attention should be paid to articulation markings. The broad difference between legato and staccato is especially important, but one might also take the opportunity to discuss how certain articulations might be implemented on various instruments (legato on trombone, for example) and to discuss the interpretation of various instrument-specific articulations (spiccato on strings or the vocal portamento, for example).

Various dynamic accents, including symbols (for example, >) and abbreviated terms (for example, *sfz*) should be encountered and interpreted by readers.[31] (Here there is some necessary and interesting overlap between accent and articulation.) In addition, no opportunity should be lost to add such accents where musically appropriate. The use of agogic accents should also be explained and encouraged as a means of shaping musical expression.

---

30. See chapter 1 for an introductory discussion of tempo in listening.
31. See the discussion of symbols and terms for accents in Read (1979), 260–65.

The art of musical phrasing must be nurtured continually from the earliest days of aural skills training. This includes the reading and proper interpretation of printed phrase markings in the music, as well as sensitivity to the extranotational aspects of hypermeter and phrasing. Perhaps most important is the choice of musically appropriate places to breathe. This is simple enough in music that includes phrase markings (but often easily ignored unless the expectation to observe such markings is unmistakably unequivocal) but requires a great deal of examination in music without such markings (for example, Baroque music or some transcriptions of folk melodies). In addition to breathing, the other components of musical expression—tempo, dynamics, articulation, and accent—should be brought into service in executing phrasing.

By this point—with the inclusion of tempo, dynamics, articulation, accent, and phrasing—we run the risk of overloading readers. This is one reason that some aural skills texts and curricula downplay these very features in favor of concentrating exclusively on rhythm and pitch. However, these features play such an important role in shaping the musical experience that they can be ignored only at the risk of producing unmusical sight readers.

Readers must sing exercises and excerpts, whether prepared or at sight, with a sense of musical purpose. They must shape phrases through proper breathing and the judicious addition of musically appropriate changes in tempo, dynamics, articulation, and accent. All readings can serve as springboards for discussion of suitable and convincing interpretations. The best aural skills instructors never let a musically flat performance go by without making suggestions for how it could be shaped, and they never let well-executed interpretations go by without offering acknowledgment and praise.

Prepared Materials and Sight Reading

There exists in the minds of some aural skills instructors and students an uncertain relationship between sight singing and prepared work. Why memorize scales, sequentials, exercises, and excerpts when the goal of training in sight singing is to become better at reading at sight, not through preparation? The answer to this question lies in part in the fact that we are generally unable to perform at sight that which we have not yet learned. To become better sight readers we must indeed do lots of sight reading; but to be able to read, interpret, and perform new musical figures we must first encounter such figures in a variety of settings and work them out in practice sessions during which they can be isolated from one or more other musical parameters so as to focus on the very thing to be learned. Quine (1990) put it this way: "Isolate the basic technical problem first, before working on it. Reducing difficulties to their simplest form makes practising them both more meaningful and more rewarding" (p. 83). Sandor (1981) wrote: "Conscious practicing is analogous to a spotlight that focuses on a relatively small area and illuminates it thoroughly. It then proceeds to other problem areas and finally is able to integrate the examined areas" (p. 186). This insight is applicable to many kinds of musical elements, be they a few beats or measures, a rhythmic figure, or a pitch pattern. By isolating, working out, and reintegrating such elements, readers arm themselves with the skills necessary to execute those elements at sight in the future.

Some skills are essentially the same regardless of whether they are performed through preparation or at sight. These skills include the preperformance activities discussed in chapter 6: establishing collection, tonic, pulse, tempo, and meter. The actual performance of musical passages (not reading or understanding the notation) in real time is essentially the same for prepared materials and for sight reading. For example, regardless of how the message "skip to the leading tone" reaches the brain, the actual execution of this skip is a similar process. Of course, there is a difference between encountering musical figures in new contexts and merely reciting a memorized tune. Herein lies one important danger in aural skills training. Readers who simply memorize prepared materials without making constant associations with the specific figures under current study will not reap much benefit in the future, since they are not memorizing the figures *as figures*. Readers must be supplied with the tools, made aware of their applicability in prepared materials, and taught to bring forward and apply the tools appropriate to specific circumstances during sight reading.

The nature and importance of other skills differ significantly depending upon whether they are used while preparing materials or while sight reading. For example, the types of eye movements necessary for sight reading (more and shorter fixations) are essentially different from those used while reading prepared music (Goolsby 1994a). As another example, consider the difference between figuring out a melody's harmonic implications while studying and practicing at leisure and scanning ahead to discover such implications in real time while sight reading. The differences between these behaviors are particularly marked during early stages of training. Finally, consider the types of practice techniques necessary to prepare materials. Although efficient and effective practice skills are crucially important to success in aural skills training and valuable for their extensibility to other practice situations (such as practice for studio lessons), they are relatively unimportant during sight reading.

Instructors and students alike should be keenly aware of the most appropriate circumstances for learning specific skills. For example, the quick reading ahead necessary for good sight reading cannot be practiced on materials that have already been prepared. With this in mind, when certain skills are to be introduced, discussed, drilled, and assessed, they should be placed in the most appropriate context.

Another important issue is the *balance* between the amount of time and effort spent on prepared materials on the one hand and sight reading on the other. Consider the two extremes posed by the following imaginary curricula: (1) a course during which new exercises and excerpts are assigned for every meeting, new ideas and concepts are constantly introduced, and no reading at sight is practiced whatsoever (even the final exam consists entirely of prepared materials); and (2) a course during which every minute of every meeting is taken up by sight reading, before which no concepts are introduced, no preparatory exercises assigned, and no illustrative excerpts learned. While these descriptions have been set up hyperbolically as straw men, there are in fact courses that come quite close to each extreme. One way to strike a balance between these poles is to design curricula so that during any critical period (a unit of study, a semester, even an entire curriculum) the number of new concepts and prepared materials declines in inverse proportion to the amount of music offered up for sight reading. Another way is to begin a measured amount of sight reading after a minimal amount of concepts and skills have been learned, keeping the sight-reading materials at a level sufficiently behind the new materials being introduced and thereafter keeping the amount of sight reading steady throughout the course of study. In either case, the guiding principle is that new concepts and prepared materials should ultimately feed into the experience of sight reading, so that the process of reading music extemporaneously relies more and more on the informed mind of a skilled reader.

In the long run, it seems that the factors that contribute most significantly to sight-reading ability are (1) understanding of notation and various musical concepts, (2) experience with reading and performing a wide variety of music literature, and (3) the amount of time and effort spent on sight reading (as opposed to preparing) music. Lehmann and Ericsson (1996) concluded that "the acquisition of sight-reading skill is more similar to the majority of other types of expert performance than the acquisition of solo performance where the musicians spend months or years to prepare for the performance of specific pieces. In the sight-reading of music (and many other types of expert performance), individuals prepare for unknown situations" (p. 24). In addition, Lehmann and Ericsson found that differences in sight-reading ability are *not* directly attributable to innate talent for music or instrumental technique. In an earlier study, they concluded that "the ability to sight-read does not increase with higher general instrumental skill" (Lehmann and Ericsson 1993, 192). Therefore, sight reading involves a set of skills to be learned in and of itself.

Transferal to Instruments

The art and craft of sight singing is most certainly applicable to vocal training in general. Singers who study sight singing will find it can greatly benefit their primary mode of expression. But instrumentalists, too, can reap great advantages in applying the skills and concepts learned through sight-singing study to their own instruments. Various studies have shown the transferal of aural skills from vocal training to instrumental performance (Brick 1984 offers a summary of some). Elliott (1982) found that a particularly "strong positive relationship exists between wind instrumentalists' general sight-reading ability and the ability to sight-read rhythm patterns" (p. 13). Luce (1965) found a significant correlation between sight reading and reproducing music by ear. McPherson (1995) found a similar link between the ability to "play by ear" (to play music previously learned only through listening) and the ability to improvise. Brick (1984) reported a transfer of skills from aural training (with the *Pitch Master*) to instrumental performance (on the trombone).

There is a long tradition of valuing the relationship between sight singing and instrumental performance. C. P. E. Bach ([1753/1762] 1949) advocated that "it is a good practice to sing instrumental melodies in order to reach an understanding of their correct performance" (pp. 151–52). Wagner ([1869] 1940) wrote of the advantages held by musicians who have "been taught to approach music mainly through the medium of the human voice" (p. 18). Scherchen (1933) stated: "To sing is the life-function of music. Where there is no singing, the forms of music become distorted and they move in a senseless time-order imposed from without" (p. 29), and, "All music both in conception and in actualization is singing" (p. 31). White (1981) wrote that "singing is basic to all music. Cellists, pianists, trombonists, bassoonists, and timpanists—all of them are (or should be) inwardly singing when they perform. It is for this reason that singing is so important in the development of basic musicianship skills" (p. 25). Most emphatically, Baillot ([1835] 1991) implored: "Learn solfège before beginning the violin. Before one begins the study of the violin, it is indispensable for him to learn solfège. The knowledge of notes, values, meters, clefs, and all the signs, and the application made of all this knowledge by singing or naming the notes and dividing the beat, demand too much attention for the student to be able to divert part of his attention to the details of instrumental technique," and, "To have the student undertake the study of the violin before he has learned solfège is to condemn him to reading music without understanding it" (p. 448).

Whereas adult learners rarely have the luxury of beginning music training through solmization and only later applying this to instrumental study, we can at least guide these musicians to incorporate what they learn from aural skills training into their primary performing media. One way is to include instrumental performance in various aural-skills activities, such as instrumental playbacks, clef reading, transposition, and general sight reading. Another is to encourage the incorporation into studio instruction and instrumental practice of the use of various aural skills, such as solmization, singing before playing[32] (with attention to details such as intonation, rhythm accuracy, and phrasing), effective eye movements while reading, and (when possible) conducting.[33]

From their earliest days of study, instrumental and vocal performers can learn to apply their aural skills in various circumstances, such as practicing, rehearsing, performing, coaching, and teaching.

32. One investigation (Elliott 1974) found that when students regularly vocalized the materials they were studying, there was a "significant [positive] effect on the sense of pitch" (p. 127).

33. Perhaps not surprisingly, Rogers and Watkins (1986) found some effects in the opposite direction as well: college students with more prior instrumental or vocal training achieved higher scores on tests of aural discrimination.

8

More Complex
Reading Skills

This chapter goes beyond the basic music-reading and performing skills examined in chapters 6 and 7. It begins by exploring some specific skills involved in negotiating chromaticism, modulation, and proportional tempo and meter changes. It also examines approaches appropriate for reading, auralizing, and performing various clefs and transpositions. Finally, it investigates how reading skills can be applied to score reading, conducting, and reading Schenkerian graphs.

Chromaticism

From a sight singer's point of view, there are five fundamental kinetic contexts for chromatic pitches in tonal music:[1] (1) as a neighboring tone, (2) as a chromatic passing tone, (3) as a chromatically altered part of a stepwise pattern, (4) as prefix neighbors, and (5) as part of a functional chromatic arpeggiation. The types of skills readers must employ in order to read, understand, auralize, and perform a given chromatic pitch depend to a great extent on which of these contexts that chromatic occurs in.

As a Neighboring Tone

For many, among the easiest chromatic pitches to auralize are lower chromatic neighbors. Once musicians have internalized the diatonic collection

---

1. As for most of the pitch materials in this book, these discussions of chromaticism are restricted to tonal contexts.

Example 8.1. Schubert, German Dance No. 5, D. 89, Trio II, mm. 1–4.

to the point that it becomes comfortably referential, changing lower neighbor whole-step figures into half steps is usually a simple task. This is in one sense a simple extension of one of the fundamental skills discussed in chapter 6: singing whole and half steps above and below any given pitch. Thus, the lower chromatic neighbor notes in mm. 1 and 2 of Example 8.1 can be executed by substituting half steps in place of the referential diatonic whole steps. Pitch patterns and exercises, such as the two sequentials shown in Example 8.2, can also pave the way for readers to master lower chromatics in musical contexts.

Upper chromatic neighbors, although not as common as lower ones, are nonetheless important as well. Example 8.3 shows ↓$\hat{7}$ as an upper neighbor to $\hat{6}$ (see m. 27). And Example 8.4 shows ↓$\hat{6}$ as an upper neighbor to $\hat{5}$ (see mm. 85 and 87).

Pitch patterns and exercises, such as sequentials that invert the pattern in Example 8.2, can help to develop readers' facility at recognizing and performing upper chromatic neighbors.

Incomplete chromatic neighbor notes of the suffix variety present little additional challenge for most sight readers: they are approached in exactly the same manner as complete neighbor-note figures but left without returning directly to the diatonic neighbor. Incomplete chromatic neighbor notes of the prefix variety will be discussed later.

As a Chromatic Passing Tone

Another rather simple context for chromatic pitches fills the space between two diatonically adjacent pitches. For example, Schubert places

Example 8.2. Sequentials that drill diatonic and chromatic lower neighbors.

Example 8.3. J. S. Bach, *Well-Tempered Clavier*, book 1, Fugue IX, BWV 854, mm. 25 (beat 4)–29.

chromatic passing tones between $\hat{1}$ and $\hat{2}$, $\hat{2}$ and $\hat{3}$, $\hat{4}$ and $\hat{5}$, and $\hat{5}$ and $\hat{6}$ in Ecossaise No. 3, D. 299 (Example 8.5).

Work on contextual passing chromatics (both ascending and descending) can also be preceded by preparatory exercises. Example 8.6 shows an appropriate sequential.[2]

Although, for some, slightly more challenging than lower chromatic neighbors, chromatic passing tones can be mastered if readers are certain to focus on the diatonic pitches that surround the chromatic ones and fix those diatonic pitches as anchor points.

As a Chromatically Altered Part of a Stepwise Pattern

This context for chromatic pitches differs from the chromatic passing tones discussed in the last section in that these chromatic pitches do not appear contiguously after their diatonic counterparts but rather as a *substitution* for those counterparts in a unidirectional three-note setting (not as neighbor notes or chromatic passing tones). The most common of these is the substitution of ↑$\hat{4}$ for $\hat{4}$ in the major mode. For example, consider the fugue subject and its extension shown in Example 8.7. The entire four-sharp diatonic collection is presented in mm. 1–2. In the third measure, $\hat{4}$ is replaced momentarily by ↑$\hat{4}$, which returns to $\hat{4}$ at the end of

Example 8.4. Janáček, *Lašské Tance* [Lachian Dances], No. 1, mm. 75–87.

2. Kazez (1992) offers a similar sequential (p. 28).

Example 8.5. Schubert, *Zwölf Ecossaisen*, D. 299, No. 3 (complete).

the measure. Here the chromatically raised fourth scale degree substitutes for its diatonic referent, requiring readers to make a temporary local change to the diatonic collection. (Another way to approach this passage is to think of the momentary tonicization of B in m. 3, but we will defer such considerations until later in this chapter.)

Other such substitutions in stepwise contexts in major are ↓$\hat{7}$, ↓$\hat{3}$ (although this can also be treated as a change of mode), and (rarely) ↑$\hat{1}$. In minor, these substitutions appear as ↑$\hat{3}$ (again, also a change of mode), ↓$\hat{2}$ (the Neapolitan), ↑$\hat{6}$, and ↓$\hat{5}$ (these last two almost always involved in modulations). Drills and excerpts designed to familiarize readers with these figures—particularly the more common ones—help to equip them with the skills necessary to execute this special kind of chromaticism and pave the way for modulatory materials. In addition, the triadic modulatory pitch patterns under " 'Common-Tone' Modulations" later in this chapter can help to arm musicians with the requisite skills for these chromatics.

As a Prefix Neighboring Tone

For many sight singers, the most challenging context for chromatic pitches occurs when they are approached by leap. Note the leap to ↑$\hat{4}$ in m. 7 of the second movement from Haydn's Symphony No. 94 (Example 8.8).

Example 8.6. Chromatic passing-tone sequential.

Example 8.7. Bach, *Well-Tempered Clavier*, book 2, Fugue IX, BWV 878, mm. 1–4.

One way of approaching such leaps (where appropriate) is auralizing them as prefix neighbors to diatonic pitches. Measures 7–8 in Figure 8.8 can be practiced by first replacing the F♯ with a quarter rest, then (when that has been mastered) replacing the quarter rest with two eighths on G and F♯ (in that order), and finally (when *that* has been mastered) returning to the music as written. In this way, readers learn to hear the G, not the F♯, as the aim point, while the F♯ earns its tonal status only as a chromatic neighbor to G. Exercises can be designed to help readers auralize leaps to chromatic pitches as prefix neighbors. See the two sequentials in Example 8.9, in this case focusing on ↑4̂ to 5̂.

As Part of a Functional Chromatic Arpeggiation

Certainly many chromatic pitches function as applied pitches (usually leading tones) as parts of various chromatic harmonies. For example, the F♯ in Example 8.8 can also be auralized as part of a secondary dominant or leading tone to V. But when the resolution of such pitches is either delayed or evaded, their context usually becomes part of a functionally chromatic arpeggiation—which demands somewhat different skills from sight readers.

Example 8.10 shows one such context. In mm. 12 and 14, the pitches D♯ and F♯ form an arpeggiated V/V, neither pitch resolving immediately after its initial statement. One might argue that this constitutes a modulation, but in any view the experience of the sight reader is the same on first encountering these pitches: approaching and leaving chromatic pitches by leap.

Readers can be prepared for such eventualities through preparatory exercises and carefully chosen excerpts (such as the passage from *Die schöne Müllerin* in Example 8.10). Preparatory exercises can include chord arpeggiations similar to those shown in chapter 7 under "Arpeggiating Chord Progressions" but including applied dominant and leading-

Example 8.8. Haydn, Symphony No. 94, mmt. 2, mm. 1–8.

Example 8.9. A pair of sequentials designed to help listeners auralize leaps to chromatics as prefix neighbors.

tone chords. In addition, the triadic modulatory pitch patterns under " 'Common-Tone' Modulations" later in this chapter are helpful.

Modulation

In order to sing music that modulates, sight singers must be able to execute changes in pitch structure in real time. The decision to *sight sing* any given passage by understanding it in terms of modulation must be distinguished from the similar kinds of decisions made for the purposes of academic analysis. Analysts seek to make well-reasoned conclusions about pitch structure based on decisions (often well-pondered ones) about local, middleground, and background parameters, as well as a host of other factors such as style, form, motivic content, and rhetoric. Sight readers must make split-second decisions about which ways of understanding a passage will render it most easily executable. Analysts have the luxury of considering and revising their conclusions over relatively long periods of time and justifying those decisions through the use of language and symbology. Sight readers must make conclusions in real time and do so without discussion or explanation. Analysts seek deep understanding and defensible, lasting truths about pitch structure. Sight singers need to get the job done (but nonetheless done intelligently and musically) and move on.

Example 8.10. Schubert, *Die schöne Müllerin*, Op. 25, D. 795, No. 5, "Am Feierabend," mm. 7–15.

Example 8.11. Yiddish folk melody, "A Geneyve."

To this end, we will see that some tools used to execute certain passages might be at odds with the kinds of sophisticated, thought-out analyses produced in books and journals and even in well-taught theory classes. Particularly notable is the fact that sight singers who read by tonal function generally make more frequent changes of tonic (and use more fragments of various scales) than one would find in any rigorous academic analysis.

In order to sight sing music that makes changes in tonic, mode, or both, musicians must be skilled at recognizing in notation certain characteristic features of pitch that cause these changes. The general rubric "modulation" is not specific enough, not faceted in ways that help readers make sense of the various kinds of modulations they might encounter. Unfortunately, many of the kinds of classifications found in many theory texts are also not skills-driven. Those classifications—such as "diatonic," "chromatic," "closely related," and "foreign"—tell us more about theoretical relationships between two keys than how to execute the change from one key to another. In order to facilitate the task of reading, understanding, and performing music that modulates, we will examine the two most important factors in such music—changes in tonic and changes in pitch collection—and explore various ways music makes such changes and the appropriate kinds of skills necessary to perform them.

Change of Tonic; No Change of Collection

Readers must learn to shift the placement of the tonic within a diatonic collection. This occurs most frequently between relative minor and major keys.

Example 8.11 shows one such melody. This entire melody consists of pitches taken solely from the one-sharp collection. This melody is unambiguously in E minor, but it contains an important local tonicization of G in mm. 9–12. This shift of tonicization, although brief, occurs without a single change in the prevailing diatonic collection and thus affords an excellent opportunity to focus on changing the tonic without changing the collection. To read and perform this melody accurately and musically, readers do well to understand the local tonicization of G (and return to E) effected without changing the locations of the diatonic half steps.

Certain kinds of folk musics (particularly Eastern European) frequently exhibit such fluctuations between relative minors and majors. This consistency of collection is similar to that in some Renaissance music, wherein a single diatonic collection supports internal cadences on various local finals.[3] (For these types of contexts—particularly pre-tonal modality—some readers may find that a relative-based solmization system is appropriate, since such systems explicitly model the *collection* rather than any tonal function.) Common-practice-period music displays similar behavior in moves between relative major and minor keys (but for tonal music many may wish to employ functional solmization in order to model tonal structure). In all these cases, the applicable aural skills involve maintaining the interval structure of a single diatonic collection while shifting the tonic to a new position within that collection.

The presence of raised sixth and seventh scale degrees in minor—or of any local nondiatonic accidentals in any mode—does not change the fundamental skills required to make changes between these conditions but only adds one: the need to make chromatic changes to the prevailing diatonic collection. Example 8.12 shows a passage that modulates from tonic major to relative minor, introducing first $\uparrow\hat{7}$ (in m. 14) and $\uparrow\hat{6}$ (in m. 19). In this passage, the reader's fundamental task is shifting the tonic from G to E. The local chromaticism in mm. 14 and 19–21 merely heightens that tonicization and presents yet another task for the reader.

Exercises designed to focus on retaining a diatonic collection while tonicizing its various members can help prepare readers for these kinds of modulations. This work can begin with drills that take place entirely within a single diatonic collection but shift between relative major and minor tonics (see Example 8.13 (a) for an example), and this can expand to tonicizations of other relative modes, if desired (Figure 8.13(b)). Chromatic leading tones (and $\uparrow\hat{6}$ with $\uparrow\hat{7}$ in minor) can be added to these

---

3. In Renaissance theory, "regular" or "natural" cadences appear on certain modal steps, "irregular" or "contrary" cadences on other pitches, all within a single diatonic collection (with possible alterations through *musica ficta*). For example, Zarlino's ([1558] 1983) discussions of the individual modes include enumerations of the regular and irregular cadence points for each mode (pp. 54–89); see—as a specific example—his two-voice example for the second mode, which contains cadences on D, A, and F (pp. 59–60). Perkins (1973, 200–201) includes a table that summarizes Renaissance views of modal characteristics, including several acceptable cadence points for each mode.

Example 8.12. Jean Baptiste Loeillet (de Gant), Sonata in G major for Flute and Continuo, Op. 3, No. 4, mmt. 4, mm. 1–22.

drills ad libitum. Of course, such drills need not always begin by tonicizing major. And—being unrhythmicized—such drills are not as convincing in terms of *how* they tonicize various members of the diatonic collection. For more persuasive instances of modal permutation within a single diatonic collection, see any one of many examples of the kind of pre-tonal modality and Eastern European folk music mentioned earlier. From this point, readers benefit most from exposure to, preparation of, and familiarity with a variety of excerpts that make such diatonic modulations.

Change of Collection; No Change of Tonic

In order to isolate and focus on the skill of changing the diatonic collection, it is helpful to provide readers with exercises and excerpts that

Example 8.13. Drills that shift between relative modes: (a) Between major and minor; (b) Among other modes.

Example 8.14. Haydn, String Quartet, Op. 76, No. 3, mmt. 3, Trio, mm. 29–44.

change between parallel modes. Although this does not truly constitute a "modulation" to many (since the tonic has not changed), it nonetheless lays bare a skill crucial to reading and auralizing many modulations.

Example 8.14 shows a passage carefully excerpted from Haydn's Op. 76, No. 3, to isolate this kind of parallel key relationship. The rather wide range of this excerpt notwithstanding, it provides a good opportunity for readers to become accustomed to reading and singing music that changes from one diatonic collection to another.[4]

Changes among other modes can be instilled by using folk tunes that appear in both modal and tonal versions (for example, "Greensleeves," which appears in Dorian and minor versions), various "parody" or "imitation" Mass settings of a particular melody (for example, compare the respective Kyrie settings of the "L'Homme armé" melody by Dufay and Ockeghem, the former Dorian/minor and the latter Mixolydian), and melodies that change mode internally (for, instance, the first five-measure phrase of the Beatles' "Eleanor Rigby," which changes from Dorian to minor).

Change of Collection and Tonic

Most typically, modulations involve changes of both collection and tonic. In such cases, the two skills learned in isolation earlier must be combined to make the change of key. See Example 8.15, in which both the prevailing diatonic collection (three flats) and the tonic (E♭) must be changed in progressing from (E♭) major to G minor. The collection undergoes alteration first, in m. 4, from three flats to two. At this point, from the sight reader's point of view, it is uncertain whether the chromatic pitch that effects this change is a local nondiatonic pitch or the first instance of a more lasting change of diatonic collection. As the reader progresses through m. 5, a change of tonic from E♭ to G becomes more apparent.

---

4. Many other similar changes between parallel major and minor modes can be found (for example, the song "Come Back to Sorrento," by Ernesto De Curtis).

Example 8.15. Brahms, "Wenn du nur zuweilen lächelst," Op. 57, No. 2, mm. 1–7.

Measures 6 and 7 reiterate A♮ to the exclusion of A♭, clarifying the move to the two-flat collection. These measures also restate the G-tonicization figure, making the new sphere of G minor unequivocal.

Such changes are, in general, more difficult to execute if an altered pitch is first approached by leap. This condition, although not generally as common in the literature as stepwise approaches, is quite prevalent in recitatives. Example 8.16 shows a recitative from Handel's *Samson*. As this excerpt modulates from A to B♭, the "new" pitches B♭ and E♭ are introduced in mm. 2 and 5, respectively. This forces sight readers to rethink the diatonic collection twice, using subsets from the one-flat collection (or F-major/D-minor, thinking tonally) for mm. 2–4 and the two-flat collection (B♭-major/G-minor) for mm. 5–6. Note that the two altered pitches B♭ and E♭ are both approached by leap (and even the G is an altered pitch, if one begins with the A-major duet that precedes this recitative). In each case, the *leap* to the altered pitch increases the difficulty of execution. Once again, the path to such figures can be prepared through drill and practice with the kinds of triadic modulatory pitch patterns under " 'Common-Tone' Modulations" later in this chapter. In addition, as Lake (1993) noted, such "tonally vague" passages can be quite appropriately managed through a more atomistic, acontextual intervallic strategy.

Many sight-singing texts offer exercises, composed melodies, and excerpts for practice in modulation. The most extensive set of such excerpts

Example 8.16. Handel, *Samson*, No. 46, recitative.

Example 8.17. Schubert, "Kennst du das Land," D. 321, mm. 1–11.

appears in Thomson ([1969] 1975): pages 28–55 and 74–105 contain progressively more complex modulations; pages 106–131 contain excerpts of "ambiguous tonality."

Recognizing Changes in Collection and Tonic

In some cases, composers or publishers supply a new key signature at the point of change, thereby making the change of collection (if not tonic) explicitly obvious. Other collection changes are effected through the use of accidentals. Readers should learn to recognize changes in collection and tonic in real time.

Consider the excerpt shown in Example 8.17. Much of the difficulty in reading this modulation (and others) in real time lies in (1) recognizing the change of collection from three sharps to no sharps/flats and (2) recognizing the local displacement of the tonic from A to C. Readers must become facile at scanning music and rapidly determining new diatonic collections and tonics.[5]

Exercises and excerpts that isolate these two features can help readers focus the appropriate reading and auralization skills on the task. For example, the excerpt shown in Example 8.18 is taken from a passage in

Example 8.18. Mahler, Symphony No. 2, mmt. 2, reh. 9, mm. 5–8.

5. John Buccheri has isolated this as a distinct skill in courses at Northwestern University. He asks students to identify the various key areas of a composition rapidly by picking up visual cues about collection and tonicization. Two software applications—*Imager* and *ScoreScan*, both co-written by Buccheri and Roland Telfeyan—afford drill and practice in these skills.

Example 8.19. Mozart, Symphony No. 40, K. 550, mmt. 1, mm. 56–62.

which (1) the local diatonic collection (four flats) is a product of accidentals that cancel the original one and replace it with a new set of intervallic structures and (2) the local tonic (A♭) is a product of the new pitch relationships therein.

In fact, material of this type is profitably studied *before* any work with changing collections or tonics is undertaken. Series of pitch patterns and collections of excerpts carefully constructed or extracted to exhibit a single diatonic collection and tonic unrelated to the printed key signature allow readers to concentrate on the skills necessary for reading and establishing collections and tonics without having to make changes in either of these parameters while singing. Aural skills textbooks are curiously bereft of such exercises, with one notable exception: Cole and Lewis (1909) composed twenty-six melodies (pp. 145–47) the diatonic collections for which are arrived at through accidentals that effectively alter each of the prevailing key signatures.

An important distinction to make here is the difference between *accidentals* and *chromatic pitches*. "Accidentals" are those pitch-inflecting symbols (♭, ♯, ♭♭, ✕, ♮, ♮♭, ♮♯, and ♮♮) that appear immediately before pitches in the course of printed music. (The symbols ♯ and ♭, when part of a key signature, are not accidentals—there is nothing "accidental" or "incidental" about them there—they *globally* affect all pitches in that staff.) The term "chromatic" refers not to any symbol but rather to the status of a pitch vis-à-vis the prevailing diatonic collection. Therefore, it is possible for accidentals to create either chromatic or diatonic pitches and for pitches without accidentals to be either diatonic or chromatic as well.

Consider the passage shown in Example 8.19. The key signature of no sharps or flats is operative for this passage. However, the diatonic collection during this passage contains one sharp—F♯—effected through the consistent use of accidentals to raise F one half step. Although they are achieved through accidentals, those F♯s are diatonic in the local one-sharp collection. Compare those F♯s with the pitches G♯ (m. 56) and C♯ and D♯ (m. 61). These latter three pitches are also achieved through accidentals, but their status is fundamentally different from that of the F♯s: they are chromatic in the local 1-sharp collection.

Example 8.20. Liszt, *Les Preludes*, mm. 370–77.

Sight singers must be able to distinguish whether accidentals result in diatonic or chromatic pitches and sing them accordingly. Some accidentals make nondiatonic (chromatic) changes within a diatonic collection, whereas other accidentals change one diatonic collection into another. For example, compare Examples 8.1 and 8.2 (in which every accidental is chromatic) with Example 8.18 (in which every accidental is diatonic). Readers' approaches to these two different types of accidentals must be fundamentally different.

Notes without accidentals also enjoy these two different statuses. On the one hand, it should be self-evident that most notes without accidentals are diatonic. On the other, there are some instances (admittedly few) of notes without accidentals that are nonetheless chromatic.

Example 8.20 shows a model-and-sequence passage from Liszt's *Les Preludes* that tonicizes C for its first four bars, then jumps directly to a tonicization of E♭ for the next four bars. Note that the D♯s and C♯s in mm. 370 and 372, respectively, require accidentals to achieve their chromatic status (↑2 and ↑1, respectively). When this model is transposed to E♭ major, we find that ↑2 is effected through the use of an accidental (F♯) in m. 374, but that ↑1 (in m. 376) requires no accidental since the pitch E♮ (although now locally chromatic) is provided by the key signature.

Chromatic pitches without accidentals are more common as raised $\hat{6}$ and raised $\hat{7}$ in the minor mode. For example, the diatonic collection for the passage in Example 8.21 is the three-flat collection, but the B♮s in m. 3—which would carry accidentals were the key signature of three flats printed at the beginning of the staff—require no accidentals since they are already present by virtue of the no-sharp/flat signature.

The use of so-called incomplete key signatures requires similar attention on the part of the reader. Example 8.22 shows an example of the Baroque practice of notating certain minor keys with a "missing" final flat. Note that both raised $\hat{6}$ and raised $\hat{7}$ appear in m. 1, but that only raised $\hat{7}$ requires an accidental; raised $\hat{6}$ is supplied by the incomplete signature. Conversely, the diatonic form of $\hat{6}$ can only be achieved in an incomplete signature through the use of an accidental: see the A♭ in m. 7.

Example 8.21. Schubert, Quintet for Strings in C, D. 956 (op. post. 163), mmt. 4, mm. 1–6.

"Common-Tone" Modulations

Some modulations make obvious use of a single pitch that serves one function in the preceding key and another function in the succeeding one—a common tone. From a melodic point of view, such modulations are analogous to what are called pivot-chord or common-chord modulations in multiple-voice harmony.

Example 8.23 shows an example of a common-tone modulation. The pitch E in mm. 83–85 serves as $\hat{3}$ in C major (the key of the concluding section) but becomes $\hat{5}$ in A major (the key of the ensuing section). The skills necessary to make such modulations involve altering the diatonic collection and reinterpreting a single pitch's function in real time.

Drills that isolate the use of common tones between key areas can help to focus on the changes of diatonic collection and scale-degree function needed to execute common-tone modulations. Example 8.24 shows two sets of such drills: one using stepwise motion and the other using arpeggiation. These diatonic five-note patterns are designed to be learned as separate entities (with or without attendant solmization), at first sung in the order shown from a single common pitch (the role G serves in the stepwise example shown), then in various orders, and finally each from a different starting pitch. Of course, other diatonic patterns may be added to these, which simply form a core from which many modulations can be made and afford ample opportunity to practice the basic skills in-

Example 8.22. Corelli, *Sonata da camera a tre*, Op. 4, No. 11, Corrente, mm. 1–9.

Example 8.23. Dvořák, *Slavonic Dances*, Op. 46, No. 1, mm. 80–88 (with octave adjustments for sight singing).

volved. For many, beginning work on modulation with the common-tone variety seems to clarify the task at hand and the requisite skills involved.

"Gradual" Modulations

Some modulations announce themselves rather clearly in notation, through the use of a new key signature or a bevy of accidentals. Others are more subtle, occurring gradually over a succession of pitches that might be interpreted in either key area (or might even faintly suggest yet a third key during these intervening pitches[6]).

For example, the passage from *Winterreise* shown in Example 8.25(a) moves from C minor in mm. 37–42 to E♭ major in m. 45. But the scalar passage that connects them—particularly the pitches in m. 43—might be thought of in either key. Example 8.25(b) shows the passage in mm. 42–45, with functional movable-*do* syllables printed below. The first line of

a.

b.

Example 8.24. Drills that prepare readers to make common-tone modulations: (a) Stepwise; (b) Via arpeggiation.

---

6. Sometimes referred to as "transient" or "passing" modulations. See, for example, Aldwell and Schachter (1989, 426).

a.

In   ei - nes Köh-lers   en - gem Haus hab   Ob - dach ich   ge - fun - den;

doch mei - 'ne Glie - der   ruhn nicht aus;   so   bren-nen ih - re   Wun - den.

b.

Do   Do   Ti   Do   Re   Me   Fa   Sol   Le   Te
                            Do   Re   Mi   Fa   Sol   Le   Sol   La   Ti   Do   Do

Example 8.25. Schubert, *Winterreise*, Op. 89, D. 911, No. 10, "Rast"; (a) Mm. 37–45 with text; (b) Mm. 42–45 with solmization.

syllables interprets the passage in C minor for as long as possible; the second line interprets it in E♭ major from the downbeat of m. 43 to the end. Different readers might mutate from the top set to the bottom at different places in m. 43, but—because of the subtlety of gradual modulations—they must be careful to recognize the modulation at all and make it before it becomes too late (particularly to make sense of the C♭ in m. 44).

"Unprepared" Modulations

Unprepared modulations typically appear at the beginning of a new phrase or section and are therefore also known as "direct" modulations and sometimes "phrase" or "sectional" modulations. These modulations are abrupt, although often quite elegant and even subtle. For purposes of definition by skill (from the point of view of the sight singer), they are unconnected by common tone or gradual change of collection or tonic.

Example 8.26 shows one such modulation. The first eight measures of the excerpt are unequivocally in D minor. After the double bar, the music jumps directly to F major. Although the move from tonic minor to relative major can be a rather easy one to navigate, its incarnation here is particularly diabolical for several reasons. First, as a sectional modulation, it begins abruptly without preparation immediately after the half-cadence in m. 8. Second, the pitch C (which has been chromaticized as the leading-tone C♯ for the entire preceding phrase) is approached through the leap

Example 8.26. Giovanni Bononcini, *Divertimento da camera* No. 2 in D minor, for Violin or Recorder and Continuo, Vivace, mm. 1–16.

of a *diminished octave*—not one of the more easily auralized relationships in tonal music. In this case, many readers will benefit from auralizing a motion to C5 in m. 8 (either chromatically down from C♯ or via a resolution to D and then to C) before leaping up to C6. Wherever possible, such interpolated auralizing can help ease the difficulties in negotiating unprepared modulations. In addition, it helps if readers can auralize the general shift from tonic minor to relative major that underlies this passage. Readers who, at the cadence in m. 8, imagine the initial tonic (D) and feel a shift to the relative major (F) can proceed to the dominant pitch of that new key for the beginning of m. 9. This ability to auralize underlying tonal shifts, particularly for certain typical modulations, is a very valuable tool.

Typical Key Relationships

Because they occur so frequently in tonal music, the following modulations should be treated as important cases, focused on, and practiced most carefully in a variety of guises: (1) tonic minor to relative major, (2) tonic major to relative minor, (3) tonic to dominant, and (4) dominant back to tonic. As each of these modulations can be made through any one of several of the means described previously and chromatics can be introduced in any of the various ways addressed at the beginning of this chapter, these typical modulations should be encountered and practiced in many of these different ways in order to acclimate readers to their various incarnations.

Example 8.27. Jean-Marie Leclair, Sonata for Violin and Basso Continuo, Op. 2, No. 5, I, mm. 28–50.

Solmization during Modulations

One of the arguments against using functional solmization centers on difficulties presented by modulatory materials. For example, *The Juilliard Report on Teaching the Literature and Materials of Music* referred to students who "have been 'contaminated' by the very limited 'movable *do*' system used in public schools and cannot cope with modulations" (Juilliard School of Music 1953, 112). One might argue, however, that functional solmization is precisely the right tool to assist in auralizing modulations. Functional solmization makes explicit the changes in collection and tonic sight singers must read, understand, and auralize in order to perform modulations with comprehension and musicality. Readers who muddle through modulatory passages without such explicit comprehension are likely to make more mistakes and will certainly communicate little musical understanding.

Example 8.27 shows a passage that requires functional readers to conceive of several different keys as they navigate its twenty-three measures. (Note that this passage would need to be transposed lower for most singers.) The movable-*do* syllables printed beneath the staves show one way sight singers might solmize this passage. The first important tonal interpretation readers must make is the key area for the opening measures. Although the printed signature is one sharp, the passage tonicizes D (with C♯ being implied but no Cs being stated through m. 34). This tonicization would be more obvious to readers who approach this passage via the opening twenty-seven measures of the movement (which modulate from G to D and include the addition of C♯ in mm. 13–27), but they must be able to recognize such tonicizations without such obvious cues as well.

Particularly subject to varying interpretations are the pivot points in mm. 35 and 44. Upon first reading, some might solmize m. 35 as *di–ti–la–re"* and attempt to continue into the following measures without changing tonic. This would soon become awkward and nonfunctional, however. Once readers become adept at making frequent syllable mutations, they can apply whatever syllable segments are practical in modulating from one stable area to another (perhaps even "mumbling" through a few pitches in transitions) as long as the locally stable areas are appropriately solmized. The mutation in m. 44 could just as easily be made in the preceding measure or perhaps even in the following measure (upon encountering the F♮). Once again, as long as the new local tonicization is recognized it matters little exactly *how* and precisely *when* the transition is made.

Proportional Tempo and Meter Changes

When tempos change in a specific, proportional manner and when meters change without pause, readers must be prepared to read, interpret, and perform these changes accurately. For example, the instruction *doppio movimento* requires a precise doubling of speed. Similarly, the instruction *l'istesso tempo* requires that the duration of the beat remain constant while the meter changes—say from $\frac{2}{4}$ to $\frac{6}{8}$ so that the dotted quarter in $\frac{6}{8}$ moves at the same pace as the quarter in $\frac{2}{4}$. The important skills involved here are the ability to maintain a steady pulse (or double or halve that pulse) and to alter the subdivision of that pulse, if necessary. For example, in the case of making the *l'istesso tempo* change from $\frac{2}{4}$ to $\frac{6}{8}$, readers maintain a steady pulse while shifting from duple to triple divisions.

Many meter changes, particularly those in much common-practice-period music, take place without further performance indications. In these cases, it is incumbent on the reader to understand the implications of the specific metric symbols involved based on stylistic considerations and current notions of performance practice.[7]

A more recent notational development has brought clarity and specificity to the situation: the explicit indication of the relationship between a rhythmic value in the "old" meter or tempo and one in the "new." This takes the form of an equation, such as ♩=♩., that equates the two durations in their respective contexts. This type of proportional tempo change

---

7. Rudolf (1994, 281–94) offers a comprehensive discussion of various representative changes of meter and tempo, illustrated with twenty-four excerpts from music literature.

is sometimes referred to as "metrical modulation" or, more simply, "metric modulation."

As readers familiarize themselves with various indications for tempo and meter changes, they must learn to carry out their specific instructions with as much accuracy as possible. Such materials can be learned via clapping (difficult with faster rhythms), tapping (with one hand or two), vocalizing on a neutral syllable ("taah"), or using rhythmic solmization. These skills can be contextualized by introducing melodic materials containing such meter and tempo changes, to be sung on pitches in rhythm.

Clef Reading

Musicians must learn to be fluent in various clefs for a variety of reasons. Perhaps the most immediately obvious reason is the need to read music printed in diverse clefs. Modern notation is for the most part restricted to four clefs: treble, bass, alto, and tenor. Many textbooks and curricula are restricted to these four as well.[8] Certainly training in treble and bass clefs goes without discussion. The frequent appearance of alto and tenor clefs in modern scores and parts makes them indispensable for most musicians as well. The alto clef bears the distinction of being the only C clef used as a default in twentieth-century practice—for the viola. It also appears occasionally in scores and parts for trombones and even less frequently for English horns. The tenor clef appears in some modern scores and parts only when certain bass-clef instruments—bassoon, trombone, cello, and occasionally even double bass—move into a higher register.

These reasons alone are sufficient to mandate the ability to read treble, bass, alto, and tenor clefs. But there are other reasons as well, and those reasons extend to the use of all seven traditional clefs (and perhaps even a few others). Many editions of early music, in transcribing older notation, maintain the various clefs of the original notation (see the various *Denkmäler*, which use seven clefs liberally). And even if there exists a modern transcription of such notation that uses only treble and bass clefs, any musician who wishes to consult the original notation must still be able to read the original clefs. The practice of writing with various clefs extended well into the eighteenth century, so that—for example—the curious musician wishing to inspect Bach's manuscript for the C-major Invention must be able to read soprano clef for the right hand. In addition, musicians who wish to transpose by using clefs need to be fluent in treble,

---

8. For example, among some traditionally or currently popular sight-singing texts, McHose and Tibbs (1945), Benjamin, Horvit, and Nelson (1994), Ottman (1996), and Berkowitz, Fontrier, and Kraft (1997) all exclude soprano, mezzo-soprano, and baritone clef (McHose and Tibbs do refer to the use of these clefs in transposition). Benward and Carr (1999) include only a scant few instances of printed C clefs but do include a few brief narrative instructions for using various clefs for transposition.

bass, alto, tenor, soprano, mezzo-soprano, and baritone clefs (see the discussion under "Transposition," later in this chapter).

To become fluent in any particular clef, musicians must first understand the mechanism of the clef itself (does it symbolize the placement of middle C? Of F3? G4?). Then they must pursue a period of acclimation, during which they read extensively in that clef. This must be done in a manner that ensures they are reading the actual note names: either by singing with a fixed solmization system or by playing on an instrument. Methods that progressively combine various clefs at the keyboard—such as Morris and Ferguson (1931)—are particularly effective in this regard.

Clef training also develops an understanding of the *system* of clef notation in general. Musicians fluent in several clefs possess an intimate sense of the matrix formed by the lines and spaces on which Western music notation takes place, regardless of which specific clef they are reading at any given time, so that the kinds of skills used to read one clef are generally extensible to reading others. Thus, the ability to recognize specific patterns (scalar passages, triads, etc.), the kinds of eye movements successful sight readers use, the application of solmization, and even the various kinds of preperformance orientation skills discussed in chapter 6 all project with equal practicality onto the various clefs.

Finally, it should be noted that readers who read any particular clef *not in that clef* but as some other clef displaced by a certain number of steps (for example, reading alto clef as a treble clef "one step higher") have not learned to read that clef at all but rather have learned to transpose (see the next section in this chapter). Whereas transposition is a worthy skill in its own right, it is not a universally serviceable substitution for clef reading and should not be practiced as such.

Transposition

Musicians need to be able to transpose in order to undertake several different kinds of important musical tasks. These include the simple act of moving a piece from one key to another (to accommodate an individual's range or to transpose an accompanying part to match an instrument with a different transposition), reading from instrumental scores and parts, playing a transposing part on a C instrument (or on an instrument with yet another transposition), and composing or arranging music for transposing instruments.

All the various kinds of transposition tasks can be grouped into one of five broad categories. They are as follows: (1) transposing from one specific key to another (for example, playing a melody—originally in D—in the key of E); (2) transposing up or down by a particular interval (for example, playing a melody a perfect fifth lower); (3) performing, at concert pitch, a part written for a transposing instrument (for example, playing a part for alto sax on piano at concert pitch); (4) performing, on a transposing instrument, a part written at concert pitch (for example, performing a violin melody at concert pitch on a B♭ clarinet); and (5) performing, on a transposing instrument, a part written for an instrument with a different transposition (for example, playing a part for French horn in F on an A cornet).

Each of these five types of tasks makes special demands on readers. They must understand the nature of transposition, the transpositions of various instruments (both interval *and* direction of transposition), and the specific types of instructions that lead to each of these categories.

Among the various methods for transposing, the most widely used are transposition by *sighting*, by *interval*, by *tonal function*, and by *clef*. Sighting involves visualizing a new key signature and reading pitches a fixed number of lines or spaces above or below the written pitches (adjusting for accidentals using the interval method). The interval method requires readers to calculate the precise interval of transposition (number and quality) from each written pitch. Transposition by tonal function involves translating the tonal functions—scale degrees, scalar passages, sequences, and harmonic functions—from the written key to a new key. Transposition by clef uses clef substitution to effect pitch changes. For example, to transpose a melody in E minor in the treble clef to the key of G minor, one substitutes bass clef (and makes the necessary key signature and accidental changes[9]). Readers must be fluent in all seven clefs in order to use clefs to make all the various kinds of transpositions.

Some musicians, particularly those who use clefs, adhere vehemently to a single method of transposition. Others use whatever method is most appropriate for the kind of music to be transposed (for example, tonal function for simple tonal music, sighting for transpositions by second or third, clefs for fourths and fifths). Still others use a combination of approaches on every piece, perhaps beginning with tonal function and shifting into sighting when such functions become less obvious. No matter which particular methods readers use, they must learn to use these methods fluently.

Learning to transpose on an instrument forces readers to read the notes as actual transposed pitches. In contrast, it is possible for singers (at least those without AP) to transpose music with no more effort than that required to perform at the original pitch. Put another way, singers have no need to know the concert pitches of the sounds they produce, only the functional relationships between them. Therefore, in order for aural training to ensure that readers are in fact learning to transpose, those readers must perform transposition tasks in one or both of two ways: (1) on an instrument, and (2) singing with a fixed solmization sys-

---

9. For a complete description of key signature and accidental changes for transposition by clef, see Levin and Martin (1988a, 235–39, 459–60). McHose and Tibbs (1945, 3–4) offer a more concise, less exegetic set of guidelines.

tem (typically either fixed-*do* or on letter names). If such a system has been employed since the earliest days of training (at least after notation has been introduced), then applying it to this new task is a relatively painless matter.

Score Reading

Up to this point, we have explored how readers take in only a single line at a time. Most aural skills textbooks operate under the same restriction. Even when multiple-part singing is included, readers are required to attend to only one part at a time. But music reading involves much more than following a single part.

How can we develop and test readers' abilities to track the simultaneous layers of activity in a score for string quartet, chorus, orchestra, or other ensemble? The traditional answer in many courses of study is to include some form of score reading at the keyboard.[10] This is a venerable tradition, the results of which—when successful—are quite impressive. Score-reading study typically begins with two staves and progressively adds more and necessarily incorporates clef reading and transpositions as well. An important practical skill—and one that has concomitant aural benefits—is the ability to infer harmonies from as little information in the printed score as possible. Perhaps the reader only glances at the bass line for a few beats or sees only the goal at the upcoming downbeat but supplies correct or appropriate music. (This is the kind of skill Morris and Ferguson [1931] were referring to when they remarked that score reading "in its highest form has always an air of genuine wizardry" [pp. iii–iv].) One means of achieving this end is to involve readers in studying the realization of figured and (especially) unfigured basses. In so doing, they can develop an intuitive, real-time sense of voice leading and harmonic motion. In general, score reading at the keyboard is a very effective way of developing readers' abilities to follow multiple layers of musical activity from a score.[11]

Several problems are involved in using the keyboard to develop score-reading abilities. First, because score reading involves a significant degree of keyboard proficiency, it is typically delayed until late in the curriculum, when it is too late to offer benefits where they are needed most: in classes such as theory, history, and aural skills. Second, there are those students whose keyboard skills are so deficient as to impede any visual and aural benefits score reading might deliver. Third, there is no certain carryover from *playing* a score to *auralizing* it (just because pianists can play some-

---

10. The standard texts for studying this discipline include Morris and Ferguson (1931), Taylor (1967, 1970), and Melcher and Warch (1971).

11. Fiske (1958, 6–9) offers some brief but helpful guidelines that concern this task.

Example 8.28. Beethoven, Symphony No. 8, mmt. 1, mm. 1–8.

thing doesn't mean they can auralize it). Nonetheless, the benefits of score reading at the keyboard are manifold and such study should retain its place in the curriculum. But—particularly in light of the preceding caveats—we should seek ways to include score-reading skills in the aural skills curriculum as well.

As a means of achieving a kind of transitional skill, getting readers accustomed to taking in music from a multiple-part score, they can be asked to sing prominent lines from full score. For example, when faced with the score page shown in Example 8.28 and asked to sing the melody for mm. 1–8, readers should follow the first violin part in mm. 1–4, then move (seamlessly in rhythm) to the clarinet part for mm. 5–8 (making the necessary transposition). Of course, octave adjustments are often necessary when reading from instrumental parts. In the case of Example 8.28, either the entire melody will have to be lowered an octave or at least the violin part will, followed by the clarinet part at pitch. Such octave adjustments must become part of the score reader's repertoire of

Example 8.29. Haydn, Symphony No. 103, mmt. 4, mm. 1–12.

skills.[12] Although the reader is still attending to only one line at a time, this kind of activity does acclimate the eye toward scanning a score for important details and segmenting it into multiple layers of activity.

To further facilitate and contextualize reading from scores, pairs or groups of readers can perform multiple parts simultaneously. Example 8.29 shows the opening of the Finale from Haydn's Symphony No. 103. This excerpt could be sung in several different ways: (1) by two readers, with one taking the lower voice (Horn II in mm. 1–8 and Clarinet II in mm. 9–12) and the other taking the upper voice (Horn I in mm. 1–4 and Violin I in mm. 5–12); (2) by four readers, two on the "secondary" material (Horns in mm. 1–8 and Clarinets in mm. 9–12) and two on the "primary" material (Violins in mm. 5–12); and (3) by six readers—two Horns, two Violins, two Clarinets. This kind of approach often necessi-

12. See Adler (1997, xii–xiii) for further helpful suggestions about accommodating instrumental ranges with the human voice.

tates many of the kinds of decisions made by score readers at the piano (what to include, what to omit, where to change register, etc.) and goes a long way toward familiarizing readers with the task of reading music from scores. And as score-reading abilities improve, more complex scores can be dealt with in this fashion.

It still remains that an important goal is to develop individual readers' abilities to auralize multiple parts simultaneously, and reading single lines from scores will not accomplish this. Since our most direct means of testing mental representations of sounds—the human voice—is monophonic, we must seek an indirect test. The most effective and practical is for readers to perform error detection and correction from full score. Discrepancies can be introduced between score and recording, to be identified and corrected by readers. The most typical of these—errors of pitch and rhythm—are certainly the most practical, since they are the types coaches and conductors are most likely to encounter. But other discrepancies—errors of harmony, chord inversion, timbre, tempo, dynamics, articulation, and other factors—can also be employed to test readers' abilities to auralize all the components of a score simultaneously.

There are few prepared sources of such materials. Grunow and Froseth (1979) include score excerpts and accompanying tapes to be evaluated in terms of tempo, balance, tone quality, rhythm, pitch, intonation, phrasing, articulation, ornamentation, dynamics, and "ensemble" (simultaneity). A recent addition is Bailey (1992), which "is designed to integrate skills acquired in traditional ear-training courses with conducting skills" (p. v). Bailey provides 105 (mostly three- and four-part) excerpts from various common-practice-period scores along with a short list of "suggested" errors (of rhythm, tempo, pitch, intonation, dynamics, and articulation) for each excerpt to be inserted in performance.[13]

Conducting as a Set of Aural Skills

Among the musical activities that place the most demands on the greatest number of aural skills is conducting. Schuller (1997) lists "a keen, discerning ear and mind" among the "requisite talents and skills needed to be a fine, perhaps even great, conductor" (pp. 6–7). He enumerates the seven kinds of "ears" a conductor should possess. They are the following: an ear for "(1) harmony; (2) pitch and intonation; (3) dynamics; (4) timbre; (5) rhythm and articulation; (6) balance and orchestrational aspects; and (7) line and continuity" (pp. 17–18). Jones (1949) remarked that "the conductor must instantly detect rhythmic and tonal errors" (p. 59). In-

---

13. The accompanying recordings (which contain both incorrect and correct readings) are unfortunately all performed on brass instruments regardless of original instrumentation.

deed, much of what conductors do in rehearsal and performance centers on error detection and correction.

But the work conductors do *preparing* for rehearsals is deeply dependent upon their music-reading and auralizing abilities. As Scherchen (1933) remarked, "To conduct means to make manifest—without flaws—that which one has perfectly heard within oneself" (p. 3). Prausnitz (1983) noted that "the process of hearing, imagining and refining begins in quiet concentration on the score" (p. 2) and "the conductor's primary musical instrument is his own mind. Work with the orchestra, his other musical instrument, will be effective only to the extent of his success in transforming the evidence of the score into a living musical image, *before* he mounts the podium" (p. 1). Similarly, Rudolf (1994) refers to the "imaginary performance" (p. 321) conductors must prepare before rehearsal. The skills involved in "hearing within oneself," in creating this "living musical image" or "imaginary performance" through score study, are all *aural* skills. In preparing a score, conductors must read and interpret its symbols for tempo, meter, rhythm, pitch, harmony, timbre, articulation, phrasing, and other parameters through auralizing those symbols—imagining the sounds in the absence of physical sound waves. Yes, conductors can resort to score reading at the piano, but this is little help with regard to timbre, balance, articulation, and other ensemble-specific features. And listening to recordings, while helpful for *comparing* interpretations, does not do much to assist conductors in developing their own aural images of a work. No, conductors must be able to read scores and mentally hear their own performances through relying on their own aural skills.

Reading Schenkerian Graphs

Cadwallader and Gagné (1998) urge that "any analysis of a musical work should not be based solely on a visual interpretation of the score—it should be based on the sound of the piece. It may initially be played on a piano or listened to on a recording, but it should ideally be memorized and heard in one's *inner ear*" (p. vii). It takes one set of aural skills to memorize the sound of a composition by repeatedly playing it on the piano or listening to a recording of it; a somewhat different set of skills is necessary to memorize simply by reading notation. In both cases, the "inner ear" Cadwallader and Gagné refer to plays a crucial role: without the ability to auralize the sound of a composition, no analysis of it is worth very much at all.

Schenkerian analysis is first and foremost an aural activity. Schenker himself spoke of experiencing compositions "not as a sum total of measures or pages, but as entities which could be heard and perceived as a whole" (Schenker [1935] 1979, xxiii).

It is the graphic nature of Schenkerian analysis that makes it so specially aural. Cadwallader (1990) notes the following about the contributors to *Trends in Schenkerian Research*: "The authors have been diligent in preparing graphs and reductions so that one can hear the music in their examples" (p. v). Note that Cadwallader refers to hearing the music *in* the examples: the analyses themselves are thought of as music to be heard. Similarly, Forte and Gilbert (1982) refer to Schenkerian graphs as analyses "intended to make sense aurally as well as conceptually" (p. 2). Salzer (1969) concluded that Schenker developed the use of graphic notation because "words can only explain or describe one event at a time, but even the most elementary musical hearing must grasp, for example, a melody and its counterpoint at the same time" (p. 15). Therefore, for listeners to be capable of reading (let alone creating) Schenkerian graphs, they must possess such "elementary musical hearing"—specifically, the ability to read, understand, and auralize the music symbols the graphs contain.

Although this discussion appears in a chapter on music-reading skills, acclimation to Schenkerian principles is intimately tied up with listening skills as well. Forte and Gilbert (1982) encourage "listening carefully, and developing and refining the hearing capacity in a musical way" (p. 3). And as listeners learn to link up Schenkerian symbols (and the concepts they represent) with the appropriate sounds, they can begin to hear these things directly from the music. Salzer ([1952] 1962) noted that "after ample experience in the detailed approach of structural hearing has been acquired, the student in many instances can afford to omit the written work of the detailed graphs, since the motion conveys its meaning and coherence to the trained ear" (p. 258). In other words, Schenkerian analysis is a kind of ear training that, when sufficiently mastered, allows listeners to hear certain features directly through listening.[14]

It is beyond the scope of this brief discussion to examine in depth the auralization of specific Schenkerian features. Nonetheless, it may prove helpful to enumerate some of the more important ones. At the very least, listeners should be able to read, identify, and hear the note heads, stems, and slurs that represent structural consonance versus dissonance, consonant skips, and arpeggiations. Beyond that, the use of slurs (both solid and dotted) to indicate prolongations can help guide the ear, particularly to their origins and goals. Other basic symbols worth auralizing include voice exchanges and interruptions. At deeper levels, the eye can learn to hear broader linear connections and local tonicizations (longer prolon-

14. Serafine, Glassman, and Overbeeke (1989) demonstrated, through a series of experiments, the "cognitive reality of hierarchic structure in music," the perceptual link between a melody and its Schenkerian reduction, particularly after repeated hearings. See Deutsch and Feroe (1981) for a model of hierarchical pitch structure based on research in perception and cognition. Deutsch and Feroe relate and compare their model to Schenkerian principles of level and prolongation (pp. 519–20).

gations). At the deepest levels, broad prolongations (such as the prolongation of the dominant from the end of a major-mode sonata form exposition through to end of the development) and background structural points of arrival (particularly the final structural dominant and tonic) are important.

How can musicians develop this kind of "structural hearing"? Certainly training in making reductive graphs can produce a kind of Schenkerian ear training as a fortuitous by-product. But other more focused activities can help to bolster more rigorous connections between sound and Schenkerian symbol. As a basic introduction, some of the recordings in Jacobson and Koozin (1996) are linked directly to graphic analyses that scroll in real time while the music sounds. This can help less skilled readers become accustomed to following graphs and auralizing the sounds they stand for. Sight singing rhythmicized reductions while simultaneously listening to the original music is an excellent way to connect graphic analyses to compositions they represent and to link up specific analytical techniques aurally with their symbols. Simultaneous singing of two or more different structural levels by more than one reader is similarly illuminating. Through these various kinds of activities, "the eye helps the ear to integrate the analysis of tonal events on the various levels of structure" (Salzer 1969, 16).[15]

Conclusion

All of the aural skills discussed in this and previous chapters should become as generalizable and practical as possible. Musicians should be able to use both long-held and newly learned aural skills in a variety of settings. In various roles—for example, as performers, conductors composers, arrangers, students, teachers, scholars, editors, and copyists—musicians can apply their aural skills to all their musical activities. Practicing, rehearsing, performing, listening, composing, arranging, conducting, studying, and teaching are but a few of the circumstances in which musicians can draw on their aural skills. Anywhere there is music to be heard, read, or made, aural skills should be at the ready.

---

15. Compare Pierce (1994) for a rather different approach to developing connections between Schenkerian graphs and hearing.

References

Adler, Samuel (1997). *Sight singing: Pitch, interval, rhythm*. 2d ed. New York: W. W. Norton.

Adolphe, Bruce (1991). *The mind's ear: Exercises for improving the musical imagination of performers, listeners and composers*. Saint Louis, MO: MMB Music.

Albert, D. G. (1967). The effect of differential treatments on pitch acuity in solo instrumental performance. Master's thesis, Florida State University.

Alchin, Carolyn A. (1904). *Ear training for teacher and pupil*. Boston: Oliver Ditson.

Aldwell, Edward, and Schachter, Carl (1989). *Harmony and voice leading*. 2d ed. San Diego, CA: Harcourt Brace Jovanovich.

Alldahl, Per-Gunnar (1974). Teaching music theory: The European conservatory. *Journal of Music Theory* 18: 111–22.

Alvarez, Manuel (1980). A comparison of scalar and root harmonic aural perception techniques. *Journal of Research in Music Education* 28: 229–35.

Anderson, Cynthia R., and Tunks, Thomas W. (1992). The influence of expectancy on harmonic perception. *Psychomusicology* 11: 3–14.

Bach, C. P. E. ([1753/1762] 1949). *Essay on the true art of playing keyboard instruments*. Trans. William J. Mitchell. New York: W. W. Norton.

Bachem, A. (1940). The genesis of absolute pitch. *Journal of the Acoustical Society of America* 11: 434–39.

Backus, John (1977). *The acoustical foundations of music*. 2d ed. New York: W. W. Norton.

Baharloo, Siamak; Johnston, Paul A.; Service, Susan K.; Gitschier, Jane; and Freimer, Nelson B. (1998). Absolute pitch: An approach for identification of genetic and nongenetic components. *American Journal of Human Genetics* 62: 224–31.

Bailey, Wayne (1992). *Aural skills for conductors*. Mountain View, CA: Mayfield.

Baillot, Pierre Marie François de Sales ([1835] 1991). *The art of the violin*. Ed. and trans. Louise Goldberg. Evanston, IL: Northwestern University Press.

Barucha, Jamshed (1984). Anchoring effects in music: The resolution of dissonance. *Cognitive Psychology* 16: 485–518.

Beckett, Christine Alyn (1997). Directing student attention during two-part dictation. *Journal of Research in Music Education* 45: 613–25.

Benjamin, Thomas; Horvit, Michael; and Nelson, Robert (1994). *Music for sight singing.* 2d ed. Belmont, CA: Wadsworth.

Benward, Bruce, and Carr, Maureen (1999). *Sightsinging complete.* 6th ed. Boston: McGraw-Hill.

Benward, Bruce, and Kolosick, J. Timothy (1991). *Ear training: A technique for listening.* 4th ed. Dubuque, IA: Brown and Benchmark.

Benward, Bruce, and Kolosick, J. Timothy (1996a). *Ear training: A technique for listening.* 5th ed. Dubuque, IA: Brown and Benchmark.

Benward, Bruce, and Kolosick, J. Timothy (1996b). Instructor's edition to *Ear training: A technique for listening.* 5th ed. Dubuque, IA: Brown and Benchmark.

Berkowitz, Sol; Fontrier, Gabriel; and Kraft, Leo (1997). *A new approach to sight singing.* 4th ed. New York: W. W. Norton.

Berz, William L. (1995). Working memory in music: A theoretical model. *Music Perception* 12: 353–64.

Berz, William L., and Kelly, Anthony E. (1998). Research note: Perceptions of more complete musical compositions: An exploratory study. *Psychology of Music* 26: 175–85.

Best, Harold M. (1992). Music curricula in the future. *Arts Education Policy Review* 94/2: 2–7.

Bland, Leland D. (1984). *Sight singing through melodic analysis.* Chicago: Nelson-Hall.

Blombach, Ann (1990). Judging melodic dictation by computer. Paper presented to the annual meeting of the College Music Society, Washington, DC.

Boatwright, Howard (1956). *Introduction to the theory of music.* New York: W. W. Norton.

Bobbitt, Richard (1959). The physical basis of intervallic quality and its application to the problem of dissonance. *Journal of Music Theory* 3: 173–207.

Boyle, J. David (1968). The effects of prescribed rhythmical movements on the ability to sight read music. Ph.D. diss., University of Kansas.

Boyle, J. David, and Radocy, Rudolf E. (1987). *Measurement and evaluation of musical experiences.* New York: Schirmer Books.

Brady, Paul T. (1970). Fixed scale mechanism of absolute pitch. *Journal of the Acoustical Society of America* 48: 883–87.

Brick, John S. (1984). An exploratory study of the effects of a self-instructional programme utilising the *Pitch Master* on pitch discrimination and pitch accuracy in performance of young trombonists. *Psychology of Music* 12: 119–25.

Broadbent, Donald E. (1958). *Perception and communication.* New York: Pergamon Press.

Broadbent, Donald E. (1962). Attention and the perception of speech. *Scientific American* 206/4: 143–51.

Brooks, Richard, and Warfield, Gerald (1978). *Layer dictation: A new approach to the Bach chorales.* New York: Longman.

Brown, Helen (1985). The effects of set content and temporal context in musicians' aural perception of tonality. Ph.D. diss., Ohio State University.

Brown, Helen (1988). The interplay of set content and temporal context in a functional theory of tonality perception. *Music Perception* 5: 219–50.

Brown, Helen; Butler, David; and Jones, Mari Riess (1994). Musical and temporal influences on key discovery. *Music Perception* 11: 371–407.

Brown, Peter (1979). An enquiry into the origins and nature of tempo behaviour. *Psychology of Music* 7/1: 19–35.

Buccheri, John (1990). Musicianship at Northwestern. *Journal of Music Theory Pedagogy* 4: 125–45.

Bunch, Meribeth (1997). *Dynamics of the singing voice.* 4th ed. Vienna: Springer-Verlag.

Burkhart, Charles (1994). *Anthology for musical analysis.* 5th ed. Fort Worth, TX: Harcourt Brace College Publishers.

Butler, David (1989). Describing the perception of tonality in music: A critique of the tonal hierarchy theory and a proposal for a theory of intervallic rivalry. *Music Perception* 6: 219–41.

Butler, David (1992). *The musician's guide to perception and cognition.* New York: Schirmer Books.

Butler, David (1997). Why the gulf between music perception research and aural training? *Bulletin of the Council for Research in Music Education* 132: 38–48.

Butler, David (1998). Tonal bootstrapping: Re-thinking the intervallic rivalry model. Paper presented to the Fifth International Conference on Music Perception and Cognition, Seoul, Korea.

Butler, David, and Brown, Helen (1994). Describing the mental representation of tonality in music. In *Musical perceptions* (pp. 191–212). Ed. Rita Aiello with John Sloboda. New York: Oxford University Press.

Butler, David, and Lochstampfor, Mark (1993). Bridges unbuilt: Aural training and cognitive science. *Indiana Theory Review* 14: 1–17.

Byo, James L. (1997). The effects of texture and number of parts on the ability of music majors to detect performance errors. *Journal of Research in Music Education* 45: 51–66.

Cadwallader, Allen (1990). Preface to *Trends in Schenkerian research* (pp. v–vi). Ed. Allen Cadwallader. New York: Schirmer Books.

Cadwallader, Allen, and Gagné, David (1998). *Analysis of tonal music: A Schenkerian approach.* New York: Oxford University Press.

Campbell, Murray, and Greated, Clive (1988). *The musician's guide to acoustics.* New York: Schirmer Books.

Chambers, Deborah, and Reisberg, Daniel (1985). Can mental images be ambiguous? *Journal of Experimental Psychology: Human Perception and Performance* 11: 317–328.

Chambers, Deborah, and Reisberg, Daniel (1992). What an image depicts depends on what an image means. *Cognitive Psychology* 24: 145–74.

Chittum, Donald (1967). Diagnosis and therapy in interval dictation. *Music Educators Journal* 54/1: 71–73.

Chittum, Donald (1969). A different approach to harmonic dictation. *Music Educators Journal* 55/7: 65–66.

Christy, Van A., and Paton, John Glenn (1997). *Foundations in singing: A basic textbook in vocal technique and song interpretation.* 6th ed. Madison, WI: Brown and Benchmark.

Cogan, Robert, and Escot, Pozzi (1976). *Sonic design: The nature of sound and music*. Englewood Cliffs, NJ: Prentice-Hall.

Cohn, Richard (1992). Metric and hypermetric dissonance in the *Menuetto* of Mozart's Symphony in G minor, K. 550. *Intégral* 6: 1–33.

Cole, Samuel W., and Lewis, Leo R. (1909). *Melodia: A comprehensive course in sight-singing (solfeggio)*. Boston: Oliver Ditson.

Cone, Edward T. (1968). *Musical form and musical performance*. New York: W. W. Norton.

Cook, Nicholas (1987a). Musical form and the listener. *Journal of Aesthetics and Art Criticism* 46: 23–29.

Cook, Nicholas (1987b). The perception of large-scale tonal closure. *Music Perception* 5: 197–205.

Cook, Nicholas (1990). *Music, imagination and culture*. New York: Oxford University Press.

Cooper, Grosvenor, and Meyer, Leonard B. (1960). *The rhythmic structure of music*. Chicago: University of Chicago Press.

Copp, Evelyn Fletcher (1916). Musical ability. *Journal of Heredity* 7: 297–305.

Costall, Alan (1985). The relativity of absolute pitch. In *Musical structure and cognition* (pp. 189–208). Ed. Peter Howell, Ian Cross, and Robert West. London: Academic Press.

Croonen, W. L. M., and Kop, P. F. M. (1989). Tonality, tonal scheme, and contour in delayed recognition of tone sequences. *Music Perception* 7: 49–68.

Cross, Ian; Howell, Peter; and West, Robert (1985). Structural relationships in the perception of musical pitch. In *Musical structure and cognition* (pp. 121–42). Ed. Peter Howell, Ian Cross, and Robert West. London: Academic Press.

Crowder, Robert G. (1993). Auditory memory. In *Thinking in sound: The cognitive psychology of human audition* (pp. 113–45). Ed. Stephen McAdams and Emmanuel Bigand. Oxford: Clarendon Press.

Crozier, John B. (1997). Absolute pitch: Practice makes perfect, the earlier the better. *Psychology of Music* 25: 110–19.

Cuddy, Lola L. (1970). Training the absolute identification of pitch. *Perception and Psychophysics* 8: 265–69.

Dahlhaus, Carl (1982). *Esthetics of music*. Trans. William W. Austin. Cambridge: Cambridge University Press.

Damrosch, Frank (1894). *Popular method of sight-singing*. New York: G. Schirmer.

Dannhäuauser, Adolphe L. (1891). *Solfége des solfèges*. 3 vols. Trans. J. H. Cornell. New York: G. Schirmer.

Davidson, Lyle, and Welsh, Patricia (1988). From collections to structure: The developmental path of tonal thinking. In *Generative processes in music: The psychology of performance, improvisation, and composition* (pp. 260–85). Ed. John A. Sloboda. Oxford: Clarendon Press.

Davies, Ann, and Roberts, Emlyn (1975). Poor pitch singing: A survey of its incidence in school children. *Psychology of Music* 3/2: 24–36.

Davies, John Booth (1978). *The psychology of music*. Stanford, CA: Stanford University Press.

Davies, John B., and Yelland, Anne (1977). Effects of two training procedures on the production of melodic contour, in short-term memory for tonal sequences. *Psychology of Music* 5/2: 3–9.

Dawe, Lloyd A.; Platt, John R.; and Racine, Ronald J. (1994). Inference of metrical structure from perception of iterative pulses within time spans defined by chord changes. *Music Perception* 12: 57–76.

Deese, J., and Hardman, G. W. (1954). An analysis of errors in retroactive inhibition of rote verbal learning. *American Journal of Psychology* 67: 299–307.

Deliège, Irène, and Mélen, Marc (1997). Cue abstraction in the representation of musical form. In *Perception and cognition of music* (pp. 387–412). Ed. Irène Deliège and John Sloboda. East Sussex: Psychology Press.

Deutsch, Diana (1970a). The deterioration of pitch information in memory. Ph.D. diss., University of California at San Diego.

Deutsch, Diana (1970b). Tones and numbers: Specificity of interference in short-term memory. *Science* 168: 1604–5.

Deutsch, Diana (1977). Memory and attention in music. In *Music and the brain: Studies in the neurology of music* (pp. 95–130). Ed. Macdonald Critchley and R. A. Henson. London: William Heinemann Medical Books.

Deutsch, Diana (1980). The processing of structured and unstructured tonal sequences. *Perception and Psychophysics* 28: 381–89.

Deutsch, Diana (1999). The processing of pitch combinations. In *The psychology of music* (pp. 349–411). 2d ed. Ed. Diana Deutsch. New York: Academic Press.

Deutsch, Diana, and Feroe, John (1981). The internal representation of pitch sequences in tonal music. *Psychological Review* 88: 503–22.

DeVoto, Mark (1992). *Mostly short pieces: An anthology for harmonic analysis*. New York: W. W. Norton.

DeWitt, Lucinda A., and Crowder, Robert G. (1986). Recognition of novel melodies after brief delays. *Music Perception* 3: 259–74.

Donato, Anthony ([1963] 1977). *Preparing music manuscript*. Westport, CT: Greenwood Press. [Reprint of the 1963 Prentice-Hall edition.]

Dowling, W. Jay (1973a). The perception of interleaved melodies. *Cognitive Psychology* 5: 322–37.

Dowling, W. Jay (1973b). Rhythmic groups and subjective chunks in memory for melodies. *Perception and Psychophysics* 14: 37–40.

Dowling, W. Jay (1978). Scale and contour: Two components of a theory of memory for melodies. *Psychological Review* 85: 341–54.

Dowling, W. Jay (1986). Context effects on melody recognition: Scale-step versus interval representations. *Music Perception* 3 (1986): 281–96.

Dowling, W. Jay (1990). Expectancy and attention in melody perception. *Psychomusicology* 9: 148–60.

Dowling, W. Jay (1993). Procedural and declarative knowledge in music cognition and education. In *Psychology and music: The understanding of melody and rhythm* (pp. 5–18). Ed. Thomas J. Tighe and W. Jay Dowling. Hillsdale, NJ: Lawrence Earlbaum Associates.

Dowling, W. Jay (1994). Melodic contour in hearing and remembering melodies. In *Musical perceptions* (pp. 173–90). Ed. Rita Aiello with John Sloboda. New York: Oxford University Press.

Dowling, W. Jay, and Bartlett, James C. (1981). The importance of interval information in long-term memory for melodies. *Psychomusicology* 1: 30–49.

Dowling, W. Jay, and Harwood, Dane L. (1986). *Music cognition*. London: Academic Press.

Durham, Thomas L. (1994). *Beginning tonal dictation*. Prospect Heights, IL: Waveland Press.

Edlund, Lars (1964). *Modus novus: Studies in reading atonal melodies*. Stockholm: Nordiska Musikförlaget.

Edlund, Lars ([1967] 1974). *Modus vetus: Sight singing and ear-training in major/minor tonality*. Trans. Alan Stout. Stockholm: Nordiska Musikförlaget.

Educational Testing Service (1993). *Practicing to take the GRE music test*. 2d ed. Princeton, NJ: Educational Testing Service.

Educational Testing Service (1998). *Released exam: 1998 AP music theory*. Princeton, NJ: Educational Testing Service.

Elliott, Charles A. (1974). Effects of vocalization on the sense of pitch of beginning band class students. *Journal of Research in Music Education* 22: 120–28.

Elliott, Charles A. (1982). The relationships among instrumental sight-reading ability and seven selected predictor variables. *Journal of Research in Music Education* 30: 5–14.

Elliott, Charles A. (1996). Music as intelligence: Some implications for the public schools. In *Ithaca conference '96: Music as intelligence* (pp. 65–75). Ed. Verna Brummett. Ithaca, NY: Ithaca College.

Elliott, David (1993). Musicing, listening, and musical understanding. *Contributions to Music Education* 20: 64–83.

Ellis, Mark C. (1991). Research note. Thresholds for detecting tempo change. *Psychology of Music* 19: 164–69.

Ellis, Mark (1995). Research note: Field dependence-independence and texture discrimination in college non-music majors. *Psychology of Music* 23: 184–89.

Farnsworth, Paul R. (1969). *The social psychology of music*. 2d ed. Ames: Iowa State University Press.

Fétis, François-Joseph ([1840] 1994). *Esquisse de l'histoire de l'harmonie: An English-language translation of the François-Joseph Fétis history of harmony*. Trans. Mary I. Arlin. Stuyvesant, NY: Pendragon Press.

Fish, Arnold, and Lloyd, Norman (1964). *Fundamentals of sight singing and ear training*. New York: Dodd, Mead.

Fiske, Roger (1958). *Score reading*. Book 1, *Orchestration*. London: Oxford University Press.

Fletcher, Stanley (1957). Music-reading reconsidered as a code-learning problem. *Journal of Music Theory* 1: 76–96.

Fogarty, Gerard A.; Buttsworth, Louise M.; and Gearing, Phillip J. (1996). Assessing intonation skills in a tertiary music training programme. *Psychology of Music* 24: 157–70.

Forte, Allen, and Gilbert, Steven E. (1982). Instructor's manual for *Introduction to Schenkerian analysis*. New York: W. W. Norton.

Freedman, Eric G. (1999). The role of diatonicism in the abstraction and representation of contour and interval information. *Music Perception* 16: 365–87.

Friedman, Milton M. (1981). *A beginner's guide to sightsinging and musical rudiments*. Englewood Cliffs, NJ: Prentice-Hall.

Friedmann, Michael (1990). *Ear training for twentieth-century music*. New Haven, CT: Yale University Press.

Gabrielsson, Alf (1982). Performance and training of musical rhythm. *Psy-*

chology of Music (Special issue: Proceedings of the ninth international seminar on research in music education): 42–46.

Gabrielsson, Alf (1988). Timing in music performance and its relations to music experience. In *Generative processes in music: The psychology of performance, improvisation, and composition* (pp. 27–51). Ed. John A. Sloboda. Oxford: Clarendon Press.

Gaffurius, Franchinus ([1496] 1968). *Practica musicae.* Trans. Clement A. Miller. Dallas, TX: American Institute of Musicology.

Gardner, Howard (1985). *Frames of mind: The theory of multiple intelligences.* New York: Basic Books.

Gardner, Howard (1993). *Multiple intelligences: The theory in practice.* New York: Basic Books.

Gauldin, Robert (1996). A different approach to teaching melodic dissonance. *Journal of Music Theory Pedagogy* 10: 79–90.

Geringer, John M., and Sogin, David W. (1988). An analysis of musicians' intonational adjustments within the duration of selected tones. *Contributions to Music Education* 15: 1–6.

Gillespie, Jeffrey L. (1993). Difficulty factors in melodic perception. *Journal of Music Theory Pedagogy* 7: 41–53.

Gjerdingen, Robert O. (1994). Apparent motion in music? *Music Perception* 11: 335–70.

Goodacre, Royston; Neal, Mark J.; and Kell, Douglas B. (1996). Quantitative analysis of multivariate data using artificial neural networks: A tutorial review and applications to the deconvolution of pyrolysis mass spectra. *Zentralblatt für Bakteriologie — International Journal of Medical Microbiology, Virology, Parasitology and Infectious Diseases* 284: 516–39.

Goolsby, Thomas W. (1989). Computer applications to eye movement research in music reading. *Psychomusicology* 8: 111–26.

Goolsby, Thomas W. (1994a). Eye movement in music reading: Effects of reading ability, notational complexity, and encounters. *Music Perception* 12: 77–96.

Goolsby, Thomas W. (1994b). Profiles of processing: Eye movements during sightreading. *Music Perception* 12: 97–123.

Gordon, Edwin (1993). *Learning sequences in music: Skill, content, and patterns.* Chicago: GIA Publications.

Gottschalk, Arthur, and Kloeckner, Phillip (1997). *Functional hearing: A contextual method for ear training.* New York: Ardsley House.

Grave, Floyd (1995). Metrical dissonance in Haydn. *Journal of Musicology* 13: 168–202.

Gregory, Andrew H. (1990). Listening to polyphonic music. *Psychology of Music* 18: 163–70.

Gregory, Andrew H. (1994). Timbre and auditory streaming. *Music Perception* 12: 161–74.

Gromko, Joyce Eastlund (1993). Perceptual differences between expert and novice listeners: A multidimensional scaling analysis. *Psychology of Music* 21: 34–47.

Grunow, Richard F., and Froseth, James O. (1979). *MLR instrumental score reading program.* Chicago: GIA Publications.

Guido of Arezzo ([n.d.] 1998). Epistle concerning an unknown chant [*Epistola de ignoto cantu*]. In *Source readings in music history* (pp. 214–18). Ed. Oliver Strunk. Rev. ed. Ed. Leo Treitler. New York: W. W. Norton.

Halpern, Andrea R.; Bartlett, James C.; and Dowling, W. Jay (1998). Perception of mode, rhythm, and contour in unfamiliar melodies: Effects of age and experience. *Music Perception* 15: 335–55.

Handel, Stephen (1989). *Listening: An introduction to the perception of auditory events*. Cambridge: MIT Press.

Hantz, Edwin (1984). Studies in musical cognition: Comments from a music theorist. *Music Perception* 2: 245–64.

Harris, Clement Antrobus (1918). The war between the fixed and movable doh. *Musical Quarterly* 4: 184–95.

Harris, Clement Antrobus (1931). The element of repetition in nature and the arts. *Musical Quarterly* 17: 302–18.

Hasty, Christopher F. (1997). *Meter as rhythm*. New York: Oxford University Press.

Henry, Earl (1997). *Sight singing*. Upper Saddle River, NJ: Prentice-Hall.

Henry, Earl, and Mobberley, James (1986). Instructor's manual for *Musicianship: Ear training, rhythmic reading, and sight singing*. Englewood Cliffs, NJ: Prentice-Hall.

Hershman, Daniel P. (1995). Rhythmic factors in tonality. *Psychomusicology* 14: 4–19.

Heussenstamm, George (1987). *The Norton manual of music notation*. New York: W. W. Norton.

Hindemith, Paul (1949). *Elementary training for musicians*. 2d ed. New York: Associated Music Publishers.

Hoffman, Richard; Pelto, William; and White, John W. (1996). Takadimi: A beat-oriented system of rhythm pedagogy. *Journal of Music Theory Pedagogy* 10: 7–30.

Hofstetter, Fred T. (1980). Computer-based recognition of perceptual patterns in chord quality dictation exercises. *Journal of Research in Music Education* 28: 83–91.

Hofstetter, Fred T. (1981). Computer-based recognition of perceptual patterns and learning styles in rhythmic dictation exercises. *Journal of Research in Music Education* 29: 265–77.

Horacek, Leo, and Lefkoff, Gerald (1989). *Programmed ear training*. 2 vols. 2d ed. San Diego, CA: Harcourt Brace Jovanovich.

Houlahan, Micháel, and Tacka, Philip (1992). The Americanization of solmization: A response to the article by Timothy A. Smith, "A comparison of pedagogical resources in solmization systems." *Journal of Music Theory Pedagogy* 6: 137–51.

Houlahan, Micháel, and Tacka, Philip (1994). Continuing the dialogue: The potential of relative solmization for the music theory curriculum at the college level. *Journal of Music Theory Pedagogy* 8: 221–25.

Houle, George (1987). *Meter in music: 1600–1800*. Bloomington: Indiana University Press.

Howe, Hubert S. (1975). *Electronic music synthesis: Concepts, facilities, techniques*. New York: W. W. Norton.

Huron, David (1989). Voice denumerability in polyphonic music of homogeneous timbres. *Music Perception* 6: 361–82.

Huron, David, and Parncutt, Richard (1993). An improved model of tonality perception incorporating pitch salience and echoic memory. *Psychomusicology* 12: 154–71.

Jacobson, Daniel, and Koozin, Timothy (1996). *The Norton CD-ROM masterworks*, vol. 1. New York: W. W. Norton.

Jenkins, J. G., and Dallenbach, K. M. (1924). Oblivescence during sleep and waking. *American Journal of Psychology* 35: 605–12.

Jeppesen, Knud ([1946] 1970). *The style of Palestrina and the dissonance.* Rev. ed. Trans. Margaret Hamerik. New York: Dover. [Reprint of the 1946 Oxford University Press edition.]

Jersild, Jörgen (1966). *Ear training: Basic instruction in melody and rhythm reading.* Copenhagen: Wilhelm Hansen.

Johnson-Laird, Philip N. (1991). Rhythm and meter: A theory at the computational level. *Psychomusicology* 10: 88–106.

Jones, Mari Riess (1990). Learning and the development of expectancies: An interactionist approach. *Psychomusicology* 9: 193–228.

Jones, Vincent (1949). *Music education in the college.* Boston: C. C. Birchard.

Juilliard School of Music (1953). *The Juilliard report on teaching the literature and materials of music.* New York: W. W. Norton.

Karno, Mitchell, and Konečni, Vladimir (1992). The effects of structural interventions in the first movement of Mozart's Symphony in G Minor K. 550 on aesthetic preference. *Music Perception* 10: 63–72.

Karpinski, Gary S. (1981). A manual of basic music theory, dictation, and solfeggio. Typescript.

Karpinski, Gary S. (1990). A model for music perception and its implications in melodic dictation. *Journal of Music Theory Pedagogy* 4: 191–229.

Karpinski, Gary S. (1993). Reviews of recent textbooks in theory and musicianship: 3. Aural skills. *Music Theory Spectrum* 15: 241–56.

Karpinski, Gary S. (1997). A perceptual basis for implementing a solmization system. Paper presented to the third U.S. conference of the Society for Music Perception and Cognition, Cambridge, MA.

Kauffman, William H., and Carlsen, James C. (1989). Memory for intact music works: The importance of music expertise and retention interval. *Psychomusicology* 8: 3–20.

Kazez, Daniel (1992). Solfege drills. *Journal of Music Theory Pedagogy* 6: 19–34.

Keele, Steven W., and Neill, Trammell (1978). Mechanisms of attention. In *Handbook of perception. Vol. 9, Perceptual processing.* New York: Academic Press.

Kelly, Steven N. (1993). An investigation of the effects of conducting instruction on the musical performance of beginning band students. Ph.D. diss., University of Kansas.

Kendall, Roger (1986). The role of acoustic signal partitions in listener categorization of musical phrases. *Music Perception* 4: 185–214.

Killam, Rosemary; Lorton, Paul V.; and Schubert, Earl D. (1975). Interval recognition: Identification of harmonic and melodic intervals. *Journal of Music Theory* 19: 212–34.

Killam, Rosemary; Lorton, Paul V.; and Schubert, Earl D. (1976). Perception of triads. Paper presented to the meeting of the Acoustical Society of America, San Diego, CA.

Kirnberger, Johann Philipp ([1771–79] 1982). *The art of strict musical composition.* New Haven, CT: Yale University Press.

Kivy, Peter (1993). *The fine art of repetition: Essays in the philosophy of music.* Cambridge: Cambridge University Press.

Koch, Heinrich Christoph ([1787/1793] 1983). *Introductory essay on composition: The mechanical rules of melody, sections 3 and 4.* From Ver-

such einer Anleitung zur Composition, vol. 2 (1787) and vol. 3 (1793). Trans. Nancy Kovaleff Baker. New Haven, CT: Yale University Press.

Komar, Arthur (1971). *Theory of suspensions: A study of metrical and pitch relations in tonal music*. Princeton, NJ: Princeton University Press.

Kostka, Stefan, and Payne, Dorothy (2000). *Tonal harmony with an introduction to twentieth-century music*. 4th ed. Boston: McGraw-Hill.

Kraft, Leo (1999). *A new approach to ear training*. 2d ed. New York: W. W. Norton.

Kramer, Jonathan (1988). *The time of music: New meanings, new temporalities, new listening strategies*. New York: Schirmer Books.

Krebs, Harald (1987). Some extensions of the concept of metrical consonance and dissonance. *Journal of Music Theory* 31: 99–120.

Krebs, Harald (1992). Review of "Rhythm and linear analysis" by Carl Schachter, and *Phrase rhythm in tonal music* by William Rothstein. *Music Theory Spectrum* 14: 82–87.

Kreter, Leo (1976). *Sight and sound: A manual of aural musicianship*. 2 vols. Englewood Cliffs, NJ: Prentice-Hall.

Krumhansl, Carol L. (1990). *Cognitive foundations of musical pitch*. New York: Oxford University Press.

Krumhansl, Carol L., and Kessler, Edward J. (1982). Tracing the dynamic changes in perceived tonal organization in a spatial representation of musical keys. *Psychological Review* 89: 334–68.

LaBerge, David (1995). Attentional processing in music listening: A cognitive neuroscience approach. *Psychomusicology* 14: 20–34.

Laden, Bernice (1994). Melodic anchoring and tone duration. *Music Perception* 12: 199–212.

Lake, William E. (1993). Interval and scale-degree strategies in melodic perception. *Journal of Music Theory Pedagogy* 7: 55–67.

Larson, Steve (1989). Solfège systems and integrated music learning. Paper presented to the twelfth annual meeting of the Society for Music Theory, Austin, TX.

Larson, Steve (1993a). Scale-degree function: A theory of expressive meaning and its application to aural skills pedagogy. *Journal of Music Theory Pedagogy* 7: 69–84.

Larson, Steve (1993b). The value of cognitive models in evaluating solfege systems. *Indiana Theory Review* 14: 73–116.

Larson, Steve (1995). "Integrated music learning" and improvisation: Teaching musicianship and theory through "menus, maps, and models." *College Music Symposium* 35: 76–90.

Larson, Steve (1997). The problem of prolongation in *tonal* music: Terminology, perception, and expressive meaning. *Journal of Music Theory* 41: 101–36.

Lawson, Robert F. (1970). Scientific approaches to problems of aural perceptivity. *Michigan Academician*, Summer: 7–18.

Lee, Christopher S. (1991). The perception of metrical structure: Experimental evidence and a model. In *Representing musical structure* (pp. 59–127). Ed. Peter Howell, Robert West, and Ian Cross. San Diego, CA: Academic Press.

Lehmann, Andreas C., and Ericsson, Anders (1993). Sight-reading ability of expert pianists in the context of piano accompanying. *Psychomusicology* 12: 182–95.

Lehmann, Andreas C., and Ericsson, Anders (1996). Performance without preparation: Structure and acquisition of expert sight-reading and accompanying performance. *Psychomusicology* 15: 1–29.

Lerdahl, Fred, and Jackendoff, Ray (1983). *A generative theory of tonal music*. Cambridge: MIT Press.

Lester, Joel (1986). *The rhythms of tonal music*. Carbondale and Edwardsville: Southern Illinois University Press.

Levarie, Siegmund, and Levy, Ernst (1980). *Tone: A study in musical acoustics*. 2d ed. Kent, OH: Kent State University Press.

Levin, Robert D., and Martin, Louis (1988a). *Sight singing and ear training through literature*. Englewood Cliffs, NJ: Prentice-Hall.

Levin, Robert D., and Martin, Louis (1988b). Teacher's manual for *Sight singing and ear training through literature*. Englewood Cliffs, NJ: Prentice-Hall.

Levinson, Jerrold (1997). *Music in the moment*. Ithaca, NY: Cornell University Press.

Levitin, Daniel (1994). Absolute memory for musical pitch: Evidence from the production of learned melodies. *Perception and Psychophysics* 56: 414–23.

Levitin, Daniel J., and Cook, Perry R. (1996). Absolute memory for musical tempo: Additional evidence that auditory memory is absolute. *Perception and Psychophysics* 58: 927–35.

Levy, Janet (1982). Texture as a sign in classic and early romantic music. *Journal of the American Musicological Society* 35: 482–531.

London, Justin (1996). A psychological addendum to Takadimi: A beat-oriented system of rhythm pedagogy. *Journal of Music Theory Pedagogy* 10: 31–36.

Long, Peggy A. (1977). Relationships between pitch memory in short melodies and selected factors. *Journal of Research in Music Education* 25: 272–82.

Longuet-Higgins, H. Christopher, and Lee, Christopher S. (1982). The perception of musical rhythms. *Perception* 11: 115–28.

Lorek, Mary Jo; Riggins, H. Lee; Pembrook, Randall; Lidge, Ken; and New, Laura (1991). The effect of three syllable systems—fixed do, movable do, and "lah"—on the sightsinging performance of freshmen music majors. Paper presented to the second annual conference of Music Theory Midwest, Kansas City, MO.

Luce, John R. (1965). Sight-reading and ear playing abilities as related to instrumental music students. *Journal of Research in Music Education* 13: 101–9.

Lundin, Robert W., and Allen, Joseph D. (1962). A technique for training perfect pitch. *Psychological Record* 12: 139–46.

MacKnight, Carol B. (1975). Music reading ability of beginning wind instrumentalists after melodic instruction. *Journal of Research in Music Education* 23: 23–34.

Madsen, Clifford K. (1979). Modulated beat discrimination among musicians and nonmusicians. *Journal of Research in Music Education* 27: 57–67.

Madsen, Clifford K.; Duke, Robert A.; and Geringer, John M. (1986). The effect of speed alterations on tempo note selection. *Journal of Research in Music Education* 34: 101–10.

Mangeot, Andre Louis (1953). *Violin technique: Notes for players and teachers*. London: D. Dobson.

Marple, Hugo D. (n.d.). Short term memory and musical stimuli. In *Psy-

chology and acoustics of music: A collection of papers (pp. 74–93). Ed. Edward P. Asmus, Jr. Lawrence: Division of Continuing Education, University of Kansas.

Martin, Daniel W. (1952). Do you auralize? *Journal of the Acoustical Society of America* 24: 416.

Martin, Louis (1978). Solmization: Getting the facts straight. *Theory and Practice* 3/2: 21–25.

Marvin, Elizabeth West (1995). Research on tonal perception and memory: What implications for theory pedagogy? *Journal of Music Theory Pedagogy* 9: 31–70.

Marvin, Elizabeth West, and Brinkman, Alexander (1999). The effect of modulation and formal manipulation on perception of tonic closure by expert listeners. *Music Perception* 16: 389–407.

Matthay, Tobias (1913). *Musical interpretation: Its laws and principles, and their application in teaching and performing.* Boston: Boston Music Company.

McHose, Allen Irvine (1948). *Teachers dictation manual.* New York: Appleton-Century-Crofts.

McHose, Allen Irvine, and Tibbs, Ruth Northup (1945). *Sight-singing manual.* 2d ed. New York: Appleton-Century-Crofts.

McPherson, Gary E. (1995). The assessment of musical performance: Development and validation of five new measures. *Psychology of Music* 23: 142–61.

Melcher, Robert A., and Warch, Willard F. (1971). *Music for score reading.* Englewood Cliffs, NJ: Prentice-Hall.

Meyer, Max (1899). Is the memory of absolute pitch capable of development by training? *Psychological Review* 6: 514–16.

Meyer, Max (1900). Elements of a psychological theory of melody. *Psychological Review* 7: 241–73.

Miller, Benjamin O. (1993). Time perception in musical meter perception. *Psychomusicology* 12: 124–53.

Miller, George (1956). The magical number seven plus or minus two: Some limits on our capacity for processing information. *Psychological Review* 63: 81–97.

Miller, Leon K. (1989). *Musical savants: Exceptional skill in the mentally retarded.* Hillsdale, NJ: Lawrence Erlbaum Associates.

Miller, Richard (1986). *The structure of singing: System and art in vocal technique.* New York: Schirmer Books.

Miyazaki, Ken'ichi (1989). Absolute pitch identification: Effects of timbre and pitch region. *Music Perception* 7: 1–14.

Miyazaki, Ken'ichi (1990). The speed of musical pitch identification by absolute-pitch possessors. *Music Perception* 8: 177–88.

Miyazaki, Ken'ichi (1992). Perception of musical intervals by absolute pitch possessors. *Music Perception* 9: 413–26.

Miyazaki, Ken'ichi (1993). Absolute pitch as an inability: Identification of musical intervals in a tonal context. *Music Perception* 11: 55–71.

Morris, R. O., and Ferguson, Howard (1931). *Preparatory exercises in score-reading.* Oxford: Oxford University Press.

Mull, Helen K. (1925). The acquisition of absolute pitch. *American Journal of Psychology* 36: 469–93.

Multer, Walt (1978). Solmization and musical perception. *Theory and Practice* 3/1: 29–51.

Ottman, Robert (1956). A statistical investigation of the influence of selected factors on the skill of sight-singing. Ph.D. diss., North Texas State College.

Ottman, Robert (1996). *Music for sight singing*. 4th ed. Upper Saddle River, NJ: Prentice-Hall.

Ottman, Robert W., and Dworak, Paul E. (1991). *Basic ear training skills*. Englewood Cliffs, NJ: Prentice-Hall.

Oura, Yoko (1991). Constructing a representation of a melody: Transforming melodic segments into reduced pitch patterns operated on by modifiers. *Music Perception* 9: 251–66.

Oura, Yoko, and Hatano, Giyoo (1988). Memory of melodies among subjects differing in age and experience in music. *Psychology of Music* 16: 91–109.

Peacham, Henry ([1634] 1906). *The compleat gentleman*. Oxford: Clarendon Press.

Pembrook, Randall G. (1983). The effects of contour, length, and tonality on melodic memory. Paper presented to the Southeast Regional meeting of the Music Educators National Conference, Louisville, KY.

Pembrook, Randall G. (1986). Interference of the transcription process and other selected variables on perception and memory during melodic dictation. *Journal of Research in Music Education* 34: 238–61.

Pembrook, Randall G. (1987). The effect of vocalization on melodic memory conservation. *Journal of Research in Music Education* 35: 155–69.

Pembrook, Randall G., and Riggins, H. Lee (1990). "Send help!": Aural skills instruction in U.S. colleges and universities. *Journal of Music Theory Pedagogy* 4: 231–41.

Perkins, Leeman (1973). Mode and structure in the masses of Josquin. *Journal of the American Musicological Society* 26: 189–239.

Phillips, Joel (in press). Evaluating student work using models derived from those used in nationally administrated examinations. *Journal of Music Theory Pedagogy*.

Pierce, Alexandra (1994). Developing Schenkerian hearing and performing. *Intégral* 8: 51–123.

Pierce, John R. (1983). *The science of musical sound*. New York: Scientific American.

Polanka, Mark (1995). Research note: Factors affecting eye movements during the reading of short melodies. *Psychology of Music* 23: 177–83.

Pollard-Gott, Lucy (1983). Emergence of thematic concepts in repeated listening to music. *Cognitive Psychology* 15: 66–94.

Potter, Gary (1990). Identifying successful dictation strategies. *Journal of Music Theory Pedagogy* 4: 63–71.

Pratt, George (1998). *Aural awareness: Principles and practice*. Rev. ed. Oxford: Oxford University Press.

Prausnitz, Frederik (1983). *Score and podium: A complete guide to conducting*. New York: W. W. Norton.

Pseudo-Odo of Cluny ([n.d.] 1998). Dialogue on music [*Enchiridion musices*]. In *Source readings in music history* (pp. 198–210). Ed. Oliver Strunk. Rev. ed. Ed. Leo Treitler. New York: W. W. Norton.

Quantz, Johann Joachim ([1752] 1985). *On playing the flute*. 2d ed. Trans. Edward R. Reilly. New York: Schirmer Books.

Quine, Hector (1990). *Guitar technique: Intermediate to advanced*. Oxford: Oxford University Press.

Quinn, Ian (1999). The combinatorial model of pitch contour. *Music Perception* 16: 439–56.

Radocy, Rudolf E., and Boyle, J. David (1997). *Psychological foundations of musical behavior*. Springfield, IL: Charles C. Thomas.

Rahn, Jay, and McKay, James R. (1988). The guide-tone method: An approach to harmonic dictation. *Journal of Music Theory Pedagogy* 2: 101–11.

Rameau, Jean-Philippe ([1722] 1971). *Treatise on harmony*. Trans. Philip Gossett. New York: Dover.

Rasch, Rudolf A. (1985). Perception of melodic and harmonic intonation of two-part musical fragments. *Music Perception* 2: 441–58.

Ray, Harry Burton (1964). An experimental approach to the reading of pitch notation. Ph.D. diss., Indiana University.

Read, Gardner (1979). *Music notation: A manual of modern practice*. 2d ed. New York: Taplinger.

Reitman, Judith Spencer (1971). Mechanisms of forgetting in short-term memory. *Cognitive Psychology* 2: 185–95.

Repp, Bruno H. (1994). On determining the basic tempo of an expressive music performance. *Psychology of Music* 22: 157–67.

Repp, Bruno H.; London, Justin; Cox, Arnie; Morrison, Charles D; Maus, Fred Everett; and Levinson, Jerrold (1999). *Music in the moment*: A discussion. *Music Perception* 16: 463–94.

Révész, G. (1913). *Zur Grundlegung der Tonpsychologie*. Leipzig: Veit.

Riggins, H. Lee (1988). Scale-degree vs. intervallic hearing: Toward a synthesis. Paper presented to the joint meeting of the Central Midwest Theory Society and the Great Plains Chapter of the College Music Society, Iowa City.

Risset, Jean-Claude, and Wessel, David L. (1999). Exploration of timbre by analysis and synthesis. In *The psychology of music* (pp. 113–69). 2d ed. Ed. Diana Deutsch. New York: Academic Press.

Roberts, Emlyn, and Davies, Ann (1976). A method of extending the vocal range of "Monotone" schoolchildren. *Psychology of Music* 4/1: 29–43.

Roberts, Linda A. (1986). Modality and suffix effects in memory for melodic and harmonic musical materials. *Cognitive Psychology* 18: 123–57.

Robinson, Franklin W. (1918). *Aural harmony*, part 1. New York: G. Schirmer.

Roederer, Juan G. (1995). *The physics and psychophysics of music: An introduction*. 3d ed. New York: Springer-Verlag.

Roemer, Clinton (1985). *The art of music copying: The preparation of music for performance*. 2d ed. Sherman Oaks, CA: Roerick Music.

Rogers, George L., and Watkins, Rosemary C. (1986). The relationship between prior musical training and aural discrimination skills of elementary education majors. *Contributions to Music Education* 13: 48–55.

Rogers, Michael (1983). Beyond intervals: The teaching of tonal hearing. *Indiana Theory Review* 6/3: 18–34.

Rogers, Michael (1984). *Teaching approaches in music theory: An overview of pedagogical philosophies*. Carbondale: Southern Illinois University Press.

Rogers, Michael (1996). The Jersild approach: A sightsinging method from Denmark. *College Music Symposium* 36: 149–61.

Rohwer, Debbie (1998). Effect of movement instruction on steady beat perception, synchronization, and performance. *Journal of Research in Music Education* 46: 414–24.

Rothgeb, John (1981). Schenkerian theory: Its implications for the undergraduate curriculum. *Music Theory Spectrum* 3: 142–49.

Rothstein, William (1989). *Phrase rhythm in tonal music.* New York: Schirmer Books.

Rudolf, Max (1994). *The grammar of conducting: A comprehensive guide to baton technique and interpretation.* 3d ed. New York: Schirmer Books.

Rush, Mark Alan (1989). An experimental investigation of the effectiveness of training on absolute pitch in adult musicians. Ph.D. dissertation, Ohio State University.

Salzberg, Rita A. (1980). The effects of visual stimulus and instruction on intonation accuracy of string instruments. *Psychology of Music* 8/2: 42–49.

Salzer, Felix ([1952] 1962). *Structural hearing: Tonal coherence in music.* New York: Dover.

Salzer, Felix (1969). Introduction to *Five graphic music analyses* by Heinrich Schenker. New York: Dover.

Salzer, Felix, and Schachter, Carl ([1969] 1989). *Counterpoint in composition: The study of voice leading.* New York: Columbia University Press.

Sandor, Gyorgy (1981). *On piano playing: Motion, sound, and expression.* New York: Schirmer Books.

Schachter, Carl (1976). Rhythm and linear analysis: A preliminary study. *Music Forum* 4: 281–334.

Schachter, Carl (1980). Rhythm and linear analysis: Durational reduction. *Music Forum* 5: 197–232.

Schachter, Carl (1987). Rhythm and linear analysis: Aspects of meter. *Music Forum* 6: 1–60.

Schenker, Heinrich ([1910/1922] 1987). *Counterpoint.* 2 vols. Trans. John Rothgeb and Jürgen Thym. New York: Schirmer Books.

Schenker, Heinrich (1923). *Der Tonwille*, vol. 5. Vienna: Albert I. Gutmann.

Schenker, Heinrich ([1935] 1979). *Free composition.* Trans. and ed. Ernst Oster. New York: Longman.

Scherchen, Hermann (1933). *Handbook of conducting.* Trans. M. D. Calvocoressi. London: Oxford University Press.

Schoenberg, Arnold (1967). *Fundamentals of musical composition.* Ed. Gerald Strang. London: Faber and Faber.

Schoenberg, Arnold ([1934] 1975). Problems of harmony. In *Style and idea* (pp. 268–87). Ed. Leonard Stein. Trans. Leo Black. Berkeley: University of California Press.

Schuller, Gunther (1997). *The compleat conductor.* New York: Oxford University Press.

Schumann, Robert ([1848] 1967). Musikalische Haus- und Lebensregeln. In *Im eigenen Wort* (pp. 400–414). Ed. Willi Reich. Zurich: Manesse Verlag.

Seashore, Carl (1938). *Psychology of Music.* New York: McGraw-Hill.

Seeger, Charles Louis (1930). On dissonant counterpoint. *Modern Music* 7: 25–31.

Serafine, Mary Louise (1983). Cognitive processes in music: Discoveries and definitions. *Council for Research in Music Education* 73: 1–14.

Serafine, Mary Louise (1988). *Music as cognition: The development of thought in sound.* New York: Columbia University Press.

Serafine, Mary Louise; Glassman, Noah; and Overbeeke, Cornell (1989). The cognitive reality of hierarchic structure in music. *Music Perception* 6: 397–430.

Sergeant, Desmond (1969). Experimental investigation of absolute pitch. *Journal of Research in Music Education* 17: 135–43.

Sergeant, Desmond, and Roche, Sheila (1973). Perceptual shifts in the auditory information processing of young children. *Psychology of Music* 1/2: 39–48.

Shatzkin, Merton (1981). Interval and pitch recognition in and out of immediate context. *Journal of Research in Music Education* 29: 111–23.

Sheldon, Deborah A. (1998). Effects of contextual sight-singing and aural skills training on error-detection abilities. *Journal of Research in Music Education* 46: 384–95.

Shepard, Roger N., and Jordan, Daniel S. (1984). Auditory illusions demonstrating that tones are assimilated to an internalized music scale. *Science* 226: 1333–34.

Shuter-Dyson, Rosamund, and Gabriel, Clive (1981). *The psychology of musical ability*. 2d ed. London: Methuen.

Siegel, Jane A., and Siegel, William (1977). Categorical perception of tonal intervals: Musicians can't tell sharp from flat. *Perception and Psychophysics* 21: 399–407.

Sloboda, John (1976). Visual perception of musical notation: Registering pitch symbols in memory. *Quarterly Journal of Experimental Psychology* 28: 1–16.

Sloboda, John (1978). The psychology of music reading. *Psychology of Music* 6/2: 3–20.

Sloboda, John (1985). *The musical mind: The cognitive psychology of music*. Oxford: Clarendon Press.

Sloboda, John A., and Edworthy, Judy (1981). Attending to two melodies at once: The effect of key relatedness. *Psychology of Music* 9/1: 39–43.

Sloboda, John A., and Parker, David H. H. (1985). Immediate recall of melodies. In *Musical structure and cognition* (pp. 143–67). Ed. Peter Howell, Ian Cross, and Robert West. London: Academic Press.

Smith, Alan (1973). Feasability of tracking musical form as a cognitive listening objective. *Journal of Research in Music Education* 21: 200–213.

Smith, Melville (1934). Solfège: An essential in musicianship. *Music Supervisors Journal* 20/5: 16–17, 58, 60–61.

Smith, Timothy A. (1991). A comparison of pedagogical resources in solmization systems. *Journal of Music Theory Pedagogy* 5: 1–23.

Smith, Timothy A. (1992). Liberation of solmization: Searching for common ground. *Journal of Music Theory Pedagogy* 6: 153–68.

Smith, Timothy A. (1994). Ending the dialogue: Imaginary solutions are no solution. *Journal of Music Theory Pedagogy* 8: 227–30.

Smyth, David H. (1990). Large-scale rhythm and classical form. *Music Theory Spectrum* 12: 236–46.

Smyth, David H. (1992). Patterning beyond hypermeter. *College Music Symposium* 32: 79–98.

Steedman, Mark J. (1977). The perception of musical rhythm and metre. *Perception* 6: 555–69.

Steele, Janet, and McDowell, Bonney (1982). *Elementary musicianship: An introduction to theory, sight-singing, and ear training*. New York: Alfred A. Knopf.

Stone, Kurt (1980). *Music notation in the twentieth century: A practical guidebook*. New York: W. W. Norton.

Surace, Joseph A. (1978). "Transposable *do*" for teaching aural recognition of diatonic intervals. *Theory and Practice* 3/2: 25–27.

Takeuchi, Annie H., and Hulse, Stewart H. (1991). Absolute-pitch judgments of black- and white-key pitches. *Music Perception* 9: 27–46.

Takeuchi, Annie H., and Hulse, Stewart H. (1993). Absolute pitch. *Psychological Bulletin* 113: 345–61.

Tallarico, P. T. (1974). A study of the three phase concept of memory: Its musical implications. *Council for Research in Music Education* 39: 1–15.

Taylor, Eric (1967). *Playing from an orchestral score*. Oxford: Oxford University Press.

Taylor, Eric (1970). *An introduction to score playing*. Oxford: Oxford University Press.

Taylor, Jack A., and Pembrook, Randall G. (1983). Strategies in memory for short melodies: An extension of Otto Ortmann's 1933 study. *Psychomusicology* 3: 16–35.

Terhardt, Ernst, and Ward, W. Dixon (1982). Recognition of musical key: Exploratory study. *Journal of the Acoustical Society of America* 72: 26–33.

Thomson, William ([1969] 1975). *Advanced music reading*. Tucson: Sonora Music.

Thomson, William E., and DeLone, Richard P. (1967). *Introduction to ear training*. Belmont, CA: Wadsworth.

Thurlow, Willard R., and Erchul, William P. (1977). Judged similarity in pitch of octave multiples. *Perception and Psychophysics* 22: 177–82.

Trubitt, Allen R., and Hines, Robert S. (1979). *Ear training and sight-singing: An integrated approach*. New York: Schirmer Books.

Tunks, Thomas W.; Bowers, Dennis R.; and Eagle, Charles T. (1993). The effect of stimulus tempo on melodic error detection. *Psychomusicology* 12: 41–51.

Unyk, Anna M., and Carlsen, James C. (1987). The influence of expectancy on melodic perception. *Psychomusicology* 7: 3–23.

Van Egmond, René, and Butler, David (1997). Diatonic connotations of pitch-class sets. *Music Perception* 15: 1–29.

Vennard, William (1967). *Singing: The mechanism and the technic*. 5th ed. Boston: Carl Fischer.

Vernon, Philip E. (1977). Absolute pitch: A case study. *British Journal of Psychology* 68: 485–89.

Vos, Piet G. (1999). Key implications of ascending fourth and descending fifth openings. *Psychology of Music* 27: 4–17.

Wagner, Richard ([1869] 1940). *On conducting*. Trans. Edward Dannreuther. 4th ed. London: William Reeves.

Walker, Robert (1981). Teaching basic musical concepts and their staff notations through cross-modal matching symbols. *Psychology of Music* 19: 31–38.

Wapnick, Joel (1980). The perception of musical and metronomic tempo change in musicians. *Psychology of Music* 8/1: 3–12.

Wapnick, Joel (1984). Undergraduate and graduate music majors' perceptions of cross-rhythms. *Psychology of Music* 12: 60–66.

Wapnick, Joel; Bourassa, Gary; and Sampson, Joanne (1982). The perception of tonal intervals in isolation and in melodic context. *Psychomusicology* 2: 21–37.

Ward, W. Dixon (1992). Early learning and absolute pitch. Paper presented at the Second International Conference on Music Perception and Cognition, UCLA.

Ward, W. Dixon (1999). Absolute pitch. In *The psychology of music* (pp. 265–98). 2nd ed. Ed. Diana Deutsch. New York: Academic Press.

Ware, Clifton (1998). *Adventures in singing: A process for exploring, discovering, and developing vocal potential.* 2d ed. Boston: McGraw-Hill.

Warfield, Gerald ([1977] 1986). *How to write music manuscript: A workbook in the basics of music notation.* New York: Schirmer Books. [Reprint of *How to write music manuscript (in pencil).* New York: D. McKay, 1977.]

Waters, Andrew J., and Underwood, Geoffrey (1998). Eye movements in a simple music reading task: A study of expert and novice musicians. *Psychology of Music* 26: 46–60.

Welch, Graham (1979). Poor pitch singing: A review of the literature. *Psychology of Music* 7/1: 50–58.

Welch, Graham (1989). Developing voice skills in children: Results with a new microcomputer-based system for real time visual feedback. *Psychology of Music* 17: 83–85.

Welch, Graham; Howard, D. M.; and Rush, C. (1989). Real-time visual feedback in the development of vocal pitch accuracy in singing. *Psychology of Music* 17: 146–57.

Wennerstrom, Mary H. (1989). The undergraduate core music curriculum at Indiana University. *Journal of Music Theory Pedagogy* 3: 153–76.

West, Robert J., and Fryer, Roz (1990). Ratings of suitability of probe tones as tonics after random orderings of notes of the diatonic scale. *Music Perception* 7: 253–58.

White, Bernice (1935). *Melodic dictation.* New York: American Book Company.

White, John D. (1981). *Guidelines for college teaching of music theory.* Metuchen, NJ: Scarecrow Press.

Williams, David (1975). Short-term retention of pitch sequence. *Journal of Research in Music Education* 23: 53–66.

Williams, David (1980). A study of tonal strength and its influence on melodic memory. In *Proceedings of the research symposium on the psychology of acoustics and music* (pp. 45–61). Ed. M. V. May. Lawrence: University of Kansas, Department of Music Education and Music Theory.

Winnick, William (1987). Hybrid methods in sight-singing. *Choral Journal* 28: 24–30.

Wittlich, Gary E., and Humphries, Lee (1974). *Ear training: An approach through music literature.* New York: Harcourt Brace Jovanovich.

Wright, James K., and Bregman, Albert S. (1987). Auditory stream segregation and the control of dissonance in polyphonic music. *Contemporary Music Review* 2: 63–92.

Wuthrich, Carol E., and Tunks, Thomas W. (1989). The influence of presentation time asynchrony on music interval perception. *Psychomusicology* 8: 31–46.

Yeston, Maury (1976). *The stratification of musical rhythm.* New Haven, CT: Yale University Press.

Zarlino, Gioseffo ([1558] 1968). *Le Istitutioni Harmoniche*. Part 3, *The art of counterpoint*. Trans. Guy A. Marco and Claude V. Palisca. New York: W. W. Norton.

Zarlino, Gioseffo ([1558] 1983). *Le Istitutioni Harmoniche*. Part 4, *On the Modes*. Trans. Vered Cohen. New Haven, CT: Yale University Press.

Zuckerkandl, Victor. (1973). *Sound and Symbol*. Vol. 2, *Man the Musician*. Trans. Norbert Guterman. Princeton, NJ: Princeton University Press.

Index